LIBERTY IN ACTION

LIBERTY IN ACTION

BILL VINCENT

CONTENTS

1. Legal Disclaimer — 1
2. Introduction: The Power of Free Expression — 3
3. Chapter 1: The Origins of the First Amendment — 7
4. Chapter 2: Free Speech: The Foundation of Democrac — 27
5. Chapter 3: The Freedom of the Press — 49
6. Chapter 4: The Right to Assemble — 69
7. Chapter 5: The Freedom to Petition the Government — 89
8. Chapter 6: The Establishment Clause: Separation of — 109
9. Chapter 7: The Free Exercise of Religion — 129
10. Chapter 8: The Internet Age: A New Frontier for th — 149
11. Chapter 9: The Global Perspective on Free Speech a — 167
12. Chapter 10: The Ongoing Battle for First Amendment — 189
13. Chapter 11: Case Studies of First Amendment Heroes — 207
14. Chapter 12: The Future of the First Amendment — 225

15 Chapter 13: First Amendment Auditors: Guardians of 245

16 Conclusion: Liberty in Action — 263

17 Appendix: Important Documents and Resources — 279

Copyright © 2024 by Bill Vincent

All rights reserved. No part of this book may be reproduced in any manner whatsoever without written permission except in the case of brief quotations embodied in critical articles and reviews.

First Printing, 2024

CHAPTER 1

Legal Disclaimer

The information contained in this book, "Protecting Our Rights: The Role of First Amendment Auditors," is provided for informational purposes only. While every effort has been made to ensure the accuracy and completeness of the information presented, the authors and publishers make no representations or warranties of any kind, express or implied, about the accuracy, reliability, suitability, or availability with respect to the book or the information, products, services, or related graphics contained in the book for any purpose. Any reliance you place on such information is therefore strictly at your own risk.

The authors and publishers are not engaged in rendering legal, professional, or other advice or services. If legal or other expert assistance is required, the services of a competent professional should be sought. The content of this book is not intended to be a substitute for professional advice, diagnosis, or treatment. Always seek the advice of your attorney or other qualified professional with any questions you may have regarding a legal matter.

The authors and publishers disclaim any liability for any direct, indirect, incidental, consequential, or other damages arising out of or in connection with the use of this book or the information contained herein. This book is sold with the understanding that the authors and publishers are not engaged in rendering legal, professional, or other advice or services.

By using this book, you agree to the terms of this disclaimer. If you do not agree to these terms, please do not use this book.

CHAPTER 2

Introduction: The Power of Free Expression

The First Amendment is the cornerstone of American democracy, enshrining the fundamental freedoms that allow individuals to express their beliefs, challenge authority, and shape society. As the first of ten amendments in the Bill of Rights, it represents the values of liberty and personal autonomy that form the foundation of the United States. By guaranteeing the rights to free speech, a free press, peaceful assembly, petition, and the free exercise of religion, the First Amendment ensures that individuals have the ability to voice their thoughts, hold their government accountable, and live in accordance with their beliefs.

The significance of the First Amendment cannot be overstated. It is the mechanism by which democracy breathes, ensuring that public discourse remains open and vibrant. Without the protections it affords, voices of dissent could be silenced, minority beliefs could be oppressed, and the ability to challenge unjust laws and practices would be severely limited. From landmark Supreme Court decisions to everyday acts of speaking one's mind, the First Amendment stands as a shield against tyranny and a safeguard for freedom.

Historically, the development of the First Amendment emerged from the struggles the early American colonists faced under British rule. The suppression of speech, press, and religion in the colonies led to a fierce determination among the Founding Fathers to prevent such abuses in the new nation. Influenced by Enlightenment philosophers who championed individual liberties, the framers of the Constitution crafted the First Amendment to ensure that freedom of expression would remain an unalienable right for all Americans. The debates over its exact wording and meaning reflected deep concerns about the balance between liberty and government power—a tension that continues to shape its interpretation today.

This book, *Liberty in Action: Embracing the First Amendment*, is an exploration of the core freedoms guaranteed by the First Amendment: freedom of speech, press, assembly, petition, and religion. Each of these rights plays a unique role in sustaining democracy, but they are also deeply interconnected. Through historical context, landmark legal battles, and contemporary challenges, this book will explore how these rights have evolved over time and how they continue to influence modern society.

We will delve into the nature of free speech and its role as the foundation of democratic discourse, examine the press's critical function as the "fourth estate" in holding power accountable, and explore how the rights to assemble and petition have fueled social movements and sparked change. We will also investigate the tension between the "Establishment Clause" and "Free Exercise Clause" in shaping religious liberty in America. As technology reshapes communication and public space, we will confront the new challenges that the internet age presents for these time-honored freedoms.

The First Amendment remains as relevant today as it was in the 18th century. In a world increasingly divided by ideology, misinformation, and competing claims to truth, the protections afforded by the First Amendment are more essential than ever. Yet these freedoms are not guaranteed to endure without vigilance. From local protests to national movements, individuals must actively engage in exercising and protecting their rights.

This book is a call to action. Understanding the First Amendment is the first step in appreciating its power, but it is also crucial to actively safeguard these liberties. Readers are encouraged not only to reflect on the historical importance of these freedoms but to participate in their preservation. Whether through speaking out, holding public institutions accountable, or advocating for religious freedom, the legacy of the First Amendment depends on the actions of those who cherish it.

By exploring the First Amendment through its legal, historical, and societal impacts, *Liberty in Action* invites you to embrace your role as both a beneficiary and a protector of these rights. Together, we can ensure that the power of free expression continues to inspire and strengthen the democratic fabric of the nation for generations to come.

CHAPTER 3

Chapter 1: The Origins of the First Amendment

Colonial Struggles and Suppression of Expression
In the early days of the American colonies, the concept of free expression was far from the liberty Americans enjoy today. British colonial rule was marked by strict control over speech, the press, and religion, as the Crown sought to maintain order and loyalty in its overseas territories. The colonial experience with repression became a powerful driving force behind the eventual development of the First Amendment. To understand how these liberties took root, we must first examine the struggles the colonists faced under British authority and how these hardships shaped their desire for freedom of expression.

One of the most significant forms of control was the licensing of printed materials. In many colonies, particularly those under direct royal control, the press was tightly regulated. Newspapers had to be licensed by the colonial government, and failure to obtain such a license could result in hefty fines or even imprisonment. Printers who dared to publish without approval risked having their operations shut down. This form of censorship was designed to suppress dissent and ensure that the only information disseminated to the public was in line with the Crown's interests.

A defining moment in the fight for press freedom in the colonies came with the trial of John Peter Zenger in 1735. Zenger, a printer for *The New York Weekly Journal*, published articles criticizing the corrupt practices of the colonial governor, William Cosby. Although Zenger was arrested and charged with libel, his defense argued that truth should be a defense against libel. The jury ultimately acquitted Zenger, setting a powerful precedent for the freedom of the press. The case demonstrated that colonial juries, and by extension the public, were willing to stand up against government overreach and support the principle of holding public officials accountable through the press. While the legal system was still aligned with British law, Zenger's victory planted the seeds for what would later become a hallmark of American democracy: a free press that could operate without fear of retribution from the government.

Religious persecution was another significant form of repression in the colonies, particularly in regions with established state churches. In Massachusetts, for instance, the Puritans imposed strict religious conformity, and dissenters, including Quakers and Baptists, faced fines, imprisonment, and even death for practicing their faith. This pattern of religious intolerance was replicated across many of the colonies, where the official church of England was often the only legally sanctioned religious body. Religious minorities were not only persecuted for their beliefs but were also barred from holding public office or participating fully in civic life.

The harshness of these conditions led many colonists to flee to areas where greater religious tolerance was allowed, such as Pennsylvania, founded by the Quaker William Penn, who famously promoted religious freedom in his colony. Penn's vision of a society where individuals could worship without interference from the government became a blueprint for the broader push for religious liberty that would eventually be codified in the First Amendment.

These experiences of repression in the press and religion were not isolated incidents but part of a broader colonial system that sought to suppress any potential for dissent. The Crown viewed free expression as a threat to its control over the colonies, and it responded by enacting laws and regulations that stifled public debate, discouraged criticism, and enforced religious uniformity. These policies, however, had the opposite effect, galvanizing colonial resistance and solidifying the belief that freedom of expression was essential to the well-being of society. The more the British authorities tried to clamp down on speech, press, and religious freedom, the more the colonists began to see these rights as indispensable to their future. Each act of suppression deepened the resolve of the colonists to create a system of government that would not only tolerate but actively protect these liberties.

By the mid-18th century, the tension between the colonies and Britain had escalated. The restrictions on free expression were part of a broader pattern of control that included harsh taxation and authoritarian rule. The American Revolution was as much a battle for the rights to speak, publish, worship, and protest as it was for independence from British rule. Pamphlets, newspapers, and public speeches became tools of the revolutionaries, allowing them to communicate revolutionary ideas, rally support for independence, and criticize the British government without fear of immediate retribution.

This struggle for freedom of expression during the colonial period laid the groundwork for the ideals that would shape the First Amendment. The colonists had lived under a system where speaking out could lead to arrest, where publishing dissent could ruin livelihoods, and where worshipping according to one's conscience could result in persecution. As the revolution unfolded, it became clear that any new government formed after the war would need to guarantee that such repression would never happen again.

The colonial experience with British censorship and religious persecution was instrumental in shaping the Founding Fathers' views on liberty. They had seen firsthand the dangers of unchecked government power and the importance of safeguarding the public's right to speak, publish, and worship freely. These struggles provided the foundation for the First Amendment's protections, ensuring that future generations would not face the same tyranny the colonists had endured.

In this context, the First Amendment was not simply an abstract ideal—it was a direct response to the lived experiences of the American colonists. It emerged as a solution to the oppressive controls that had stifled their expression and faith, offering a framework for a new society where the government would be the servant of the people, not their master. The birth of the First Amendment, as we will see, was the culmination of decades of struggle and resistance to the forces of repression, and its legacy continues to shape American democracy to this day.

The Revolutionary Era and the Call for Rights

The American Revolution was more than a fight for independence—it was a battle over ideas, particularly the rights and freedoms that would define the new nation. During the Revolutionary era, the colonies were not just struggling for political autonomy from Britain, but for fundamental rights that they believed were being unjustly denied. Central to this was the belief in the right to free expression, which played a crucial role in the lead-up to and during the revolution. As tensions between the colonies and Britain grew, the importance of being able to speak, write, and protest against government authority became even more apparent. This era laid the foundation for the First Amendment by demonstrating the indispensable role of free expression in the fight for liberty.

One of the most powerful examples of free expression during this period was the use of pamphlets to spread revolutionary ideas. These small, inexpensive booklets circulated widely throughout the colonies, helping to build a sense of shared purpose and resistance. Perhaps the most famous pamphlet of all was Thomas Paine's *Common Sense*, published in January 1776. In plain and forceful language, Paine argued that it was both necessary and just for the colonies to break away from British rule. He attacked the idea of monarchy and hereditary succession and made the case for an independent republic based on equality and individual rights. *Common Sense* was a sensation, selling hundreds of thousands of copies, and is often credited with galvanizing public support for the cause of independence.

The success of *Common Sense* demonstrated the power of the written word in shaping public opinion. It also highlighted the crucial role that freedom of the press played in the revolutionary movement. Without the ability to print and distribute these ideas freely, the revolution might never have gained the widespread support it needed. At a time when the British government controlled much of the press in the colonies and sought to suppress dissenting voices, the free exchange of ideas became an act of rebellion in itself. Revolutionary leaders understood that the ability to express and share ideas was key to building the consensus necessary to fight for independence.

Alongside pamphlets, newspapers also played a significant role in spreading revolutionary ideals and challenging British authority. Colonial newspapers, like *The Boston Gazette* and *The Pennsylvania Journal*, became hubs of revolutionary activity, publishing editorials, essays, and letters that called for resistance to British policies. These papers not only informed the public but also provided a forum for debate on the pressing issues of the day. The free flow of information was critical in shaping the political consciousness of the colonists and in organizing resistance efforts, such as the boycotts of British goods and the formation of the Continental Congress.

The Declaration of Independence itself is a testament to the importance of free expression during the revolutionary era. Drafted by Thomas Jefferson and approved by the Continental Congress in 1776, the Declaration articulated the colonies' grievances against the British Crown and proclaimed the colonies' right to independence. It asserted that all men are endowed with "unalienable Rights" to "Life, Liberty, and the pursuit of Happiness," and that governments derive their power from the consent of the governed. These ideas were deeply influenced by Enlightenment thought, particularly the writings of John Locke, who emphasized the rights of individuals to speak freely and challenge unjust authority. The Declaration was not just a statement of political separation; it was a profound expression of the colonists' belief in the natural rights of all people, including the right to free expression.

However, the road to securing these rights was far from easy. Throughout the revolutionary period, British authorities sought to silence dissent and crush the revolutionary movement. Loyalists, or colonists who remained loyal to Britain, often faced persecution, censorship, and suppression from both sides of the conflict. British officials tried to prevent the spread of revolutionary propaganda, arresting printers and writers who published anti-British material. These actions reinforced the colonists' belief that a government that did not respect free expression was tyrannical and must be overthrown.

As the war progressed, the necessity of protecting free speech and the press became increasingly clear to the revolutionaries. They recognized that, in order to build a new nation, these rights would need to be enshrined in law. While the Articles of Confederation, the first governing document of the United States, did not include explicit protections for free expression, the experiences of the Revolutionary War made it clear that these rights would need to be a cornerstone of the future Constitution.

The Revolutionary era was a time of profound transformation, not only in terms of political independence but also in the understanding of individual rights. The colonists' fight against British repression of speech, press, and assembly highlighted the essential role these freedoms play in a healthy democracy. The ability to criticize the government, spread revolutionary ideas, and organize for change proved to be crucial tools in the fight for independence. As the new nation began to take shape, it was clear that the protection of these rights would be central to the vision of a free and democratic society.

In the years following the revolution, these ideals would be put to the test as the young United States grappled with the task of creating a stable and just government. The lessons of the Revolutionary War—the importance of free expression, the dangers of government censorship, and the need for a free press—would directly inform the drafting of the Bill of Rights, and ultimately, the First Amendment. As the nation moved from revolution to governance, the call for rights that had been born out of resistance to tyranny would become a defining feature of the American identity.

The Constitutional Convention and Debates Over Free Speech

After the Revolutionary War, the newly independent American colonies faced the monumental task of building a stable and functional government. The Articles of Confederation, which had loosely bound the states during the war, proved to be weak and ineffective in addressing the needs of a growing nation. In response, delegates from the thirteen states convened at the Constitutional Convention in Philadelphia in 1787 to draft a new constitution. While the convention was primarily focused on creating a more robust federal government, the question of individual rights, particularly free speech and free press, was hotly debated. The absence of explicit protections for these rights in the original draft of the Constitution would eventually lead to the inclusion of the Bill of Rights, with the First Amendment at its core.

At the heart of the debates over the new Constitution was the tension between two political factions: the Federalists and the Anti-Federalists. The Federalists, led by figures like Alexander Hamilton, James Madison, and John Jay, argued for a strong central government that could effectively manage the country's affairs. They believed that the Constitution, as written, provided a sufficient framework for governance and that additional protections for individual rights were unnecessary. Federalists were wary of including a Bill of Rights, fearing that listing specific freedoms might imply that other, unlisted rights were not protected.

The Anti-Federalists, on the other hand, were deeply concerned about the potential for government overreach and the infringement on individual liberties. Leaders like Patrick Henry and George Mason insisted that the new Constitution should explicitly protect the rights of the people, particularly freedom of speech, freedom of the press, and freedom of religion. They argued that the experience of living under British rule had shown the dangers of unchecked governmental power and the need for safeguards against tyranny. The Anti-Federalists feared that, without clear protections, the new federal government could easily become as oppressive as the British monarchy they had fought to escape.

One of the key issues raised during the debates was the role of free speech and a free press in a democratic society. Anti-Federalists pointed to the colonial period, when the British government had suppressed criticism through censorship and harsh penalties for those who spoke out against the Crown. They argued that the ability to freely criticize the government was essential to maintaining a healthy republic and ensuring that public officials remained accountable to the people. Without protections for free speech, they contended, the new government could use its power to silence dissent and control public opinion.

James Madison, who would later become known as the "Father of the Constitution," initially opposed the idea of including a Bill of Rights, believing that the Constitution itself was a sufficient safeguard. However, as the debate over ratification intensified, Madison recognized the growing demand for explicit protections of individual freedoms. The Anti-Federalists were gaining traction by arguing that the new Constitution failed to protect the people from government tyranny, and several states made it clear that they would not ratify the Constitution without the promise of a Bill of Rights.

One of the most vocal advocates for the inclusion of a Bill of Rights was Thomas Jefferson, who was serving as the U.S. minister to France during the Constitutional Convention. In his correspondence with Madison, Jefferson expressed his concern that the Constitution lacked sufficient protections for individual liberties. He argued that even the wisest and most benevolent government could be corrupted over time, and that explicit safeguards for free speech, press, and religion were necessary to prevent abuses of power. Jefferson's influence was instrumental in convincing Madison to champion the cause of a Bill of Rights.

The debates over free speech and free press were not just philosophical—they were rooted in practical concerns about the future of the republic. The newly independent states had already seen the power of the press in mobilizing public opinion during the Revolutionary War. Newspapers and pamphlets had been vital tools for spreading revolutionary ideas and organizing resistance against British rule. Anti-Federalists believed that a free press would continue to play a critical role in holding government officials accountable and ensuring that the people remained informed about their leaders' actions.

Despite Madison's initial reluctance, he became a leading advocate for the Bill of Rights after the Constitution was ratified. In 1789, during the first session of the new Congress, Madison introduced a series of amendments that would eventually become the Bill of Rights. Among these was what would later be known as the First Amendment, which explicitly protected the freedoms of speech, press, assembly, petition, and religion. Madison's amendments were designed to address the concerns of the Anti-Federalists and to reassure the public that the new federal government would not infringe on their rights.

The process of drafting the Bill of Rights was not without challenges. Some Federalists continued to argue that the amendments were unnecessary, while others believed that they did not go far enough in protecting individual freedoms. However, Madison and his supporters succeeded in persuading Congress to adopt the amendments, and by December 1791, the Bill of Rights was ratified by the states.

The debates over the inclusion of free speech and press protections in the Constitution reflected a fundamental question about the nature of government and the role of the people in a democracy. The Federalists believed that a strong central government was necessary to ensure stability and order, while the Anti-Federalists feared that without explicit protections, the government would become too powerful and suppress individual liberties. Ultimately, the inclusion of the First Amendment was a recognition that free expression was essential to the functioning of a democratic society. It ensured that the new government would be held accountable to the people and that citizens would have the right to express their opinions without fear of censorship or punishment.

The Constitutional Convention and the subsequent debates over the Bill of Rights were pivotal moments in the creation of the First Amendment. They revealed the deep-seated concerns about government power that had been forged during the colonial period and underscored the importance of free expression in maintaining a free society. The inclusion of the First Amendment in the Bill of Rights marked a major victory for the advocates of individual liberty and laid the foundation for the robust protections of speech and press that would become hallmarks of American democracy.

Enlightenment Philosophy and Intellectual Foundations

The First Amendment did not emerge in a vacuum—it was profoundly shaped by the philosophical currents of the Enlightenment, a period in the 17th and 18th centuries when thinkers across Europe began to challenge traditional authority and emphasize the power of reason, individual rights, and the potential for human progress. The intellectual foundations of the First Amendment were laid by the writings of Enlightenment philosophers, who argued that freedom of thought and expression was essential for the flourishing of society. The Founding Fathers, deeply influenced by these ideas, saw free speech, freedom of the press, and religious liberty as fundamental human rights that had to be protected in the new American republic.

Among the most influential of these Enlightenment thinkers was John Locke, the English philosopher whose writings on natural rights and government would have a profound impact on the development of American political thought. Locke argued that all individuals possessed certain inalienable rights by virtue of their humanity—chief among these were life, liberty, and property. Locke's *Two Treatises of Government* (1689) made the case that legitimate governments derive their authority from the consent of the governed, and that any government that infringes on individual rights loses its legitimacy. Locke's vision of a social contract between the government and the people—where the protection of individual rights was paramount—was a major influence on the Founding Fathers.

Locke also emphasized the importance of freedom of expression as a natural right. He believed that for individuals to fulfill their potential, they needed to be free to express their thoughts, question authority, and engage in public debate. Locke's ideas on freedom of conscience, especially in matters of religion, were revolutionary in their time. He argued that religious belief was a deeply personal matter and that no government had the right to dictate what its citizens should believe or how they should worship. This principle of religious tolerance would later become a key element of the First Amendment's guarantee of religious freedom.

The Enlightenment belief in the power of reason was central to the development of the idea that free speech and a free press were necessary for the progress of society. Thinkers like Voltaire, the French philosopher known for his sharp wit and unrelenting criticism of authority, championed the cause of free expression. Voltaire famously declared, "I disapprove of what you say, but I will defend to the death your right to say it," a sentiment that captured the spirit of Enlightenment thought on free speech. Voltaire believed that the ability to criticize those in power was essential to protecting liberty and preventing tyranny. His belief that open discourse, even when offensive or unpopular, was critical to the advancement of knowledge and justice resonated deeply with the architects of the American Constitution.

Another key figure was Montesquieu, whose *The Spirit of the Laws* (1748) argued for the separation of powers in government to prevent any one branch from becoming too powerful. Montesquieu's ideas on checks and balances influenced the structure of the U.S. government, but his broader belief in the need for free and open communication between citizens and their rulers also informed the Founding Fathers' views on the importance of a free press. Montesquieu argued that in a functioning republic, the people needed access to information and the freedom to discuss political issues without fear of retribution. This concept of the "marketplace of ideas," where different views could be freely expressed and debated, was central to the development of the First Amendment.

The Founding Fathers, particularly figures like Thomas Jefferson, Benjamin Franklin, and James Madison, were steeped in Enlightenment philosophy and saw free expression as essential to the creation of a just and prosperous society. Jefferson, a passionate advocate of individual liberty, was heavily influenced by Locke's writings on natural rights and religious freedom. He believed that a well-informed citizenry was the cornerstone of democracy and that a free press was necessary to ensure that the people could hold their government accountable. Jefferson's *Virginia Statute for Religious Freedom* (1786) laid the groundwork for the First Amendment's protection of religious liberty, arguing that "no man shall be compelled to frequent or support any religious worship, place, or ministry" and that "all men shall be free to profess, and by argument to maintain, their opinions in matters of religion."

Madison, too, was influenced by the Enlightenment's emphasis on reason and individual rights. As the chief architect of the Bill of Rights, Madison sought to enshrine the protections of free speech, press, and religion into the Constitution to safeguard against government overreach. He was particularly concerned with protecting the minority from the tyranny of the majority, a theme that ran through Enlightenment thought. Madison believed that a free press would serve as a "bulwark of liberty," ensuring that the government remained transparent and accountable to the people. His belief in the power of free expression to prevent the abuse of power was central to the drafting of the First Amendment.

The influence of Enlightenment philosophy on the First Amendment is perhaps most evident in its framing of rights as universal and inalienable. The Founding Fathers viewed freedom of speech, press, and religion not merely as privileges granted by the government, but as inherent rights that all individuals possessed by virtue of their humanity. These rights were not subject to the whims of rulers or the majority, but were fundamental to the dignity and autonomy of the individual. The Founders believed that protecting these rights was essential to creating a society where people could think, speak, worship, and organize freely without fear of persecution.

In many ways, the First Amendment can be seen as the practical realization of the Enlightenment's bold vision of human liberty. It embodies the belief that a free and open society is one where individuals can express their ideas, challenge authority, and pursue truth without interference from the government. The marketplace of ideas, a concept rooted in Enlightenment thought, holds that the best ideas will rise to the top through free and open debate, and that suppressing speech only leads to ignorance and tyranny.

The Enlightenment's emphasis on reason, natural rights, and the necessity of free expression provided the intellectual foundation for the First Amendment. The Founding Fathers, drawing on the writings of Locke, Voltaire, Montesquieu, and others, understood that a healthy democracy required the protection of speech, press, and religion. They believed that a government committed to liberty must protect these rights, not as favors granted by the state, but as fundamental elements of human dignity and freedom. This vision of liberty in action—where individuals could speak their minds, practice their faiths, and challenge authority—became the bedrock of American democracy, and it continues to shape the nation's understanding of freedom today.

The Road to Ratification: The Bill of Rights and the First Amendment

The path to ratifying the Bill of Rights, and in particular the First Amendment, was fraught with debate, compromise, and political maneuvering. While the Constitution established the framework of the new American government, it initially lacked specific guarantees of individual freedoms. The omission of these protections sparked intense concern among many citizens and political leaders who feared that a strong federal government could infringe upon their hard-won liberties. The demand for a Bill of Rights became a central issue in the ratification of the Constitution, and the eventual inclusion of the First Amendment marked a significant victory for those who sought to safeguard freedom of expression and other fundamental rights.

In the immediate aftermath of the Constitutional Convention in 1787, the battle lines were drawn between two opposing camps: the Federalists, who supported the new Constitution as it was written, and the Anti-Federalists, who demanded amendments to protect individual rights. The Federalists, including influential figures like Alexander Hamilton and James Madison, argued that the Constitution already provided sufficient checks on government power. They believed that since the government was designed to be one of limited powers, there was no need to explicitly list the rights of the people, as doing so might suggest that any unlisted rights were not protected.

However, the Anti-Federalists, led by men like Patrick Henry and George Mason, were deeply suspicious of centralized authority. They believed that without clear protections for freedoms like speech, press, religion, and assembly, the new government could easily become tyrannical. Many states, including Massachusetts, Virginia, and New York, expressed reluctance to ratify the Constitution unless it was accompanied by a promise to add a Bill of Rights. The Anti-Federalists were particularly concerned about the potential for government overreach in the realm of free expression, having lived through the years of British repression when speaking out against the Crown was met with harsh punishment.

The demand for a Bill of Rights grew louder during the ratification process. In state ratifying conventions, delegates from a wide range of political perspectives voiced their concerns that the new federal government could become as oppressive as the British monarchy if individual liberties were not explicitly protected. Several states only agreed to ratify the Constitution on the condition that amendments would be introduced to address these concerns. In Virginia, for instance, the Anti-Federalist Patrick Henry led the charge against ratification, warning that the federal government, with its power over the army, taxes, and trade, would inevitably infringe on the people's rights unless explicit safeguards were put in place.

James Madison, initially skeptical of the need for a Bill of Rights, eventually came to recognize its political necessity. As the push for ratification grew, he saw that adding protections for individual rights was crucial not only for securing the support of key states but also for ensuring the long-term legitimacy of the new government. Madison took up the cause of drafting amendments, drawing on a wide range of proposals from the states, as well as the principles enshrined in state constitutions and declarations of rights. His vision was to create a set of amendments that would protect the most fundamental freedoms, while avoiding the pitfalls of an overly detailed or restrictive list of rights.

In 1789, during the first session of the U.S. Congress, Madison introduced a series of amendments that would eventually become the Bill of Rights. He aimed to address the core concerns of the Anti-Federalists while maintaining the integrity of the Constitution. The proposed amendments focused on protecting individual liberties, including the freedom of speech, press, religion, and assembly, which were seen as essential to maintaining a free and democratic society.

The First Amendment, as drafted by Madison, was a response to the central concerns of the revolutionaries: that the government should never have the power to silence dissent, control the press, or impose a state-sponsored religion. It was designed to protect not only individual freedoms but also the broader principles of democracy by ensuring that the government would remain open to scrutiny and accountability. Madison believed that a free press and the ability to criticize the government were vital to preventing tyranny and preserving the republic.

The final text of the First Amendment reads: "Congress shall make no law respecting an establishment of religion, or prohibiting the free exercise thereof; or abridging the freedom of speech, or of the press; or the right of the people peaceably to assemble, and to petition the Government for a redress of grievances." In these few words, the Founders laid the foundation for a society in which individuals could speak their minds, practice their faith, and challenge their leaders without fear of retribution.

The process of ratifying the Bill of Rights was not without its challenges. Some members of Congress and state legislators continued to argue that the amendments were unnecessary or that they did not go far enough in protecting individual freedoms. Others believed that the Constitution itself was sufficient and that listing specific rights might open the door to endless legal disputes over the scope and application of these rights. Despite these objections, the Bill of Rights was ratified by the necessary number of states in December 1791, becoming the first ten amendments to the Constitution.

The inclusion of the First Amendment in the Bill of Rights was a historic moment, one that marked a decisive shift in the relationship between the government and the governed. It reflected the Founders' commitment to creating a system of government that would be responsive to the people and respectful of their fundamental rights. The ratification of the Bill of Rights, and particularly the First Amendment, was a victory for the Anti-Federalists and all those who had fought for explicit protections of individual liberties.

The First Amendment's protections of free speech, press, assembly, petition, and religion were groundbreaking in their scope. Unlike many other nations at the time, where governments tightly controlled the flow of information and restricted political dissent, the United States embraced a model in which the free exchange of ideas was not only tolerated but encouraged. The Founders understood that a vibrant democracy required an informed and engaged citizenry, and they believed that the best way to ensure this was by protecting the rights of individuals to speak their minds, publish their ideas, and gather in protest.

The road to ratification of the Bill of Rights, and the First Amendment in particular, was shaped by the experiences of the American Revolution and the philosophical currents of the Enlightenment. The Founders, influenced by the ideas of John Locke, Montesquieu, and other Enlightenment thinkers, believed that the protection of individual liberties was essential to the success of the new republic. They recognized that free speech and a free press were not mere privileges, but fundamental rights that would enable the people to hold their government accountable and participate fully in the democratic process.

The ratification of the First Amendment was the culmination of years of debate, struggle, and compromise. It enshrined in law the principles that had been at the heart of the American Revolution—the belief that individuals had the right to think, speak, and worship freely, and that the government should serve the people, not suppress them. This foundational amendment continues to be a cornerstone of American democracy, shaping the nation's identity as a land of liberty, where the free exchange of ideas is seen as essential to the pursuit of truth and justice.

CHAPTER 4

Chapter 2: Free Speech: The Foundation of Democrac

The Philosophy of Free Speech and Its Role in Democracy
The right to free speech is more than just a legal guarantee—it is the cornerstone of any functioning democracy, rooted in centuries of philosophical thought and debate. Its importance lies in the role it plays in fostering an environment where ideas can be freely exchanged, where individuals can question authority, and where society can progress through reasoned discourse. Free speech is not simply about allowing people to say what they want; it is about creating the conditions under which truth can emerge, power can be checked, and democratic principles can thrive. This understanding of free speech has been shaped by the work of philosophers, particularly during the Enlightenment, who argued that the freedom to express ideas was essential for human development, political freedom, and societal advancement.

One of the earliest and most influential philosophers to champion free speech was John Locke, whose ideas about natural rights laid the groundwork for modern liberal democracy. Locke argued that all individuals possess certain inalienable rights, including the right to life, liberty, and property. For Locke, liberty was not only the freedom to act but also the freedom to think and speak. He believed that government existed to protect these rights, and that any government that sought to suppress speech was overstepping its bounds. In Locke's view, free speech was a natural extension of personal liberty, necessary for individuals to explore ideas, debate with others, and contribute to the collective good of society.

Locke's ideas heavily influenced the development of the American Constitution, but the philosophical defense of free speech did not stop there. Another pivotal figure in the evolution of free speech was John Stuart Mill, a 19th-century philosopher who provided one of the most enduring arguments for the importance of free expression in his seminal work, *On Liberty* (1859). Mill argued that the free exchange of ideas is critical not only for individual development but also for the well-being of society as a whole. His famous "marketplace of ideas" concept suggests that in a free and open exchange, good ideas will ultimately prevail over bad ones. Mill warned that suppressing any viewpoint, no matter how unpopular or offensive, deprives society of the opportunity to challenge and refine its understanding of the truth.

Mill's argument was grounded in the belief that no individual or government can be certain of possessing the absolute truth. As such, every opinion, even those that seem misguided or wrong, has value because it forces others to think critically and defend their own views. This, Mill believed, is how truth emerges—not from the silencing of dissent but from the clash of competing ideas. In a society that values free speech, individuals are constantly engaged in this process of questioning, debating, and refining their understanding, which Mill saw as essential for intellectual and moral progress.

Another key figure in the defense of free speech was the French Enlightenment philosopher Voltaire. Voltaire was a fierce critic of religious and political authority, often facing persecution for his writings. Yet, he is famously credited with the quote, "I disapprove of what you say, but I will defend to the death your right to say it." While the attribution of this exact phrase to Voltaire is debated, it nonetheless encapsulates the spirit of his advocacy for free speech. Voltaire believed that the freedom to speak out against tyranny, injustice, and dogma was essential for the pursuit of truth and the advancement of human knowledge. His works inspired many of the revolutionary ideas that would shape modern democracies, including the belief that a society must allow dissenting voices to be heard, even if they are unpopular or controversial.

The central idea shared by these thinkers is that free speech is vital for democracy because it empowers individuals to think independently, challenge authority, and engage in public discourse. In a democratic society, the people are sovereign, and their ability to make informed decisions relies on access to a wide range of viewpoints. This is where the marketplace of ideas becomes particularly important. In an open society, individuals are free to express their thoughts, opinions, and criticisms, and through this exchange, ideas are tested, refined, and either accepted or rejected. The ability to critique those in power, to challenge the status quo, and to propose new ideas is essential for democratic governance.

This philosophical foundation underscores the role of free speech in maintaining a healthy democracy. Without the ability to freely express ideas, citizens cannot fully participate in the democratic process. Elections, public debates, and civic engagement all depend on the flow of information and the ability to discuss issues openly. If speech is restricted, so too is the people's power to hold their leaders accountable. The Founding Fathers of the United States, deeply influenced by these philosophical arguments, recognized the dangers of government censorship and enshrined the right to free speech in the First Amendment to protect against the rise of tyranny.

Furthermore, free speech serves as a check on government power. In democratic systems, governments derive their legitimacy from the consent of the governed. Free speech allows citizens to express their dissatisfaction, advocate for change, and demand accountability from their leaders. Without the freedom to speak, governments could operate without transparency, shielded from criticism, and insulated from the will of the people. History has shown time and again that authoritarian regimes, in their efforts to maintain power, often target free speech first, silencing dissenting voices to stifle opposition and control public discourse.

In addition to its political importance, free speech is also essential for personal autonomy. The ability to express oneself is tied to the development of one's identity and beliefs. People discover who they are, what they believe, and how they relate to others through the process of articulating their thoughts and engaging in dialogue. In this sense, free speech is not just about the exchange of ideas in the public sphere, but about the very essence of what it means to be human. It is a right that allows individuals to grow intellectually, morally, and socially.

In summary, the philosophy of free speech, as articulated by thinkers like John Locke, John Stuart Mill, and Voltaire, establishes its fundamental role in democracy. Free speech allows for the discovery of truth, the protection of individual liberty, and the prevention of tyranny. It ensures that democratic societies remain open, dynamic, and responsive to the needs and voices of their citizens. This intellectual tradition laid the groundwork for the First Amendment's protection of free speech, and it continues to influence the modern understanding of why free expression is indispensable to a thriving democracy.

Legal Foundations and Supreme Court Rulings on Free Speech

The First Amendment's guarantee of free speech is a cornerstone of American democracy, but its scope and limitations have been defined and refined over centuries, primarily through landmark Supreme Court rulings. While the text of the First Amendment is clear—"Congress shall make no law... abridging the freedom of speech"—it does not explicitly delineate what constitutes speech, nor does it specify which forms of speech are protected, limited, or restricted. It has fallen to the courts, and especially the Supreme Court, to interpret the extent of this fundamental right. The legal history of free speech in the United States is marked by a delicate balance between protecting individual expression and addressing concerns for national security, public order, and the prevention of harm.

The earliest interpretations of the First Amendment were limited. For much of the 19th century, the courts were hesitant to apply the First Amendment broadly. It wasn't until the early 20th century, during a period of heightened political tensions and World War I, that the Supreme Court began to engage seriously with cases involving free speech. One of the most pivotal early rulings was *Schenck v. United States* (1919), in which the Court introduced the "clear and present danger" test. This case arose when Charles Schenck, a socialist, was convicted under the Espionage Act of 1917 for distributing leaflets opposing the draft during World War I. Schenck argued that his conviction violated his First Amendment right to free speech, but the Supreme Court, in a unanimous opinion written by Justice Oliver Wendell Holmes, upheld the conviction.

Justice Holmes introduced the idea that speech could be restricted if it posed a "clear and present danger" to the country's interests, famously stating, "The most stringent protection of free speech would not protect a man in falsely shouting fire in a theatre and causing a panic." This ruling marked the first time the Court explicitly set limits on free speech, acknowledging that certain expressions could be curtailed if they threatened public safety or national security. The "clear and present danger" test became a key standard for determining when speech crossed the line from protected to unprotected.

In subsequent years, however, the Court began to adopt a more protective stance on free speech. A major shift occurred with *Brandenburg v. Ohio* (1969), which overturned the "clear and present danger" standard in favor of a stricter test known as the "imminent lawless action" standard. Clarence Brandenburg, a Ku Klux Klan leader, had been convicted under Ohio law for advocating violence in a speech at a Klan rally. The Supreme Court ruled in Brandenburg's favor, stating that the government could only restrict speech that was "directed to inciting or producing imminent lawless action" and was "likely to incite or produce such action." This ruling significantly narrowed the scope of speech that could be punished and set a higher bar for government interference in free expression.

The *Brandenburg* decision marked a crucial turning point in American free speech law, emphasizing that advocacy, even of unpopular or offensive ideas, was protected unless it directly incited immediate illegal activity. This ruling was rooted in the Court's growing recognition that free speech plays a vital role in the functioning of democracy, and that the suppression of speech—especially political speech—posed a greater threat to democratic institutions than the potential harms caused by allowing controversial or inflammatory rhetoric.

Throughout the 20th century, the Supreme Court continued to grapple with the boundaries of free speech, often in cases involving political dissent, artistic expression, and symbolic speech. In *Texas v. Johnson* (1989), the Court confronted the issue of whether flag burning constituted protected speech under the First Amendment. Gregory Lee Johnson had been convicted of desecrating a flag during a political protest at the 1984 Republican National Convention. Johnson argued that his act was a form of political expression, protected by the First Amendment, while the state of Texas maintained that flag burning was an act of public disorder and disrespect for a national symbol.

In a 5-4 decision, the Supreme Court sided with Johnson, ruling that flag burning, while deeply offensive to many, was a form of symbolic speech protected by the First Amendment. Justice William Brennan, writing for the majority, stated, "If there is a bedrock principle underlying the First Amendment, it is that the government may not prohibit the expression of an idea simply because society finds the idea itself offensive or disagreeable." This decision reaffirmed the Court's commitment to protecting even the most controversial forms of speech, recognizing that the suppression of symbolic acts could lead to broader restrictions on political expression.

Another significant ruling that expanded the scope of free speech was *New York Times Co. v. United States* (1971), often referred to as the "Pentagon Papers" case. In this case, the Nixon administration sought to prevent the *New York Times* and the *Washington Post* from publishing classified documents detailing the United States' involvement in the Vietnam War, arguing that the release of this information posed a threat to national security. The newspapers countered that the government was attempting to censor the press, violating the First Amendment's protection of freedom of the press. The Supreme Court ruled in favor of the newspapers, holding that the government had failed to meet the heavy burden of proof required for prior restraint—the suppression of material before it is published. The decision was a landmark victory for press freedom and underscored the importance of a free and independent media in holding the government accountable.

As the Supreme Court continued to refine the boundaries of free speech, it also addressed the question of whether certain categories of speech could be regulated without violating the First Amendment. For example, in *Chaplinsky v. New Hampshire* (1942), the Court ruled that "fighting words"—speech that is likely to incite immediate violence—are not protected by the First Amendment. This case arose when Walter Chaplinsky, a Jehovah's Witness, was convicted for calling a city marshal a "damned Fascist" during a public altercation. The Court held that certain categories of speech, including fighting words, obscenity, and libel, could be restricted without violating the Constitution because they did not contribute to the exchange of ideas or serve any essential function in democratic discourse.

However, even with these exceptions, the Supreme Court has consistently favored a broad interpretation of free speech protections. Cases like *Snyder v. Phelps* (2011) demonstrate the Court's ongoing commitment to safeguarding speech, even when it is deeply offensive to many. In *Snyder*, the Court ruled in favor of the Westboro Baptist Church, which had picketed the funeral of a U.S. Marine with signs bearing hateful messages. The Court held that while the speech was undoubtedly hurtful, it was related to matters of public concern and therefore protected under the First Amendment.

Through these rulings, the Supreme Court has built a robust legal framework that upholds the principle that free speech, particularly political speech, must be fiercely protected in a democratic society. While the Court has recognized certain limitations—such as incitement to violence, threats, and defamatory speech—the overwhelming trend in American jurisprudence has been to err on the side of protecting free expression, even when it is unpopular, offensive, or disruptive. This legal foundation reflects the belief that the free exchange of ideas, however contentious, is essential to the preservation of democracy, allowing individuals to engage in the kind of open debate that leads to a more informed and just society.

Free Speech and Social Movements: A Tool for Change

Free speech has long been one of the most powerful tools for social change, enabling marginalized voices to challenge injustice, protest inequality, and demand reforms. From the early days of abolitionism to the fight for civil rights, women's suffrage, LGBTQ+ rights, and beyond, the ability to speak freely has empowered individuals and movements to confront entrenched systems of power. Without the protection of free expression, many of the most transformative moments in American history would never have occurred. This chapter examines how free speech has fueled social movements and served as a catalyst for change, showing that the First Amendment is not just a legal guarantee but a vital instrument for democratic progress.

One of the earliest examples of free speech being used as a force for change was the abolitionist movement in the 19th century. Abolitionists, such as Frederick Douglass, William Lloyd Garrison, and Harriet Beecher Stowe, used their right to free speech to speak out against the horrors of slavery and to demand its abolition. At the time, speaking publicly against slavery was not only unpopular in many parts of the country, but it was also dangerous. Abolitionists were often met with violent opposition, censorship, and legal challenges, especially in the South. Yet, they persisted, using newspapers, pamphlets, speeches, and public gatherings to spread their message.

Frederick Douglass, a former slave who became one of the most eloquent voices of the abolitionist movement, understood the power of free speech better than most. His speeches, often delivered to hostile crowds, were not just a means of personal expression; they were a tool for moral suasion, designed to awaken the conscience of a nation. Douglass believed that the right to speak freely was indispensable to the struggle for justice, famously declaring, "Liberty is meaningless where the right to utter one's thoughts and opinions has ceased to exist." Through his words, Douglass was able to expose the brutality of slavery and argue for its abolition, demonstrating how free speech could be used to challenge the moral failings of society.

The women's suffrage movement also made powerful use of free speech to advance its cause. For decades, suffragists like Susan B. Anthony, Elizabeth Cady Stanton, and Sojourner Truth delivered speeches, organized rallies, and published writings advocating for women's right to vote. In a time when women were largely excluded from public and political life, the act of speaking out was itself a form of resistance. Suffragists faced intense opposition, with many critics arguing that women lacked the intellectual capacity for political participation. Yet, through the relentless exercise of free speech, suffragists were able to build a movement that ultimately succeeded in securing the passage of the 19th Amendment in 1920, granting women the right to vote.

Perhaps one of the most iconic examples of free speech fueling social change is the Civil Rights Movement of the 1950s and 1960s. Leaders like Martin Luther King Jr., Malcolm X, and John Lewis used their voices to challenge the systemic racism that had long oppressed Black Americans. King's speeches, in particular, are remembered for their rhetorical power and their ability to inspire both Black and white Americans to join the struggle for equality. His "I Have a Dream" speech, delivered during the 1963 March on Washington, is one of the most famous examples of free speech being used to advocate for justice. King understood that speech could move people to action, and he used his platform to not only articulate the goals of the movement but also to call for nonviolent resistance in the face of violent repression.

The Civil Rights Movement relied heavily on the First Amendment to protect the right to protest, assemble, and speak out against injustice. In *New York Times Co. v. Sullivan* (1964), the Supreme Court strengthened the protection of free speech in the context of civil rights activism. The case arose when a public official in Alabama sued the *New York Times* for libel after it published an advertisement criticizing the treatment of civil rights protesters. The Court ruled in favor of the *Times*, holding that public officials could not sue for libel unless they could prove that false statements had been made with "actual malice"—a difficult standard to meet. This ruling was a major victory for the Civil Rights Movement, as it ensured that activists and the press could freely criticize government officials without fear of legal retribution.

Another crucial aspect of the Civil Rights Movement was the role of symbolic speech. In cases like *Tinker v. Des Moines Independent Community School District* (1969), the Supreme Court expanded the definition of free speech to include nonverbal expression, such as wearing armbands or participating in sit-ins. The *Tinker* case arose when students in Des Moines, Iowa, were suspended for wearing black armbands to protest the Vietnam War. The Court ruled that the students' actions were protected by the First Amendment, stating that students do not "shed their constitutional rights to freedom of speech or expression at the schoolhouse gate." This decision affirmed that symbolic acts of protest, which had been central to the Civil Rights Movement, were just as deserving of protection as spoken or written words.

As the 20th century progressed, the LGBTQ+ rights movement emerged as another powerful example of free speech being used to fight for equality. From the early days of the Gay Liberation Front to the fight for marriage equality, activists used their voices to challenge laws and societal norms that discriminated against LGBTQ+ individuals. The Stonewall Riots of 1969, often considered the birth of the modern LGBTQ+ rights movement, were a spontaneous act of resistance against police harassment, but they were also a symbolic declaration of the right to exist, to love, and to speak out without fear of persecution.

In the decades that followed, LGBTQ+ activists continued to use free speech to push for change, often in the face of significant opposition. Public protests, court challenges, and advocacy through the media were all critical tools in advancing LGBTQ+ rights. The legal battles over same-sex marriage, culminating in the Supreme Court's decision in *Obergefell v. Hodges* (2015), were built on the foundation of free speech, as activists used public discourse to shift societal attitudes and build a legal case for equality. Without the protection of free speech, these movements might have been silenced before they could gain the momentum needed to achieve lasting change.

Today, the role of free speech in social movements remains as vital as ever. From the #MeToo movement, which has used social media as a platform to expose sexual harassment and assault, to the Black Lives Matter movement, which continues the fight for racial justice, free speech remains a powerful tool for those seeking to challenge injustice. The ability to speak out, to protest, to organize, and to share stories of oppression is essential for any movement that seeks to create meaningful change. Social movements thrive when individuals are free to express their discontent, articulate their visions for a better future, and mobilize others to join their cause.

In summary, free speech has been at the heart of every major social movement in American history. From abolitionism and women's suffrage to civil rights and LGBTQ+ equality, the right to speak out against injustice has been indispensable in the struggle for freedom and equality. Without the protections afforded by the First Amendment, many of the most significant advances in human rights and civil liberties might never have been realized. Free speech is not just a tool for individual expression—it is a force for collective action, enabling society to confront its failings and strive for a more just and equitable future.

The Marketplace of Ideas: Free Speech and Democratic Debate

One of the most enduring justifications for the protection of free speech is the idea of the "marketplace of ideas." This concept, which traces its roots to Enlightenment philosophy and was later embraced by the U.S. Supreme Court, holds that the best way to reach truth or societal progress is through the free exchange of ideas. In a democracy, this open competition of ideas allows for the most convincing, accurate, or valuable beliefs to prevail, while false or harmful ideas are exposed and discredited. The marketplace of ideas assumes that when individuals are free to express their opinions and debate those of others, society as a whole benefits from the diversity of perspectives and the wisdom that emerges from such exchanges.

The marketplace of ideas is rooted in the belief that no authority, whether government, religious institution, or social elite, should have the power to dictate what is true or acceptable. This philosophy can be traced back to thinkers like John Milton and John Stuart Mill, who argued that suppressing any opinion—whether true, false, or partially true—deprives society of an opportunity to learn. John Stuart Mill, in his influential work *On Liberty* (1859), asserted that even false opinions have value, because they force individuals to critically engage with their own beliefs and strengthen the arguments for the truth. Mill warned that silencing any voice, even one that seems erroneous or offensive, is a loss for society because it stifles the possibility of discovering new insights or correcting errors in prevailing views.

This philosophy of free speech as essential to the pursuit of truth was echoed by Justice Oliver Wendell Holmes Jr. in his famous dissent in *Abrams v. United States* (1919). Holmes argued that "the best test of truth is the power of the thought to get itself accepted in the competition of the market," thus articulating the idea that truth emerges through the process of debate and scrutiny. Holmes' vision of the marketplace of ideas as central to the democratic process has since become a bedrock principle of First Amendment jurisprudence, influencing countless decisions about the limits and protections of free expression.

The concept of the marketplace of ideas is especially important in the context of political speech, which the Supreme Court has long recognized as deserving of the highest level of protection. In a democracy, the ability to discuss, criticize, and challenge government policies, leaders, and institutions is essential for informed decision-making by the electorate. Without the freedom to express political opinions, citizens are unable to hold their government accountable or advocate for change. In fact, it is the protection of political speech that lies at the heart of the First Amendment. The framers of the Constitution understood that a free and open public discourse was necessary for a functioning democracy, where power is derived from the consent of the governed.

The importance of free speech in democratic debate can be seen in the role it plays during election campaigns. Candidates for public office rely on their ability to communicate their ideas, policies, and platforms to voters. In turn, voters must have the freedom to discuss, debate, and critique these ideas in order to make informed choices at the ballot box. The Supreme Court has repeatedly emphasized the centrality of free speech in the electoral process. In *Buckley v. Valeo*

(1976), the Court ruled that political spending, including campaign contributions, is a form of protected speech because it allows individuals and groups to advocate for candidates or causes they support. This decision underscored the idea that free speech is not only about spoken or written words but also about the ability to participate in the broader marketplace of ideas that shapes political discourse.

However, the marketplace of ideas is not without challenges. One of the most significant critiques of this theory is that it assumes an idealized version of public debate, where all participants have equal access to the means of expression and where the best ideas naturally rise to the top. In reality, disparities in wealth, power, and access to media platforms can skew the marketplace of ideas, allowing certain voices to dominate while others are marginalized or drowned out. For example, in modern American politics, corporate interests, wealthy individuals, and well-funded political action committees (PACs) often have disproportionate influence on public debate through their ability to finance advertising, lobbying, and other forms of political communication.

This inequality in the marketplace of ideas can distort democratic debate by giving certain viewpoints more visibility and credibility simply because they have more resources behind them. The rise of social media and digital platforms has both exacerbated and mitigated this issue. On the one hand, social media has democratized access to public discourse, allowing individuals who might not have had a platform in traditional media to express their views and connect with like-minded communities. Movements like #BlackLivesMatter, for instance, have gained significant momentum through grassroots activism on social media, challenging mainstream narratives about race and policing.

On the other hand, the digital marketplace of ideas has also given rise to new challenges, including the spread of misinformation, conspiracy theories, and hate speech. The decentralized nature of social media platforms makes it difficult to regulate the quality of information being shared, and algorithms that prioritize sensational or polarizing content can amplify false or harmful ideas. In this new digital age, the question arises: How can we ensure that the marketplace of ideas functions in a way that promotes truth and democratic deliberation without infringing on the fundamental right to free speech?

Despite these challenges, the underlying principle of the marketplace of ideas remains a powerful defense of free expression. The solution to bad speech, as the saying goes, is more speech—not censorship. The remedy for misinformation or harmful ideas is to counter them with better ideas, more accurate information, and reasoned debate. This approach, while imperfect, reflects the deep American commitment to free speech as the lifeblood of democracy. The alternative—government control over what can be said or heard—risks stifling the very diversity of thought that makes democratic deliberation possible.

Moreover, the marketplace of ideas is not just about reaching consensus or finding the "truth" in any absolute sense. It is also about fostering a culture of open inquiry, where dissent, debate, and even disagreement are seen as essential components of democratic life. The protection of free speech ensures that no idea is ever settled beyond challenge, that no orthodoxy can calcify without being subject to question, and that individuals retain the right to think for themselves. In this sense, the marketplace of ideas is not just about outcomes; it is about the process of democratic engagement itself.

In conclusion, the marketplace of ideas is a foundational concept in First Amendment theory, emphasizing the importance of free speech in promoting truth, fostering democratic debate, and safeguarding individual liberty. While the ideal of an open, fair, and equitable marketplace of ideas is difficult to achieve in practice, it remains a crucial guiding principle for American democracy. By allowing the free exchange of ideas, society ensures that it can continually evolve, adapt, and improve in the face of new challenges and changing circumstances. The health of any democracy depends on its willingness to protect free speech, even when the ideas expressed are controversial, unpopular, or uncomfortable. Only through this ongoing process of debate and dialogue can a democracy truly thrive.

Limits on Free Speech: Balancing Rights and Responsibilities

While the First Amendment guarantees the right to free speech, it is not an absolute right without limitations. Over the years, the courts have grappled with defining the boundaries of free expression, seeking to balance individual liberties with the broader need to protect public order, safety, and the rights of others. This delicate balancing act raises important questions: What kinds of speech should be restricted, if any? When does speech cross the line from protected expression into harmful conduct? Point 5 delves into the complex legal and philosophical debates surrounding the limits on free speech, exploring key court cases and the criteria used to determine when restrictions are warranted.

One of the most well-known and widely accepted limits on free speech is the prohibition against speech that incites violence or lawless action. This principle was famously articulated in *Brandenburg v. Ohio* (1969), a landmark Supreme Court case that established the "imminent lawless action" test. The case involved Clarence Brandenburg, a Ku Klux Klan leader, who had made inflammatory remarks during a rally, calling for "revengeance" against the government. He was convicted under Ohio's criminal syndicalism law, which prohibited advocating for violence as a means of political reform. However, the Supreme Court overturned his conviction, ruling that speech could only be restricted if it is "directed to inciting or producing imminent lawless action" and is "likely to incite or produce such action."

The *Brandenburg* ruling marked a significant shift from earlier decisions, such as *Schenck v. United States* (1919), which had applied a broader "clear and present danger" standard to limit speech. In *Schenck*, the Court had upheld the conviction of a socialist leader for distributing anti-draft leaflets during World War I, reasoning that his actions posed a clear and present danger to national security. Justice Oliver Wendell Holmes Jr., in his famous opinion, likened the speech to "falsely shouting fire in a theater and causing a panic," a phrase that continues to be cited when discussing the limits of free speech. However, the *Brandenburg* decision tightened the criteria for restricting speech, emphasizing the need for a direct and immediate connection between the speech and unlawful action. Today, this standard continues to serve as the primary test for determining whether speech that advocates violence is protected or not.

Another significant area where free speech is limited is in cases of defamation—false statements that harm the reputation of others. The balance between free speech and the protection of individuals' reputations has been shaped by key rulings like *New York Times Co. v. Sullivan* (1964). This case arose when the *New York Times* published an advertisement that criticized the actions of police in Alabama during the civil rights movement. L.B. Sullivan, a city commissioner in Montgomery, sued the newspaper for libel, claiming the ad contained factual inaccuracies. The Supreme Court ruled in favor of the *New York Times*, establishing the "actual malice" standard for defamation cases involving public figures. According to this ruling, public officials and public figures must prove that false statements were made with "actual malice"—that is, with knowledge of their falsity or reckless disregard for the truth. This heightened standard aims to protect robust debate about public officials and issues, ensuring that fear of defamation lawsuits does not chill free speech in political discourse.

However, the limits of defamation law have been tested in recent years, particularly with the rise of social media and the spread of misinformation. The challenge of balancing free expression with protecting individuals from reputational harm has become more complex as digital platforms allow for the rapid dissemination of information, true or false. Courts continue to grapple with how to apply defamation laws in a world where anyone can publish content to a global audience in seconds, and where the lines between public and private figures are increasingly blurred. These issues highlight the evolving nature of the free speech debate in the digital age.

Hate speech, another contentious issue, also tests the boundaries of free expression. The United States has taken a different approach to hate speech than many other democratic countries, where such speech is often criminalized. In the U.S., hate speech is generally protected under the First Amendment, unless it directly incites violence or constitutes harassment. The Supreme Court has consistently ruled that the government cannot restrict speech simply because it is offensive, disagreeable, or discriminatory. For example, in *R.A.V. v. City of St. Paul* (1992), the Court struck down a city ordinance that prohibited cross-burning and other forms of symbolic speech that could be seen as hate speech. The Court ruled that the ordinance was overly broad and content-based, as it prohibited certain types of speech based on their viewpoint. While acknowledging the hateful nature of the expression, the Court emphasized that the government could not ban speech based on its content without violating the First Amendment.

This strong protection of hate speech in the United States contrasts sharply with countries like Germany, France, and Canada, where hate speech laws prohibit expressions that promote racial, ethnic, or religious hatred. Proponents of U.S. law argue that allowing even hateful speech is essential to protecting the broader principle of free expression. They contend that suppressing offensive speech sets a dangerous precedent, potentially leading to the restriction of political dissent or minority viewpoints. Critics, however, argue that hate speech can cause real harm to individuals and communities, particularly those that are historically marginalized. The debate over whether hate speech should be limited or protected under the First Amendment remains a deeply divisive issue, reflecting the tension between protecting free expression and ensuring the dignity and safety of all individuals.

Another significant limit on free speech involves speech that is deemed obscene. Obscenity has long been excluded from First Amendment protection, but determining what constitutes obscenity has proven to be a difficult and subjective task. The Supreme Court's approach to obscenity was most clearly defined in *Miller v. California* (1973), which established the "Miller test." According to this test, speech can be considered obscene—and therefore not protected by the First Amendment—if it meets three criteria: (1) the average person, applying contemporary community standards, would find that the work appeals to prurient interests; (2) the work depicts or describes sexual conduct in a patently offensive way; and (3) the work, taken as a whole, lacks serious literary, artistic, political, or scientific value. The *Miller* test remains the standard for determining whether speech is obscene, but it is often criticized for its reliance on subjective community standards, which can vary widely across different regions of the country.

In the digital age, questions about obscenity and pornography have taken on new dimensions, particularly in the context of internet regulation. The rise of online pornography and the accessibility of explicit material to minors have raised concerns about how to regulate such content without infringing on free speech rights. Laws like the Communications Decency Act (CDA) and the Child Online Protection Act (COPA) have attempted to address these issues, but many provisions have been struck down by the courts as unconstitutional. The ongoing challenge is how to balance the need to protect children and other vulnerable populations from harmful content while respecting the right to free expression in a rapidly changing technological landscape.

In conclusion, while free speech is a fundamental right protected by the First Amendment, it is not without limits. The courts have long wrestled with the challenge of balancing the need for free expression with the need to protect public safety, individual rights, and societal order. Speech that incites violence, defames individuals, promotes hate, or is deemed obscene can, in certain circumstances, be restricted. Yet even as these limits are defined, the overarching principle remains that any restriction on free speech must be carefully scrutinized to ensure that it does not undermine the core values of a democratic society. The ongoing debates over the limits of free speech reflect the complexities of living in a pluralistic society, where the rights of individuals must be balanced with the responsibilities of citizenship and the common good.

CHAPTER 5

Chapter 3: The Freedom of the Press

Historical Foundations of Press Freedom
The freedom of the press, as enshrined in the First Amendment, is a cornerstone of American democracy. However, its origins stretch back to a time when the concept of an independent press was radical and dangerous. To understand the significance of press freedom today, we must explore its roots in colonial America and how it evolved from a tool of resistance against British oppression into a fundamental right protected by the U.S. Constitution.

In the 17th and 18th centuries, the British Crown tightly controlled the flow of information in the colonies. Newspapers and pamphlets were subject to licensing laws, which required government approval before they could be printed. This form of pre-publication censorship ensured that only content favorable to the British government could be legally disseminated. The Stamp Act of 1765, which imposed a tax on printed materials, further restricted the ability of colonists to circulate ideas freely. These measures were part of a broader strategy to maintain control over the colonies by stifling dissent and preventing the free exchange of ideas.

Despite these restrictions, colonial printers and pamphleteers played a crucial role in challenging British authority. One of the most famous early examples of resistance to press censorship was the trial of John Peter Zenger in 1735. Zenger, a printer for the *New York Weekly Journal*, was arrested and charged with seditious libel for publishing articles critical of the colonial governor, William Cosby. At the time, the law did not distinguish between truth and falsehood in cases of libel—any criticism of the government could be considered seditious. However, Zenger's lawyer, Andrew Hamilton, argued that the truth should be a defense against libel charges. In a landmark decision, the jury acquitted Zenger, establishing an important precedent for freedom of the press and the right to criticize government officials.

The Zenger case was a turning point, but it was only the beginning of the press's role in advocating for independence. As tensions between the colonies and Britain grew, pamphleteers like Thomas Paine became instrumental in shaping public opinion. Paine's *Common Sense*, published in 1776, was a fiery call for independence and a scathing critique of monarchical rule. Written in plain language, it was accessible to ordinary colonists and quickly became one of the most widely read and influential pamphlets of the American Revolution. Paine's work exemplified how the press could be used as a tool for political mobilization, spreading revolutionary ideas far and wide, and uniting disparate colonies in their fight for liberty.

The power of the press in colonial America extended beyond pamphlets and newspapers. Broadsides—large sheets of paper printed with proclamations, advertisements, or political messages—were posted in town squares, taverns, and churches, reaching audiences who might not have had access to more formal publications. These printed materials were critical in spreading news of events like the Boston Massacre and the Boston Tea Party, fueling anti-British sentiment and rallying support for the cause of independence.

As the American Revolution unfolded, the need for an independent press became even more apparent. The British government continued its attempts to suppress dissenting voices, using laws like the Sedition Act of 1798 to punish those who criticized its policies. However, the experience of colonial printers, who had fought against British censorship, laid the groundwork for the recognition of press freedom as a fundamental right. When the framers of the Constitution gathered in 1787, they were keenly aware of the role that an unfettered press had played in the fight for independence.

The inclusion of press freedom in the First Amendment was a direct response to the oppressive measures colonists had experienced under British rule. The founders understood that a free press was essential to safeguarding liberty, ensuring that citizens could criticize their government, advocate for change, and hold power to account. In drafting the Bill of Rights, they sought to protect the press from government interference, believing that a free and open exchange of ideas was vital to the functioning of a democratic society.

The historical foundations of press freedom in America are deeply intertwined with the struggle for independence and the broader fight against tyranny. The press was not just a passive recorder of events—it was an active participant in shaping public opinion, mobilizing resistance, and fostering a culture of dissent. The lessons learned from the colonial experience with censorship and repression continue to inform contemporary debates about the role of the press in society.

As we move forward, it is crucial to remember that the freedom of the press was hard-won, born out of a fierce determination to resist oppression and advocate for liberty. It remains one of the most important protections in the First Amendment, ensuring that the government remains accountable to the people and that the marketplace of ideas remains vibrant and open. Today, as we navigate the challenges of misinformation, digital media, and changing political landscapes, the historical foundations of press freedom serve as a reminder of the essential role that a free press plays in upholding democratic values.

The Watchdog Role of the Press in a Democracy

The press is often referred to as the "fourth estate," a term that underscores its essential role in safeguarding democracy. Alongside the three branches of government—executive, legislative, and judicial—the press serves as a vital check on power, holding officials and institutions accountable to the people. In a functioning democracy, the freedom of the press ensures that citizens have access to the information they need to make informed decisions, voice their concerns, and participate in the political process. This "watchdog" function of the press is perhaps its most critical role, one that has been central to preserving democratic governance throughout American history.

The power of the press to expose government corruption and malfeasance has been demonstrated time and again, most famously in the Watergate scandal of the 1970s. Reporters Bob Woodward and Carl Bernstein of *The Washington Post* uncovered a series of illegal activities linked to the Nixon administration, leading to President Richard Nixon's resignation. Their investigative journalism, which involved relentless fact-checking, anonymous sources, and deep investigative reporting, brought to light abuses of power that might have otherwise remained hidden from the public. Watergate is often cited as one of the most striking examples of the press acting as a watchdog, showing how essential a free press is to exposing wrongdoing at the highest levels of government.

The press's role as a watchdog is not confined to presidential scandals. At all levels of government, from local to federal, the press is instrumental in uncovering instances of corruption, waste, fraud, and abuse. In the 1950s, journalist Edward R. Murrow famously took on Senator Joseph McCarthy and his infamous anti-communist crusade, exposing McCarthy's tactics of fear and intimidation. Through his program *See It Now*, Murrow provided a platform for those who had been unjustly targeted by McCarthy's accusations, and his coverage helped shift public opinion against the senator's witch hunt. Murrow's courageous reporting is an enduring example of how the press can act as a counterbalance to unchecked political power, especially in times when fear and paranoia threaten to undermine democratic values.

One of the core principles of press freedom is the ability to investigate and report without fear of government reprisal. Without this protection, journalists would be less willing to take risks in pursuing stories that expose corruption or challenge those in power. The U.S. Supreme Court has repeatedly affirmed this principle, most notably in *New York Times Co. v. United States* (1971), commonly known as the Pentagon Papers case. In this landmark decision, the Court ruled that the government could not prevent the *New York Times* or *The Washington Post* from publishing classified documents revealing the U.S. government's misleading statements about the Vietnam War. The Court emphasized that prior restraint—government censorship before publication—was a direct violation of the First Amendment, reinforcing the press's right to publish information that is of public interest, even when the government wishes to keep it secret.

The Pentagon Papers case is a powerful illustration of how the press can shine a light on government deception and ensure that the public is not kept in the dark about critical issues. It also underscores the essential tension between government interests, such as national security, and the public's right to know. In this instance, the press fulfilled its role as a watchdog by providing the public with the truth about a war that had divided the nation and caused immense loss of life. By holding the government accountable for its actions, the press empowered citizens to make informed decisions about their country's involvement in Vietnam.

Beyond political corruption and government secrecy, the press also plays a watchdog role in exposing corporate malfeasance, environmental abuses, and social injustices. Investigative journalism has been key in bringing attention to issues that would otherwise be overlooked or ignored by those in power. For example, the Boston Globe's Spotlight team conducted a thorough investigation into sexual abuse within the Catholic Church, revealing decades of abuse and cover-ups by church officials. The reporting not only led to widespread public outrage but also spurred legal reforms and investigations across the globe. This type of journalism serves the public interest by holding powerful institutions accountable and ensuring that justice is pursued, regardless of the status or influence of the individuals or organizations involved.

The press's watchdog function is rooted in its ability to ask hard questions, scrutinize those in power, and expose uncomfortable truths. While politicians and institutions may prefer to operate without this level of scrutiny, it is essential for maintaining transparency and accountability in a democracy. When the press is free to investigate and report, it serves as a vital check on power, preventing abuses that could otherwise go unchecked.

However, the press's watchdog role has come under increasing pressure in recent years. The rise of digital media, the decline of traditional news outlets, and the proliferation of misinformation have made it more difficult for journalists to fulfill this critical function. Investigative journalism is resource-intensive and time-consuming, and as many news organizations face financial challenges, the resources dedicated to in-depth reporting have dwindled. At the same time, journalists themselves have come under attack, both physically and through lawsuits aimed at silencing critical reporting. These trends pose serious threats to the press's ability to serve as an effective watchdog in the digital age.

Despite these challenges, the press's role in defending democracy remains as important as ever. In a world where misinformation spreads rapidly and public trust in institutions is waning, the need for a vigilant, independent press is paramount. Journalists who continue to investigate, report, and expose wrongdoing are carrying forward the legacy of those who fought for press freedom in earlier eras. Their work ensures that power remains accountable to the people and that the ideals of democracy are protected from corruption and abuse.

The watchdog function of the press is not just a theoretical concept—it is an ongoing, dynamic process that plays out in real-time, often with profound consequences for society. By shining a light on injustice, exposing corruption, and holding those in power accountable, the press helps ensure that democracy remains vibrant and responsive to the needs of its citizens. Without a free and independent press, the people's ability to govern themselves would be significantly diminished, and the very foundations of democracy would be at risk.

Landmark Court Cases Defining Press Freedom

The freedom of the press, though guaranteed by the First Amendment, has been defined and refined through a series of landmark court cases that have tested its boundaries. These rulings have played a pivotal role in shaping how the press operates within the American legal system, clarifying the balance between the rights of the press and the interests of the government or individuals. Through these decisions, the judiciary has reinforced the notion that a free press is essential to a functioning democracy, even as it grapples with competing concerns like privacy, national security, and defamation.

One of the most significant cases in this area is *New York Times Co. v. Sullivan* (1964), a ruling that fundamentally changed the landscape of libel law in the United States. The case arose during the civil rights movement, when the *New York Times* published an advertisement that criticized the actions of the Montgomery, Alabama, police department. The ad contained some minor factual inaccuracies, which led L.B. Sullivan, the city's public safety commissioner, to sue for libel, claiming that the advertisement defamed him personally. In Alabama, libel laws at the time favored plaintiffs, and Sullivan was initially awarded a large sum in damages.

The case eventually made its way to the U.S. Supreme Court, where the justices faced a crucial question: How should libel laws apply to public officials, particularly in the context of political speech? The Court's decision was groundbreaking. It held that public officials cannot recover damages for defamatory statements related to their official conduct unless they can prove "actual malice"—that the statement was made with knowledge of its falsity or with reckless disregard for the truth. This ruling established a high bar for public figures to claim libel, thereby protecting the press from lawsuits that might otherwise chill free speech and open debate on important public issues.

New York Times Co. v. Sullivan set a powerful precedent that still resonates today. It acknowledged that errors are inevitable in journalism, especially when reporting on contentious political issues. The Court recognized that the threat of libel suits could discourage the press from performing its vital role in exposing government misconduct or discussing public officials' actions. By requiring proof of actual malice, the decision allowed for a more robust exchange of ideas, even if that exchange included harsh or inaccurate criticisms of those in power.

Another landmark case that helped define press freedom is *Near v. Minnesota* (1931). In this case, the state of Minnesota attempted to prevent the publication of a newspaper that was accused of being "scandalous" and "defamatory." The paper, *The Saturday Press*, was known for publishing stories that accused local officials of corruption, often without substantiating its claims. The state used a law known as the "gag law" to obtain an injunction that effectively shut down the newspaper, preventing it from publishing any further issues.

When the case reached the U.S. Supreme Court, the justices ruled that the Minnesota law constituted an unconstitutional prior restraint on publication. In a decision that would become a cornerstone of First Amendment jurisprudence, the Court held that, except in extremely rare circumstances (such as matters of national security), the government could not prevent the press from publishing information. This ruling established the principle that the press has the right to publish freely without fear of censorship or preemptive government interference, affirming that prior restraint is incompatible with the values of a free and open society.

The *Near v. Minnesota* ruling has been cited in numerous subsequent cases as a key defense against attempts to censor or silence the press. One of the most famous applications of this principle came in *New York Times Co. v. United States* (1971), also known as the Pentagon Papers case. In this instance, the *New York Times* and *The Washington Post* obtained classified documents from the Department of Defense detailing the U.S. government's involvement in the Vietnam War. The documents, known as the Pentagon Papers, revealed that the government had misled the public about the progress and conduct of the war over several administrations.

When the newspapers began publishing stories based on the documents, the Nixon administration sought a court order to stop further publication, arguing that it would harm national security. The case was fast-tracked to the Supreme Court, which issued a 6-3 ruling in favor of the newspapers. The Court held that the government had failed to meet the heavy burden of proof required to justify prior restraint, ruling that the vague assertion of national security concerns could not override the First Amendment's protection of press freedom. This decision reinforced the principle that the government cannot silence the press simply to avoid embarrassment or prevent public scrutiny of its actions.

Together, these landmark cases—*New York Times Co. v. Sullivan*, *Near v. Minnesota*, and *New York Times Co. v. United States*—have established critical legal protections for the press. They ensure that journalists can investigate and report on government actions without fear of unwarranted legal reprisals. These rulings protect not just the rights of journalists, but the rights of all citizens to receive information about their government and to engage in informed debate.

However, the tension between press freedom and other societal interests remains a constant source of legal and political debate. For example, national security concerns continue to challenge the boundaries of press freedom. While the Pentagon Papers case was a victory for the press, modern whistleblower cases—such as those involving Edward Snowden and Chelsea Manning—have reignited debates about the limits of press freedom when it comes to classified information.

Similarly, the rise of the internet and social media has introduced new questions about defamation, misinformation, and the role of the press in an increasingly decentralized media environment. As courts continue to navigate these challenges, the foundational principles established in these landmark cases will remain central to the ongoing struggle to balance the rights of the press with other important societal values.

Ultimately, the legal framework established by these cases underscores the profound importance of an independent press in a democracy. By providing protections against prior restraint and unreasonable libel claims, the courts have upheld the vital role that the press plays in informing the public, promoting transparency, and holding those in power accountable.

The Challenges of Press Freedom in the Digital Age

As the world transitions into the digital era, the nature of journalism and press freedom has transformed in ways that both expand and threaten the traditional role of the press. The advent of the internet, social media, and new forms of digital media has created unprecedented opportunities for information dissemination and citizen engagement. However, these developments have also posed serious challenges to the press's ability to maintain its role as a reliable source of news, a watchdog over power, and a guardian of truth. The digital age has redefined the boundaries of press freedom, forcing societies to reconsider how to balance this essential right with the complexities of modern technology.

One of the most significant shifts in the digital age is the democratization of information. In the past, the press primarily consisted of established institutions like newspapers, magazines, and broadcast networks, which operated within a clearly defined legal and ethical framework. Today, anyone with an internet connection can publish and distribute information to a global audience. Platforms like Twitter, Facebook, YouTube, and independent blogs have empowered individuals to become "citizen journalists," providing alternative perspectives and filling gaps left by traditional media. This democratization has its advantages: marginalized voices that were once ignored by the mainstream press now have platforms to share their stories, and independent journalists can break stories that large news organizations might overlook.

However, the rise of digital media has also led to new challenges in maintaining journalistic standards and credibility. With the collapse of the gatekeeping function that traditional media once held, the internet has become a fertile ground for the spread of misinformation and disinformation. Unlike established news outlets, which are bound by editorial standards and fact-checking processes, many online sources operate without such constraints. The result is a proliferation of "fake news," conspiracy theories, and false information that can spread rapidly through social media algorithms designed to prioritize engagement over accuracy. This phenomenon has eroded public trust in the press, as many people struggle to distinguish between credible journalism and false narratives.

The problem is compounded by the business model that drives much of digital media. In the age of the internet, advertising revenue—once the lifeblood of newspapers and TV stations—has shifted dramatically to tech giants like Google and Facebook. These platforms rely on user-generated content to drive traffic, using sophisticated algorithms to curate what people see based on their behavior and preferences. The emphasis on clickbait headlines and sensational stories, which generate higher engagement and, therefore, more advertising dollars, has further undermined the integrity of online journalism. Traditional news outlets, facing declining revenues, have had to adapt to these pressures by cutting back on investigative reporting, which is resource-intensive and costly, or by chasing viral content to stay relevant.

The loss of revenue and the pressure to produce faster, more engaging content has created what some have called a "crisis of journalism." Newsrooms across the country have downsized, local newspapers have shuttered, and the quality of investigative journalism has suffered as resources dwindle. This decline in local news is particularly concerning because local journalists play a crucial role in covering city councils, school boards, and local courts—issues that may not make national headlines but have a direct impact on citizens' lives. The weakening of local journalism has created information deserts in many parts of the country, leaving communities without the scrutiny and accountability that a free press provides.

Another significant challenge to press freedom in the digital age is the rise of government surveillance and the targeting of journalists who report on sensitive issues. While the internet has made it easier for journalists to gather and share information, it has also made them more vulnerable to surveillance by both governments and private actors. Investigative journalists who work on stories related to national security, whistleblowers, or corruption often find themselves subject to state-sponsored hacking, intimidation, or even arrest. For example, Edward Snowden's revelations about the National Security Agency's (NSA) mass surveillance program raised concerns about the extent to which governments monitor not just their own citizens but also the communications of journalists. In many cases, such surveillance efforts are justified under the banner of national security, but they can have a chilling effect on press freedom, discouraging reporters from pursuing sensitive stories.

The digital landscape has also blurred the lines between platforms and publishers. While social media platforms claim to be neutral intermediaries, their role in shaping public discourse has placed them at the center of debates about press freedom and regulation. Section 230 of the Communications Decency Act, a U.S. law passed in 1996, grants platforms like Facebook and Twitter immunity from liability for the content users post. This law has allowed tech companies to grow exponentially without being held responsible for harmful or false information spread on their platforms. However, critics argue that these platforms wield enormous power over the flow of information and that their algorithms can amplify harmful content, distort public perception, and undermine democratic debate.

In response to these challenges, there have been calls for greater regulation of tech companies and more accountability for the spread of misinformation online. Proposals range from reforming Section 230 to creating new legal frameworks that would require platforms to take more responsibility for the content they host. At the same time, media literacy has become an increasingly important issue, as citizens must learn to navigate a complex and often misleading information ecosystem. The ability to critically assess sources, verify facts, and recognize bias is more important than ever in an era when misinformation can spread with the click of a button.

Despite these challenges, the digital age also offers new opportunities for press freedom. Investigative journalism has found new life on platforms like ProPublica, which uses nonprofit funding to support in-depth reporting that traditional news outlets may not have the resources to pursue. Crowdsourced journalism projects and collaborative investigations between newsrooms across the globe have produced groundbreaking stories, such as the Panama Papers, which exposed offshore tax havens used by the global elite. The internet allows for greater reach and impact, enabling important stories to transcend borders and hold powerful actors accountable on a global scale.

In conclusion, the digital age presents both extraordinary challenges and opportunities for press freedom. The internet has fundamentally changed the way journalism is produced, consumed, and distributed, often in ways that erode the press's traditional role as a reliable source of information and a watchdog over power. However, as the media landscape continues to evolve, the core principles of press freedom—the right to report without fear of censorship, intimidation, or reprisal—remain as vital as ever. To navigate these challenges, societies must find ways to protect the press while addressing the new realities of the digital world, ensuring that journalism can continue to serve its essential function in a democracy.

Global Perspectives on Press Freedom: Lessons and Challenges

As we reflect on the role of press freedom in the United States, it's important to recognize that the challenges and opportunities facing journalism are not unique to one country. Around the world, the struggle for press freedom is both a universal battle and one shaped by local contexts. In some nations, the press enjoys robust protections similar to those found in the United States, while in others, journalists risk imprisonment, violence, or death for doing their jobs. Examining global perspectives on press freedom provides valuable lessons and highlights the importance of defending this fundamental right at home and abroad.

One country that has become emblematic of the fight for press freedom is Turkey. Once considered a rising democracy, Turkey has seen a dramatic decline in press freedom over the past decade. Under the leadership of President Recep Tayyip Erdoğan, the government has systematically clamped down on independent media outlets, imprisoning journalists, shuttering newspapers, and tightening control over the internet. In 2016, following a failed coup attempt, the Erdoğan government declared a state of emergency, during which hundreds of journalists were arrested, and dozens of media organizations were closed. Those who remain have faced intimidation and the constant threat of prosecution under anti-terrorism laws, which are often used to silence critics of the government. Turkey's situation underscores how fragile press freedom can be in countries where democratic institutions are weakened, and how essential it is for the press to resist authoritarian pressures.

In contrast, nations like Finland and Norway consistently rank among the top in global press freedom indices. These countries benefit from a culture of transparency, robust legal protections for journalists, and a high level of trust in the media. In Finland, the constitution explicitly protects freedom of expression and the press, and the government actively promotes media literacy among its citizens. The country's legal framework ensures that journalists can report on sensitive issues without fear of reprisal, and there is a strong emphasis on editorial independence. The media in Finland also benefits from financial models that allow for high-quality journalism without the same level of reliance on advertising revenue that has led to sensationalism in other parts of the world. These countries demonstrate that strong legal protections, combined with a societal commitment to press freedom, can foster an environment in which the media thrives as a pillar of democracy.

However, not all democratic countries share the same level of press freedom. In India, the world's largest democracy, press freedom has come under increasing strain in recent years. While the Indian press has a long tradition of investigative journalism and public accountability, the current political climate has become more hostile to critical reporting. Journalists investigating sensitive topics such as corruption, religious violence, or environmental issues have faced lawsuits, online harassment, and even physical attacks. India's defamation laws, which allow for criminal prosecution, have been used to stifle dissent, and the rise of populist nationalism has led to an environment where independent media are often labeled as "anti-national" or "enemies of the state." The situation in India highlights the complex relationship between democracy, nationalism, and press freedom, and how easily political pressures can threaten the independence of the media.

In authoritarian regimes like China and Russia, the press operates under the constant shadow of state control. In China, the government exerts tight control over the flow of information, employing sophisticated surveillance technologies and censorship to shape public discourse. The Great Firewall, a comprehensive system of internet censorship, blocks access to foreign news sources and restricts social media platforms that could be used to organize dissent. Chinese journalists who challenge the official narrative or report on politically sensitive topics face imprisonment, forced confessions, or worse. The Chinese government also exerts significant influence over international media, using economic leverage to pressure foreign journalists and media organizations to self-censor critical reporting. In Russia, the situation is similarly bleak, with independent journalists and media outlets facing constant harassment, state interference, and violence. Under President Vladimir Putin, the Russian government has consolidated control over major media outlets, and journalists who investigate corruption, human rights abuses, or government malfeasance have been subject to physical attacks, imprisonment, or even assassination.

These examples of press repression are stark reminders of how fragile press freedom can be, even in countries that claim to respect human rights. The international community has responded to these threats in various ways, from diplomatic pressure to sanctions, but progress has been slow. Organizations like Reporters Without Borders and the Committee to Protect Journalists continue to advocate for press freedom around the world, shining a spotlight on abuses and providing support to journalists operating in hostile environments. Their work is a testament to the fact that the struggle for a free press is a global one, and it requires constant vigilance and solidarity.

Despite the challenges, there are inspiring stories of journalists around the world who continue to fight for press freedom, often at great personal risk. In countries like Mexico, which is one of the most dangerous places in the world to be a journalist due to drug cartel violence, reporters continue to expose corruption, human rights abuses, and organized crime. In countries across Africa, where press freedom is often constrained by authoritarian governments, journalists have used digital platforms to bypass state-controlled media and share stories that would otherwise go untold. These journalists embody the spirit of the First Amendment, demonstrating that the fight for truth and accountability transcends borders.

The global perspective on press freedom also underscores the interconnectedness of media in today's world. Information flows across borders, and the challenges facing journalists in one country can have ripple effects elsewhere. For example, the rise of disinformation campaigns, often orchestrated by state actors, has shown that threats to press freedom are not confined by geography. The weaponization of information—through fake news, deepfakes, or coordinated misinformation campaigns—poses a serious threat to democracies around the world, including the United States. Defending press freedom in the digital age means recognizing that the battle is not just a domestic one but a global one, requiring cooperation and a commitment to truth across nations.

Ultimately, the lessons from around the world remind us that press freedom is not a given—it is something that must be fought for, protected, and nurtured. While the United States enjoys some of the strongest legal protections for the press, it is not immune to the pressures that have eroded press freedom elsewhere. The global struggle for press freedom underscores the importance of vigilance in defending these rights at home and abroad. A free press is a cornerstone of democracy, not just in the United States but everywhere, and its defense is a universal cause that demands the attention of all who value truth, accountability, and liberty.

CHAPTER 6

Chapter 4: The Right to Assemble

The Historical Roots of Assembly Rights

The right to assemble, like many of the freedoms guaranteed by the First Amendment, has deep historical roots that trace back to the earliest days of democratic governance. Long before the United States came into existence, the concept of public assembly was already recognized as a fundamental element of civic life. It allowed people to gather, exchange ideas, and voice their collective concerns. This principle would become essential to the development of the United States, serving as a cornerstone of democratic participation during the colonial era and later solidified in the U.S. Constitution.

One of the most significant influences on the American understanding of the right to assemble comes from English common law. In medieval England, the Crown viewed large public gatherings with suspicion, associating them with rebellion and disorder. As a result, the right to gather was tightly controlled, with assemblies needing royal approval or facing punishment. However, over time, political theorists and legal scholars in England began to argue that the ability of citizens to gather peaceably was essential for a healthy society.

These ideas gradually filtered into colonial America, where settlers sought to exercise their natural rights, including the right to assemble and petition the government for redress of grievances.

In the American colonies, public assemblies became a critical means of organizing political resistance against British rule. Early examples of assembly in action can be found in the town hall meetings of New England, where citizens gathered to debate local issues and challenge colonial authorities. These gatherings were often spontaneous and informal, allowing colonists to voice their frustrations and coordinate their efforts. As tensions with Britain escalated, assemblies became more formalized, playing a key role in organizing opposition to unpopular policies like the Stamp Act and the Townshend Acts. The famous Stamp Act Congress of 1765, for instance, saw representatives from various colonies come together to craft a unified response to British taxation, demonstrating the power of collective assembly to resist tyranny.

Perhaps the most iconic example of assembly rights during this period is the Boston Tea Party of 1773. In defiance of British laws, colonists assembled to protest the Tea Act, which granted the British East India Company a monopoly on tea imports. The assembly of angry colonists, disguised as Mohawk Indians, boarded British ships and dumped tea into Boston Harbor in an act of political defiance. While technically illegal, this gathering would come to symbolize the spirit of protest and resistance that defined the American Revolution. Events like the Boston Tea Party underscored the importance of the right to assemble as a tool for citizens to express dissent and organize against oppression.

The importance of assembly rights was further demonstrated in the creation of the Continental Congresses. The First Continental Congress in 1774 and the Second Continental Congress in 1775 were both critical assemblies of colonial leaders who convened to debate how to respond to British aggression. These congresses led to the coordination of boycotts, the establishment of a Continental Army, and eventually the drafting of the Declaration of Independence. The ability to assemble was not merely a practical tool for organizing rebellion; it was seen as a fundamental right, essential to the colonies' ability to shape their future and resist authoritarian rule.

By the time the Constitution was drafted in 1787, the importance of the right to assemble was clear to the founders. Having experienced firsthand the power of collective action and the need for citizens to gather peacefully, the framers of the Constitution ensured that this right would be protected for future generations. The Bill of Rights, ratified in 1791, included the right to assemble as part of the First Amendment, cementing its place in American law and culture. It reads: "Congress shall make no law respecting an establishment of religion, or prohibiting the free exercise thereof; or abridging the freedom of speech, or of the press; or the right of the people peaceably to assemble, and to petition the Government for a redress of grievances."

The inclusion of assembly rights in the First Amendment reflected the founders' belief that democracy depends on the ability of citizens to gather, share ideas, and challenge the government. They understood that a free society must allow people to come together peacefully to express their views, whether in support of or opposition to government policies. For the founders, this was not merely an abstract principle but a lived experience, born out of the assemblies that had helped shape the nation's fight for independence.

In summary, the right to assemble in the United States has deep historical roots, tracing back to English common law and gaining critical importance during the American Revolution. The colonists' use of assemblies to resist British rule and organize the push for independence demonstrated the essential nature of this right in a democratic society. By enshrining the right to assemble in the First Amendment, the founders ensured that future generations would have the freedom to gather, voice their opinions, and challenge those in power. This right remains a foundational element of American democracy, reflecting the belief that the power of collective action is central to the preservation of liberty and justice.

Assembly and Social Movements: The Power of Collective Action

The right to assemble has not only been a historical cornerstone of American democracy but also a driving force behind some of the most transformative social and political movements in U.S. history. From the abolitionist movement to civil rights, labor activism, and women's suffrage, the power of collective action has been pivotal in pushing forward reforms that have shaped the nation. These movements harnessed the right to assemble as a vital tool for organizing protests, raising awareness, and forcing the government to confront issues of injustice and inequality.

One of the earliest and most significant examples of assembly rights in action was the abolitionist movement. Beginning in the early 19th century, a diverse coalition of activists, including former slaves, religious leaders, and political reformers, came together to demand an end to slavery. The right to assemble was crucial in allowing abolitionists to hold public meetings, organize rallies, and distribute literature that exposed the horrors of slavery. Anti-slavery gatherings, like the annual conventions of the American Anti-Slavery Society, gave voice to the growing demand for emancipation and provided a platform for leaders such as Frederick Douglass and William Lloyd Garrison to advocate for immediate abolition. These assemblies not only fostered solidarity among abolitionists but also put immense pressure on lawmakers, paving the way for the eventual passage of the 13th Amendment, which abolished slavery in 1865.

Similarly, the women's suffrage movement relied heavily on the right to assemble to challenge the exclusion of women from the political process. Beginning in the mid-19th century, women's rights activists gathered in towns and cities across the country to advocate for the right to vote. One of the most famous assemblies in American history, the Seneca Falls Convention of 1848, was a groundbreaking moment for the women's movement. Organized by activists like Elizabeth Cady Stanton and Lucretia Mott, this assembly marked the first formal demand for women's suffrage and produced the Declaration of Sentiments, which outlined the ways in which women were being denied basic rights. The convention was a watershed event, galvanizing the movement and inspiring future generations of suffragists. Over the decades, suffragists continued to assemble for marches, rallies, and conventions, including the massive 1913 Woman Suffrage Procession in Washington, D.C. These gatherings were instrumental in building public support for the cause, culminating in the passage of the 19th Amendment in 1920, granting women the right to vote.

The labor movement is another powerful example of how the right to assemble has been used to fight for justice and improve working conditions. In the late 19th and early 20th centuries, American workers faced grueling hours, dangerous working conditions, and inadequate wages. The labor movement, spearheaded by organizations like the American Federation of Labor (AFL) and the Industrial Workers of the World (IWW), used public assemblies to demand better conditions and fair pay. Strikes, picket lines, and mass demonstrations became central to the movement's strategy, allowing workers to show solidarity and leverage their collective power against employers. One of the most famous labor assemblies in U.S. history was the 1886 Haymarket Rally in Chicago, which initially began as a peaceful gathering of workers advocating for an eight-hour workday. Though it tragically ended in violence, the Haymarket affair became a symbol of the struggle for labor rights and helped galvanize support for the labor movement. Over time, these assemblies and the collective action they represented led to significant labor reforms, including the establishment of the eight-hour workday and the recognition of workers' rights to organize and bargain collectively.

The civil rights movement of the 1950s and 1960s offers perhaps the most iconic example of how the right to assemble can serve as a vehicle for social change. From the Montgomery Bus Boycott to the March on Washington, civil rights activists used public assemblies to demand an end to racial segregation and discrimination. The movement's leaders, including Martin Luther King Jr., understood the power of peaceful assembly in drawing attention to the injustices faced by African Americans. One of the defining moments of the movement was the 1963 March on Washington for Jobs and Freedom, where over 250,000 people gathered at the Lincoln Memorial to call for civil and economic rights. It was here that King delivered his historic "I Have a Dream" speech, a powerful call for racial equality and justice that reverberated across the nation. The march and other mass assemblies of the era played a critical role in pressuring lawmakers to pass landmark legislation, including the Civil Rights Act of 1964 and the Voting Rights Act of 1965.

Nonviolent resistance and civil disobedience were key strategies used by both the civil rights and labor movements. These assemblies were not just about raising awareness; they were designed to confront and disrupt systems of power. The Greensboro sit-ins of 1960, where African American college students assembled at a segregated Woolworth's lunch counter, is a prime example of how peaceful assembly can challenge oppressive laws. By refusing to leave, the students sparked a nationwide sit-in movement that forced businesses to reconsider their discriminatory practices. Similarly, the labor strikes of the early 20th century often involved workers occupying factories and other workplaces, demanding better conditions from within the very systems they sought to reform.

Throughout these movements, the right to assemble provided a critical space for marginalized voices to be heard. Assemblies allowed individuals to gather, share their stories, and develop strategies for advocacy. They were also a way to build communities of resistance, where people could find strength and solidarity in their collective struggle for justice. The success of these movements illustrates the transformative power of assembly rights, which allow ordinary citizens to stand together and demand change.

In summary, the right to assemble has been a driving force behind many of the most important social movements in American history. Whether fighting for the abolition of slavery, women's suffrage, labor rights, or civil rights, activists have relied on collective action to challenge oppression and push for progress. The ability to gather, peacefully protest, and advocate for change is essential to democracy, and it continues to empower movements for justice and equality in modern times. As history shows, when people come together, their voices can shape the future of the nation.

The Legal Limits of Assembly: Balancing Freedom and Order

While the right to assemble is a fundamental liberty enshrined in the First Amendment, it is not without its limits. Throughout American history, courts and lawmakers have had to grapple with how to balance the public's right to gather with the need to maintain peace, safety, and order. This tension has resulted in a body of laws and legal precedents that shape the boundaries of assembly rights, defining where, when, and how people can gather. The legal limits of assembly often revolve around issues of public safety, national security, and the rights of others, reflecting the complex interplay between individual freedoms and the collective well-being of society.

One of the earliest and most important cases regarding the limits of assembly rights was *Cox v. New Hampshire* (1941). In this case, a group of Jehovah's Witnesses organized a peaceful parade without obtaining a required permit, arguing that the permit requirement violated their First Amendment rights. The Supreme Court ruled against them, upholding the permit requirement and establishing the principle that governments have the authority to regulate the time, place, and manner of public assemblies, as long as the regulations are content-neutral. This ruling clarified that while the right to assemble is protected, it is subject to reasonable restrictions designed to prevent chaos and maintain public order.

The concept of time, place, and manner restrictions is now a cornerstone of assembly law. These regulations allow the government to impose limits on when and where assemblies can occur and what methods participants can use, provided the restrictions do not target the content of the assembly itself. For example, requiring permits for parades or large gatherings ensures that city officials can coordinate logistics, such as traffic management and public safety measures, without infringing on the message or purpose of the event. However, any restrictions must be applied fairly and uniformly to all groups, regardless of the content of their speech or the cause they advocate.

Another significant limit on assembly rights involves the use of public versus private spaces. The First Amendment guarantees the right to assemble in public spaces such as parks, streets, and sidewalks, but it does not extend to private property. This means that protesters cannot simply gather on private land without the owner's consent. In cases where assembly takes place on public property, the government can impose restrictions to prevent disruption to the regular use of that space. For example, a large demonstration on a busy street may require rerouting traffic or limiting the duration of the protest to avoid major disruptions to daily life. Courts have generally upheld these types of restrictions as long as they are applied equally to all groups and do not disproportionately target specific political viewpoints.

The tension between assembly rights and public safety becomes particularly pronounced during times of national crisis or heightened security concerns. For example, during the early 20th century, the U.S. government imposed significant restrictions on assemblies in response to labor strikes, wartime protests, and communist gatherings. The Espionage Act of 1917 and the Sedition Act of 1918, passed during World War I, gave the government broad authority to suppress assemblies deemed to be harmful to national security or public morale. These laws were used to crack down on antiwar protests and labor strikes, leading to the arrest and imprisonment of activists who were exercising their right to assemble. The Supreme Court upheld many of these restrictions at the time, reflecting the prevailing view that national security could outweigh individual freedoms during periods of crisis.

In the landmark case of *Edwards v. South Carolina* (1963), the Supreme Court reaffirmed the importance of protecting peaceful assemblies, even in the face of public opposition. In this case, a group of African American students had gathered on the steps of the South Carolina State House to protest racial segregation. When the peaceful assembly drew an angry crowd of counter-protesters, police ordered the students to disperse, claiming they were disturbing the peace. When the students refused, they were arrested. The Supreme Court overturned their convictions, ruling that the state had violated their First Amendment rights by dispersing a peaceful assembly without just cause. This case established that the mere presence of hostile opposition or the potential for public unrest is not enough to justify breaking up a peaceful protest.

However, the line between peaceful assembly and disruptive or violent conduct is often difficult to define, especially when assemblies escalate into civil disobedience or unrest. The government can place additional restrictions on assemblies that involve unlawful activities, such as trespassing, vandalism, or violence. In such cases, the authorities have the legal right to disperse the gathering and arrest those involved in illegal acts. The challenge lies in ensuring that the government's response is proportional and that peaceful protesters are not unfairly targeted. Law enforcement agencies have sometimes been criticized for using excessive force or broad dispersal orders that affect both peaceful demonstrators and those engaged in unlawful activities.

The legal framework surrounding assembly rights has evolved to address modern challenges as well. For instance, courts have had to consider how technology and social media affect the dynamics of public gatherings. Digital platforms now play a significant role in organizing protests and assemblies, often allowing movements to gather massive crowds with little notice. While the right to assemble remains protected, governments are grappling with how to regulate the use of digital tools to organize large-scale events that can potentially overwhelm public infrastructure. In some cases, authorities have attempted to shut down internet access or social media platforms during protests, raising new questions about the intersection of free speech, assembly, and digital rights.

In summary, while the right to assemble is a cornerstone of American democracy, it is not an absolute freedom. The government has the authority to impose reasonable limits on assemblies to protect public safety, ensure the rights of others, and maintain order. The key legal principle is that any restrictions must be content-neutral, meaning they cannot discriminate based on the message or viewpoint of the assembly. Over the years, courts have carefully navigated the tension between protecting assembly rights and allowing for reasonable regulations, ensuring that this vital freedom remains balanced with the broader needs of society. As new challenges arise, the legal framework surrounding assembly rights will continue to evolve, ensuring that this essential liberty adapts to the changing dynamics of democratic participation.

The Role of Peaceful Assembly in Democracy: Civic Engagement and Social Change

The right to assemble is not just a constitutional guarantee; it is a vital mechanism for civic engagement and the pursuit of social change. Throughout history, peaceful assembly has served as a catalyst for democratic participation, allowing individuals and communities to express their grievances, advocate for reforms, and hold those in power accountable. It is a tool that gives voice to the voiceless, empowering ordinary citizens to unite around a common cause and make their concerns heard in the public sphere. In this way, peaceful assembly functions as both a form of free expression and a critical component of a healthy, functioning democracy.

At the heart of peaceful assembly is the idea that democracy thrives when citizens actively participate in public life. The founders of the United States understood this principle well. They recognized that a government "of the people, by the people, and for the people" depends on an engaged citizenry willing to debate ideas, petition the government, and gather to protest injustices. The right to assemble, therefore, was not viewed as a mere privilege but as an essential element of democratic governance. It is through assemblies that citizens can come together, exchange ideas, and collectively advocate for their rights and interests.

One of the most important functions of peaceful assembly is its ability to shine a spotlight on issues that might otherwise be ignored. In many cases, marginalized or disenfranchised groups have used assemblies to draw attention to their struggles and demand recognition from society and the government. For example, the early labor movement in the United States relied heavily on public demonstrations to highlight the harsh conditions faced by workers in factories and mines. Without the ability to gather and protest, the plight of these workers might have remained invisible to those in power. By assembling in the streets, laborers forced the nation to confront the urgent need for reform, leading to the eventual establishment of labor rights and workplace protections.

Similarly, peaceful assemblies have played a key role in advancing civil rights and social justice throughout American history. The civil rights movement, in particular, demonstrates the power of peaceful protest to bring about meaningful change. Through sit-ins, marches, and rallies, African Americans and their allies were able to challenge deeply entrenched systems of racial segregation and discrimination. The 1965 Selma to Montgomery marches, led by figures like Martin Luther King Jr. and John Lewis, are a powerful example of how peaceful assembly can mobilize public support for a cause. The sight of thousands of men, women, and children marching for voting rights—and the violent response they faced from law enforcement—galvanized public opinion and led to the passage of the Voting Rights Act later that year.

The March on Washington in 1963 is another iconic moment in American history that illustrates the transformative potential of peaceful assembly. As over 250,000 people gathered at the Lincoln Memorial to demand racial and economic justice, the march became a symbol of the power of collective action. Martin Luther King Jr.'s "I Have a Dream" speech, delivered during this assembly, has since become one of the most famous speeches in history, capturing the aspirations of a nation longing for equality and freedom. The success of the civil rights movement demonstrates that peaceful assembly can serve as a powerful instrument for social change, offering a platform for marginalized communities to assert their rights and challenge oppressive structures.

Peaceful assemblies also play a crucial role in giving citizens a means to directly interact with their government. Public protests and demonstrations allow individuals to bypass traditional political channels, such as elections or lobbying, and directly communicate their demands to those in power. This form of direct action can be especially important when the normal political process seems unresponsive to the concerns of certain groups. When elected officials fail to address issues of injustice, peaceful assembly provides an alternative avenue for citizens to make their voices heard. This was evident during the women's suffrage movement, as activists used marches, rallies, and picketing to pressure the government to grant women the right to vote. In a political system that had excluded them for decades, these assemblies provided a way for women to assert their political power and force the issue of suffrage onto the national agenda.

The role of peaceful assembly in democracy is also evident in more recent movements. The Black Lives Matter (BLM) protests, which gained prominence following the police killings of unarmed African Americans, are a contemporary example of how assemblies can bring attention to systemic injustice. The nationwide demonstrations that erupted in 2020, after the murder of George Floyd, were some of the largest in U.S. history. These peaceful assemblies brought millions of people together to demand police reform, racial justice, and accountability for acts of violence against African Americans. The protests not only highlighted the pervasiveness of police brutality but also spurred important discussions about race, inequality, and the need for systemic change in America. While some gatherings were marred by clashes with law enforcement, the overwhelming majority of these assemblies were peaceful, underscoring the continued relevance of peaceful protest as a tool for advancing civil rights in the modern era.

Peaceful assemblies have the unique ability to create a sense of solidarity among participants, fostering a shared identity and sense of purpose. When people gather to protest or demonstrate, they are often united by a common cause or goal, whether it is fighting for labor rights, racial justice, or environmental protection. This collective experience can be empowering, offering individuals the reassurance that they are not alone in their struggles. For many participants, the act of assembly is not just a political statement but a form of community building. It creates a space where individuals can come together, share their experiences, and build a movement that is greater than the sum of its parts. In this way, peaceful assemblies not only serve as a platform for advocacy but also as a means of fostering civic engagement and empowering individuals to take an active role in shaping their society.

At its core, the right to assemble is about more than just gathering in public spaces—it is about the power of ordinary citizens to influence the course of history. By coming together in peaceful assemblies, individuals can challenge injustice, advocate for change, and hold their government accountable. This right is essential to the functioning of democracy because it ensures that the voices of the people—especially those who are marginalized or silenced—can be heard. Peaceful assembly is a reminder that in a democracy, power ultimately rests with the people, and through collective action, they can shape the future of their nation.

In conclusion, peaceful assembly plays a vital role in democracy by providing a platform for civic engagement and social change. Throughout history, assemblies have been a powerful tool for marginalized communities to advocate for their rights and push for reforms. Whether through labor strikes, civil rights marches, or modern-day protests, the ability to gather and peacefully express grievances is a fundamental aspect of democratic participation. In a society that values freedom and justice, the right to assemble must be protected as a means of ensuring that the voices of the people can always be heard.

Modern Challenges and the Future of Assembly Rights

As society evolves and the methods of organizing and protesting change, the right to assemble faces new and complex challenges. While the basic principles of assembly remain rooted in the First Amendment, the landscape of public protest has been dramatically transformed by technological advancements, shifting political climates, and increasing tensions around public safety. In the 21st century, the right to assemble must contend with both new opportunities and emerging threats, as the digital age, heightened security concerns, and social fragmentation reshape the ways people come together to express their grievances and advocate for change.

One of the most significant changes affecting the right to assemble is the rise of digital platforms and social media as tools for organizing. Platforms like Twitter, Facebook, and Instagram have revolutionized how protests are mobilized, making it easier for people to connect, share information, and plan demonstrations on a large scale. The Arab Spring uprisings, which began in 2010, are a prime example of how social media can be used to organize mass protests. Activists in Tunisia, Egypt, and other Middle Eastern countries used platforms like Facebook and Twitter to call for demonstrations, share real-time updates, and amplify their messages to a global audience. Similarly, the Black Lives Matter movement has utilized social media to coordinate protests, share stories of injustice, and build a decentralized yet powerful coalition of activists advocating for racial justice.

While digital platforms have expanded the reach and impact of assemblies, they have also introduced new challenges. Governments and law enforcement agencies now monitor social media for signs of upcoming protests, sometimes using this information to preemptively disrupt or restrict assemblies. In some cases, internet shutdowns or platform blackouts have been used as a tactic to prevent protesters from organizing. This raises important questions about the role of digital rights in relation to assembly rights. If the right to assemble is fundamental to democratic participation, then limiting access to digital tools used for organizing could be seen as an infringement on that right. Courts and lawmakers will likely need to address these issues as digital activism continues to grow in prominence.

Another modern challenge facing assembly rights is the increasing militarization of law enforcement and the use of heavy-handed tactics to control protests. In recent years, there has been growing concern about the use of military-grade equipment, such as tear gas, rubber bullets, and armored vehicles, to disperse peaceful assemblies. The 2020 Black Lives Matter protests, which followed the killing of George Floyd, saw widespread use of these tactics by police forces across the United States. While law enforcement agencies argue that such measures are necessary to maintain public order, critics contend that they often escalate tensions and lead to unnecessary violence. The images of peaceful protesters being met with tear gas and baton charges during these demonstrations have sparked debates about the appropriate use of force in policing assemblies. These confrontations highlight the delicate balance between maintaining public safety and respecting the constitutional right to peaceful assembly.

The question of what constitutes "peaceful" assembly has also become more complicated in recent years, as some protests have seen a mix of peaceful demonstrators and individuals engaging in acts of violence or vandalism. This blurring of the lines between peaceful protest and unlawful activity poses a challenge for both protesters and law enforcement. The vast majority of demonstrators may be peaceful, but the actions of a few can lead to a disproportionate response from authorities, resulting in the dispersal of entire assemblies. For example, during the 2020 protests, some cities experienced instances of looting and property damage, which were often used to justify aggressive police actions against otherwise peaceful crowds. The challenge lies in distinguishing between those exercising their lawful right to protest and those who engage in criminal behavior, without infringing on the broader right to assemble.

In addition to these practical concerns, the political climate in many countries has become increasingly polarized, which poses another challenge to the right to assemble. Public protests are often seen as inherently political acts, and as divisions in society deepen, assemblies can become flashpoints for conflict. Counter-protests, in which opposing groups gather in response to a protest, are becoming more common, leading to the risk of violent clashes. The 2017 Unite the Right rally in Charlottesville, Virginia, where white supremacists and counter-protesters violently confronted one another, is a stark example of how assemblies can devolve into violence in a highly charged political atmosphere. This polarization creates a dilemma for law enforcement, which must ensure that both sides are allowed to assemble peacefully while preventing violence. As political tensions continue to rise, the potential for assemblies to be exploited by extremist groups or devolve into violent confrontations will remain a challenge.

Despite these obstacles, peaceful assembly remains a powerful tool for social change, and there are encouraging signs that the future of this right can adapt to modern challenges. Grassroots movements continue to find innovative ways to gather and protest, even in the face of repression or restrictions. The rise of decentralized movements, such as Occupy Wall Street or the Women's March, demonstrates how technology and flexible organizing strategies can help overcome traditional barriers to assembly. In these movements, leadership is often diffuse, and organization occurs organically through social media and other digital platforms, allowing protests to grow quickly and respond to changing circumstances. These new forms of assembly are harder to suppress because they do not rely on a centralized leadership or a specific location, making them more resilient in the face of government crackdowns.

Additionally, legal protections for assembly rights have evolved alongside these changes. In some instances, courts have reaffirmed the importance of protecting the right to assemble, even in the face of modern challenges. The U.S. Supreme Court has generally taken a protective stance toward peaceful assemblies, recognizing their importance in democratic life. However, the ongoing debate over how far those protections extend, particularly in the context of digital rights and public safety concerns, will continue to shape the future of assembly law. As new legal precedents are set and the landscape of protest continues to evolve, courts will need to navigate the delicate balance between protecting assembly rights and addressing legitimate concerns about security and order.

Looking ahead, the right to assemble will likely face continued challenges, but its importance in democratic societies cannot be overstated. In an increasingly interconnected world, where citizens are more empowered than ever to organize and advocate for change, the right to assemble remains a crucial means of holding governments accountable and pushing for progress. From the streets to the digital sphere, assemblies will continue to be a fundamental expression of free speech and civic engagement, driving social movements and influencing public policy.

In conclusion, the future of assembly rights is shaped by both modern challenges and new opportunities. While technology, political polarization, and public safety concerns present obstacles, the resilience of grassroots movements and evolving legal protections offer hope that the right to assemble will remain a powerful force for social change. As societies continue to confront issues of inequality, injustice, and governance, the ability to gather and protest peacefully will remain a vital tool for advancing democracy and ensuring that the voices of the people are heard.

CHAPTER 7

Chapter 5: The Freedom to Petition the Government

The Historical Roots of Petitioning

The right to petition the government for a redress of grievances has deep historical roots, stretching back centuries before it was enshrined in the First Amendment of the U.S. Constitution. Petitioning was one of the earliest methods by which ordinary citizens could voice their concerns and seek justice from those in power, long before the advent of modern democratic institutions. This tradition, born in the medieval English legal system, provided the framework for what would eventually become a core tenet of American democracy.

In England, the right to petition was formally recognized in the Magna Carta of 1215, a historic document that limited the powers of the monarchy and established certain legal protections for English barons. Among its many provisions, the Magna Carta affirmed the right of individuals to appeal to the king for the redress of grievances. Over the centuries, this right expanded beyond the nobility, allowing common citizens to submit petitions to the government, parliament, or the crown. Petitioning became a vital avenue for addressing injustice, especially in an era when most people had little say in government. For the powerless, it was one of the few legal means available to confront the powerful.

By the 17th century, petitioning had become a significant part of English political life, particularly during times of political upheaval. The English Civil War (1642-1651), which pitted Parliament against King Charles I, saw widespread use of petitions as a way for the people to express their political allegiances and demand change. In the aftermath of the Glorious Revolution of 1688, the right to petition was formally guaranteed in the English Bill of Rights of 1689. This document not only laid the foundation for constitutional monarchy in England but also explicitly acknowledged the right of citizens to petition the monarch without fear of reprisal. Petitioning, therefore, became a symbol of the people's ability to influence the actions of their government, even in a system where most had no direct representation.

As British subjects, the American colonists inherited this tradition of petitioning. Throughout the colonial period, petitioning served as a key means by which colonists voiced their discontent with British rule. From local issues, such as disputes over land and taxes, to larger political grievances, colonists regularly petitioned British authorities to address their concerns. In the years leading up to the American Revolution, petitioning took on an increasingly central role as tensions between the colonies and the British government escalated.

One of the most famous examples of colonial petitioning occurred in 1774 when the First Continental Congress drafted the Petition to the King. In this document, colonial leaders outlined their grievances regarding British taxation and interference in colonial governance, calling on King George III to intervene on their behalf. The petition was an attempt to resolve the growing conflict through peaceful, legal means, reflecting the colonies' continued hope for reconciliation with the British Crown. However, the petition was ignored, further fueling colonial resentment and pushing the colonies closer to revolution.

The failure of petitions like the Petition to the King demonstrated the limitations of petitioning under a government that refused to recognize the rights and concerns of its subjects. For many colonists, this rejection underscored the need for independence and self-governance. As a result, when the Founding Fathers drafted the U.S. Constitution, they ensured that the right to petition would be protected as part of the broader framework of individual liberties. Enshrined in the First Amendment, the right to petition the government for a redress of grievances became a cornerstone of the new American democracy.

The importance of petitioning in early America cannot be overstated. In a time when voting rights were limited to a small segment of the population—primarily white male property owners—petitioning provided a critical means for others to participate in the political process. Women, slaves, and other marginalized groups frequently used petitions to advocate for their rights and seek redress from the government. The right to petition thus served as an important check on government power, allowing citizens to hold their leaders accountable and push for social and political change.

In the early years of the republic, petitioning remained a popular and effective tool for civic engagement. From petitions advocating for the abolition of slavery to those calling for women's suffrage, the right to petition allowed citizens to engage directly with their government. By exercising this right, ordinary Americans could influence the legislative process, ensuring that their voices were heard in the halls of power. Even those without the right to vote could petition their government, using this tool to challenge injustice and demand equal treatment under the law.

The historical roots of petitioning illustrate its significance as a means of democratic participation. What began as a privilege granted by monarchs in medieval England evolved into a powerful tool for citizens to engage with their government and advocate for change. In the context of American history, petitioning has played a crucial role in shaping the nation's political and social landscape, allowing individuals and groups to push for reforms that have fundamentally altered the course of the country's development. As the United States grew and its democratic institutions expanded, the right to petition remained a vital element of its constitutional framework, ensuring that the government remained responsive to the needs and concerns of its people.

The Constitutional Guarantee and Its Interpretation

The right to petition the government for redress of grievances, enshrined in the First Amendment, is one of the most fundamental guarantees in the U.S. Constitution. It represents the formal acknowledgment that citizens have the right to challenge their government, demand accountability, and seek remedies for injustice. Alongside freedoms of speech, religion, the press, and assembly, the right to petition underscores the First Amendment's commitment to protecting civic engagement and democratic participation.

In drafting the First Amendment, the Founding Fathers were mindful of the lessons from British rule, where petitions had been disregarded and dissent was often met with force. The early American experience, particularly the failure of colonial petitions like the Petition to the King, solidified the belief that a government should be accountable to its people. The inclusion of the right to petition in the Constitution was not merely symbolic; it was an essential guarantee that citizens would always have a voice in their government, even in the face of injustice or corruption.

While the right to petition was clearly outlined in the First Amendment, its interpretation and scope were not fully defined until later judicial rulings clarified its application. In early American history, the right to petition was understood to be a broad one, encompassing both written requests to the government and public demonstrations aimed at influencing lawmakers. However, as the country evolved, questions about the boundaries of this right arose, particularly regarding how far the government was obligated to respond to petitions and the extent to which citizens could challenge government actions without fear of reprisal.

One of the first significant cases to address the right to petition was *United States v. Cruikshank* in 1876. In this case, the U.S. Supreme Court ruled that the First Amendment, including the right to petition, only applied to the federal government and not to state governments. This decision underscored the limited scope of First Amendment protections at that time, placing many petitioners at the mercy of state governments, which were not bound by the same constitutional guarantees. However, the ruling also reaffirmed that citizens had the right to petition their government without fear of retaliation—a critical safeguard for those challenging government authority.

Another landmark case in the evolution of petition rights was *De Jonge v. Oregon* (1937). In this case, the Court extended First Amendment protections, including the right to petition, to state governments through the incorporation doctrine, which applied certain provisions of the Bill of Rights to the states via the Fourteenth Amendment. *De Jonge* involved a peaceful assembly organized by a communist group, and the Court held that the state's suppression of this assembly violated the group's right to petition.

This case was crucial in establishing the principle that state governments, like the federal government, could not infringe on a citizen's right to petition for redress.

As the right to petition became more firmly established, courts also had to address the question of what obligations the government had in responding to petitions. While the First Amendment guarantees the right to petition, it does not explicitly require the government to act on every petition it receives. This distinction became an important point of debate in subsequent legal challenges. In some cases, petitioners argued that the government's failure to respond to or acknowledge petitions constituted a violation of their rights. However, courts have generally ruled that while citizens have the right to petition, the government is not necessarily required to provide a specific response or remedy. Instead, the right to petition ensures that citizens can express their grievances without interference or punishment from the state.

One of the clearest modern interpretations of the right to petition came in the 1985 case *Minnesota State Board for Community Colleges v. Knight*. In this case, the Supreme Court ruled that while individuals have the right to petition the government, they do not have the right to compel the government to listen or respond to those petitions. The ruling reaffirmed that the First Amendment protects the act of petitioning itself but does not impose a duty on government officials to engage with or act on those petitions. This decision, while controversial, clarified the limits of the right to petition, emphasizing that it is a right to be heard, not necessarily a right to a guaranteed outcome.

Despite these limitations, the right to petition remains a powerful tool for influencing government policy. Throughout American history, petitions have played a significant role in shaping legislative action and social reforms. Even when the government does not provide a direct response, petitions often serve as catalysts for broader public debates, generating attention for issues that may have been overlooked or ignored by lawmakers. The mere act of petitioning can mobilize public support and place pressure on elected officials to address the concerns raised by their constituents.

The right to petition has also been closely linked to other First Amendment freedoms, particularly freedom of speech and assembly. Petitioning is often part of a larger effort to advocate for change, and it is common for petitioners to use public demonstrations, media campaigns, and lobbying efforts to amplify their message. In many ways, the right to petition complements these other rights, providing a formal mechanism for citizens to engage with their government. It allows individuals and groups to take their concerns directly to those in power, whether through written petitions, public hearings, or other forms of direct communication with lawmakers.

Moreover, the right to petition has been a vital tool for marginalized groups seeking to address systemic injustices. From abolitionists petitioning against slavery in the 19th century to civil rights activists petitioning for voting rights and desegregation in the 20th century, the right to petition has empowered those who were often excluded from the traditional political process. By petitioning the government, these groups were able to highlight their grievances and demand action, even when they lacked the political power to influence elections or legislation directly.

In conclusion, the right to petition, as enshrined in the First Amendment, stands as a fundamental guarantee of democratic participation. Through judicial interpretation and historical practice, this right has been shaped into a powerful tool for citizens to challenge their government and seek justice. While the government is not always obligated to respond to petitions, the act of petitioning itself remains a cornerstone of civic engagement, ensuring that the voices of the people can be heard. Whether through written appeals, public demonstrations, or digital campaigns, the right to petition continues to play a crucial role in holding the government accountable and fostering a responsive democracy.

Petitioning in Practice: Examples from U.S. History

The right to petition has been one of the most vital tools in the American democratic process, used by citizens from all walks of life to advocate for social change, challenge unjust laws, and press for government action. Throughout U.S. history, some of the most significant political movements have relied on petitions as a key strategy to promote their causes. From the abolition of slavery to the fight for women's suffrage and labor rights, petitioning has been instrumental in shaping the nation's legal and social landscape.

One of the earliest and most powerful examples of petitioning in the United States was the abolitionist movement, which sought to end the institution of slavery. By the 1830s, the practice of submitting petitions to Congress became a central tactic of abolitionists, who inundated lawmakers with thousands of petitions demanding the immediate abolition of slavery in the nation's capital and throughout the country. These petitions were often signed by ordinary citizens—both black and white—who were deeply opposed to the brutality of slavery. Women, in particular, played a prominent role in organizing petition campaigns, collecting signatures and mobilizing communities to confront lawmakers.

The sheer volume of petitions submitted by abolitionists became impossible for Congress to ignore. By 1836, so many petitions were being submitted that pro-slavery members of Congress passed the so-called "gag rule," a procedural rule that automatically tabled any petition related to slavery without debate or consideration. This rule, which was renewed several times, represented a blatant attempt to silence the growing movement against slavery. However, the gag rule only intensified the abolitionists' resolve. Leaders like John Quincy Adams, the former president who had returned to Congress, became fierce opponents of the gag rule, arguing that it violated the constitutional right to petition. Adams, who presented hundreds of abolitionist petitions in defiance of the rule, ultimately succeeded in getting it repealed in 1844.

The abolitionist petition campaigns not only raised public awareness of the evils of slavery but also helped to lay the groundwork for the eventual emancipation of enslaved people in the United States. These petitions demonstrated the power of ordinary citizens to engage directly with their government, even in the face of powerful opposition, and to persistently push for justice over time. The right to petition proved to be a critical weapon in the battle to end one of the darkest chapters in American history.

Another powerful example of petitioning in practice is the women's suffrage movement. Throughout the 19th and early 20th centuries, suffragists used petitions as a means of pressuring state and federal governments to grant women the right to vote. Much like the abolitionists before them, suffragists organized petition drives across the country, collecting millions of signatures in support of their cause. These petitions were often delivered to state legislatures or Congress, where they served as concrete evidence of the widespread public demand for women's suffrage.

One of the most notable petitioning efforts in the suffrage movement occurred in 1878 when leaders of the National Woman Suffrage Association, including Susan B. Anthony and Elizabeth Cady Stanton, presented a petition to Congress urging the passage of a constitutional amendment granting women the right to vote. Although the amendment failed to pass at that time, the petitioning effort persisted for decades, culminating in the ratification of the 19th Amendment in 1920. The suffragists' use of petitions not only helped to keep the issue of women's voting rights on the national agenda but also galvanized supporters, demonstrating the ability of a determined movement to bring about profound change through peaceful means.

In addition to these social movements, labor rights advocates also relied heavily on petitioning throughout the 19th and 20th centuries. As industrialization transformed the American economy, workers across the country began to organize and petition for better wages, safer working conditions, and the right to unionize. Labor unions frequently used petitions as a way to present their demands to employers and lawmakers, often backed by mass demonstrations and strikes. These petitions played a key role in the passage of landmark labor legislation, such as the Fair Labor Standards Act of 1938, which established minimum wage and overtime pay protections for American workers.

The power of petitioning is perhaps most evident in moments when it serves as a vehicle for marginalized groups to assert their rights and seek justice from the government. In the 1950s and 1960s, the civil rights movement, led by figures such as Martin Luther King Jr. and Rosa Parks, used petitioning as part of their broader strategy to challenge racial segregation and discrimination. Civil rights activists submitted petitions to local, state, and federal governments demanding an end to Jim Crow laws, voter suppression, and police brutality. These petitions, often accompanied by peaceful protests and legal challenges, helped to generate public pressure for the passage of civil rights legislation, including the Civil Rights Act of 1964 and the Voting Rights Act of 1965.

Even in more recent history, petitioning has continued to be a powerful tool for change. The environmental movement of the late 20th and early 21st centuries used petitions to call attention to issues such as climate change, deforestation, and pollution. Environmental advocacy groups, like Greenpeace and the Sierra Club, launched petition drives aimed at pressuring the government to enact stronger environmental protections and to hold corporations accountable for environmental degradation. These petitions, often bolstered by scientific evidence and public opinion, have played a critical role in shaping environmental policy, from the creation of the Environmental Protection Agency (EPA) in 1970 to the signing of international climate agreements.

Petitions have also become a cornerstone of efforts to address social and economic inequality in recent decades. Movements such as Occupy Wall Street and the Fight for $15 have used petitioning to raise awareness about income inequality and to push for higher wages and better working conditions for low-wage workers. These petitions have helped to build momentum for legislative initiatives, such as raising the minimum wage and expanding worker protections.

The history of petitioning in the United States is one of persistence, creativity, and determination. From the abolition of slavery to the expansion of voting rights, from labor protections to civil rights, petitioning has been a key mechanism by which citizens have engaged with their government and sought to shape the course of history. While not every petition results in immediate change, the cumulative impact of these efforts has been profound. Petitioning has not only given voice to the voiceless but has also served as a critical check on government power, ensuring that the demands of the people remain at the forefront of the democratic process.

In conclusion, petitioning in practice has proven to be a powerful instrument for social change in American history. It has empowered citizens to challenge injustice, advocate for their rights, and demand action from their government. Whether fighting for the abolition of slavery, the right to vote, or better working conditions, petitioners have left an indelible mark on the nation's legal and social fabric, proving that even in the face of opposition, the right to petition can be a catalyst for justice and progress.

Petitioning in the Digital Age

The evolution of technology has transformed how people engage with the right to petition. In the past, petitioning involved gathering physical signatures, submitting paper documents to government offices, and mobilizing communities through local networks and public meetings. However, with the rise of the internet and digital platforms, the act of petitioning has entered a new era, one defined by speed, accessibility, and reach. The digital age has fundamentally altered how citizens exercise their First Amendment right to petition, enabling millions of people to participate in the democratic process from their homes, workplaces, or even mobile phones.

One of the most visible developments in the digital age has been the proliferation of online petition platforms. Websites like Change.org, Avaaz, and MoveOn.org have become powerful tools for activists and everyday citizens to organize, promote, and share petitions with a global audience. These platforms allow users to create petitions on a wide variety of topics, from local issues such as neighborhood zoning to global concerns like climate change and human rights violations. Once a petition is created, it can be shared across social media networks, email lists, and other online platforms, exponentially increasing its visibility.

Online petitions have democratized access to the right to petition. In the past, organizing a petition drive required time, resources, and often access to specific social networks. Gathering signatures might involve door-to-door canvassing or setting up booths at public events. Today, anyone with an internet connection can start a petition, often with little more than a few clicks. This ease of access has empowered people from all walks of life to participate in civic engagement. Voices that might have been marginalized or ignored in traditional petitioning efforts are now able to reach vast audiences. A single petition, if compelling enough, can garner millions of signatures from around the world within days.

One example of the impact of digital petitions can be seen in the case of Trayvon Martin, an unarmed African American teenager who was shot and killed in Florida in 2012. In the wake of the incident, Martin's family created a petition on Change.org calling for the arrest of the man responsible, George Zimmerman, who had not initially been charged. The petition quickly went viral, collecting more than 2 million signatures. The massive public outcry, fueled in part by this online petition, led to Zimmerman's eventual arrest and trial, drawing attention to issues of racial profiling and justice that had been largely overlooked by mainstream media at the time.

Similarly, the #MeToo movement, which began as a social media campaign, also saw the use of digital petitions to hold powerful individuals and institutions accountable for sexual harassment and assault. Survivors of harassment and assault, empowered by the collective strength of their voices, used online platforms to demand action against perpetrators, leading to investigations, resignations, and policy changes across various industries. The digital petitioning efforts in this movement highlighted the power of online platforms to amplify voices that had long been silenced by societal norms and institutional barriers.

The digital age has also enabled petitions to transcend national borders, allowing people to petition governments, organizations, and corporations around the world. Global campaigns, such as those calling for action on climate change, animal rights, and humanitarian crises, have used online petitions to create transnational movements. For example, in 2014, a petition on Avaaz called for a ban on the ivory trade to protect endangered elephants. The petition garnered over 1.4 million signatures from people across the globe, helping to pressure governments and international organizations to take stronger action against poaching and the illegal ivory trade.

However, while digital petitions have expanded the reach and accessibility of petitioning, they have also raised questions about their effectiveness. Critics argue that many online petitions, particularly those with millions of signatures, can become little more than symbolic gestures—"clicktivism" or "slacktivism"—that fail to lead to meaningful action or change. Signing an online petition, while easy, often requires little commitment or effort, leading some to question whether such petitions can truly influence policy decisions or social movements in the way traditional petitions did.

Despite these concerns, there are numerous examples of digital petitions leading to tangible outcomes. In 2017, a petition on Change.org calling for net neutrality protections in the United States gathered more than 2 million signatures. The petition played a key role in raising public awareness about the Federal Communications Commission's (FCC) efforts to roll back net neutrality regulations, ultimately helping to generate widespread political pressure. Although the regulations were eventually repealed, the public outcry, amplified by digital petitions, kept the issue in the national spotlight and set the stage for ongoing legal and political battles over the future of the internet.

Another success story of digital petitioning occurred in 2019 when a petition on Change.org, started by a teenage activist in the United Kingdom, demanded that the UK government declare a climate emergency. The petition garnered more than 300,000 signatures and helped to galvanize public support for urgent climate action. Shortly after the petition gained national attention, the UK Parliament became the first in the world to declare a climate emergency, a symbolic but significant step in the global fight against climate change.

Digital petitions have also proven to be effective tools for corporate accountability. Companies, often more responsive to consumer pressure than governments are to voter demands, have faced growing scrutiny through online petitions. For example, a 2013 petition on Change.org called on Kraft Foods to remove artificial dyes from its macaroni and cheese products. The petition, signed by over 350,000 people, led to the company announcing that it would phase out synthetic food dyes from its products, demonstrating the ability of consumers to influence corporate behavior through digital activism.

The advent of social media has further magnified the power of digital petitions, allowing petitions to be shared instantly with millions of people. Platforms like Twitter, Facebook, and Instagram have enabled petition organizers to reach audiences far beyond their immediate networks. Social media campaigns often tie petitions to hashtags, videos, and viral challenges, further boosting their visibility. This has blurred the lines between petitioning and broader forms of digital activism, creating a more dynamic and interactive form of public engagement.

Despite the challenges posed by "clicktivism," digital petitions remain a valuable tool for holding governments, corporations, and other institutions accountable. In many cases, they serve as the first step in larger, multi-faceted campaigns that combine petitions with protests, lobbying efforts, and legal actions. Even when digital petitions do not result in immediate policy changes, they help to create awareness, mobilize communities, and generate the momentum needed for sustained social and political movements.

In conclusion, the digital age has transformed the right to petition, making it more accessible, faster, and far-reaching than ever before. While digital petitions are not without their limitations, they have demonstrated their ability to bring attention to critical issues, mobilize large numbers of people, and, in many cases, lead to meaningful change. As technology continues to evolve, digital petitioning will likely remain a key component of civic engagement, allowing citizens to participate in the democratic process in new and innovative ways.

Petitioning's Role in the Future of Democracy

As society continues to evolve in response to technological advancements, political shifts, and global challenges, the right to petition will undoubtedly remain a critical element of democratic engagement. However, the form and function of petitioning in the future will be shaped by the changing nature of governance, public participation, and digital innovation. In this context, petitioning is poised to take on new roles in strengthening democratic systems and ensuring that the voices of the people are heard, particularly in an era where traditional avenues of influence may feel increasingly out of reach for many citizens.

One of the most significant factors influencing the future of petitioning is the growing divide between the governed and their representatives. Across the world, people have expressed a sense of disillusionment with political institutions, feeling that their governments are no longer responsive to the needs of ordinary citizens. As partisan gridlock, corporate influence, and elite decision-making dominate political landscapes, the average person may feel powerless to effect change through conventional means like voting or direct lobbying. In this environment, petitioning offers an accessible and democratic way for people to express their concerns, rally around common causes, and demand accountability from their leaders.

In fact, petitioning may become even more critical in the coming years as an antidote to the perceived alienation of the public from political elites. By allowing individuals and groups to bypass formal channels of political power, petitions can serve as a direct line of communication between citizens and their government. They provide a platform for grassroots activism and community-based action, ensuring that even those who lack the resources or influence to engage in traditional political advocacy can still have their voices heard. The ease and immediacy of petitioning, especially in its digital form, will likely make it an indispensable tool for marginalized and disenfranchised communities seeking to address issues that may be overlooked by those in power.

One future trend that could enhance the impact of petitioning is the rise of direct democracy initiatives. In many countries and U.S. states, petitioning is a fundamental component of the initiative and referendum process, where citizens can propose new laws or demand a vote on existing legislation. As more people push for greater participation in their political systems, we may see an expansion of these mechanisms, giving petitioners the ability to place their issues directly on the ballot for a popular vote. This process empowers citizens to circumvent legislative bodies that may be unresponsive to public sentiment and creates a more direct form of democratic engagement.

For instance, many U.S. states already allow ballot initiatives on issues ranging from taxation and healthcare to environmental policy and criminal justice reform. Petition campaigns for these initiatives often begin at the grassroots level, where individuals or small organizations gather the necessary signatures to qualify their proposal for the ballot. These campaigns provide an opportunity for communities to engage in debates about policy, build coalitions, and directly shape the laws that govern their lives. In the future, as more states and countries adopt these mechanisms, petitioning could play an even more prominent role in giving citizens direct control over political decision-making.

The potential for technology to reshape petitioning is another crucial aspect of its future. Innovations in blockchain, artificial intelligence, and data analytics could transform how petitions are created, signed, and verified. Blockchain technology, for example, could be used to create secure, transparent petition platforms where signatures are verified in real-time, reducing the potential for fraud and increasing the credibility of petition campaigns. Such platforms could also ensure that petitions cannot be tampered with or manipulated by outside actors, thus enhancing the integrity of the petitioning process.

Artificial intelligence (AI) could play a role in analyzing petitions to identify trends, categorize public concerns, and even predict the success of a petition based on its content and the historical patterns of similar efforts. AI could also help petitioners craft more persuasive and impactful petitions by analyzing the language and structure of successful petitions. Additionally, AI-driven tools could facilitate engagement by suggesting petitions that align with a user's interests or by connecting like-minded individuals to work together on a cause.

The digital platforms of the future may also offer more interactive petitioning experiences, where signers can engage in discussions, share personal stories, and collaborate on solutions to the issues they care about. Virtual town halls, hosted through petition platforms, could give citizens the chance to speak directly to lawmakers or experts about the topics raised in their petitions. By creating more participatory and dynamic petitioning processes, technology can help deepen democratic engagement and make petitioning an even more powerful tool for change.

However, as the role of petitioning grows in the future, challenges and risks will also arise. The digital nature of modern petitioning makes it vulnerable to cyberattacks, misinformation campaigns, and other forms of manipulation. As we've seen in recent years, online platforms can be used to spread false information or amplify fringe causes, sometimes undermining legitimate efforts for change. Safeguarding the integrity of petition platforms will be essential to ensuring that petitioning remains a constructive and trusted part of democratic discourse. Governments, technology companies, and civil society organizations will need to work together to develop safeguards that protect petition platforms from malicious actors while maintaining their openness and accessibility.

In addition to technological risks, the challenge of "petition fatigue" may become more pronounced as petitioning becomes an increasingly common practice. With the rise of digital platforms, citizens are bombarded with petition requests on a daily basis, often leading to a sense of overwhelm or apathy. When people are asked to sign multiple petitions on numerous issues, they may become desensitized or less likely to engage with petitions in meaningful ways. Ensuring that petitions are focused, targeted, and connected to tangible action will be crucial to maintaining public interest and participation in the petitioning process.

In spite of these challenges, the right to petition will remain a cornerstone of democratic governance in the future. As the world faces complex and interconnected challenges—such as climate change, inequality, and threats to civil liberties—petitioning will continue to serve as a vital tool for citizens to raise their voices and advocate for change. It is a reminder that democracy is not a static system, but an ongoing conversation between the governed and those in power. Petitioning ensures that this conversation remains open, responsive, and inclusive, empowering individuals to play an active role in shaping the future of their societies.

As we look ahead, the right to petition will likely continue to evolve, adapting to new technologies, political realities, and social movements. But at its core, petitioning will remain a simple yet powerful act: the ability of ordinary people to come together and make their voices heard in the halls of power. Whether through traditional means or cutting-edge digital platforms, petitioning will remain a fundamental expression of democracy in action—an essential tool for ensuring that the will of the people is reflected in the decisions that shape their lives.

CHAPTER 8

Chapter 6: The Establishment Clause: Separation of

Origins and Historical Context of the Establishment Clause

The Establishment Clause, part of the First Amendment to the U.S. Constitution, has its roots in centuries of religious conflict and a desire for freedom from state-imposed religion. To understand why the Founding Fathers insisted on the separation of church and state, it's essential to first explore the historical context that shaped their thinking. Europe's long history of religious persecution, the rise of Enlightenment philosophy, and the unique experiences of early American settlers all played crucial roles in the development of this foundational principle of American democracy.

Throughout much of European history, religion and government were inseparable. Monarchs ruled with the divine right of kings, sanctioned by religious authority, and in many cases, the state imposed a singular religion on its people. In England, for example, the Church of England was established as the official state religion, and dissenters were often persecuted for their beliefs. Catholics, Protestants, and others who didn't conform to the established church faced legal penalties, social ostracism, and sometimes violence. This intertwining of church and state led to centuries of religious wars, including the Thirty Years' War (1618–1648), which devastated much of Europe and demonstrated the deadly consequences of religious intolerance.

By the 17th century, a new wave of thinkers began to challenge the notion that government should control religious belief. One of the most influential voices in this movement was the English philosopher John Locke. Locke's ideas about religious tolerance and individual rights laid the intellectual groundwork for the separation of church and state. In his seminal work, *A Letter Concerning Toleration* (1689), Locke argued that civil government should concern itself with the protection of life, liberty, and property, not the salvation of souls. He believed that religion was a personal matter, one that could not be legislated or enforced by the state. Locke's ideas resonated with many in the American colonies, where religious pluralism was already becoming a reality.

The American colonies were themselves born out of religious dissent. Many settlers came to the New World in search of religious freedom, fleeing the persecution they had experienced in Europe. Groups like the Puritans, Quakers, and Catholics sought a place where they could worship freely and establish communities based on their religious beliefs. However, even in the colonies, the relationship between religion and government was complicated. Some colonies, like Massachusetts, enforced strict religious conformity, while others, like Rhode Island, promoted religious tolerance. Rhode Island, founded by Roger Williams in 1636, became an early example of the separation of church and state. Williams, a Puritan minister, believed that government had no authority over individual religious beliefs and that a "wall of separation" should exist between the two. His radical ideas would later influence the framing of the First Amendment.

By the time of the American Revolution, the desire for religious freedom was deeply embedded in the political consciousness of the colonies. The colonists had experienced firsthand the dangers of government involvement in religion, both in Europe and in America. The Revolutionary War was not just a struggle for political independence; it was also a fight for personal liberty, including the right to worship (or not) without government interference. The Founding Fathers, many of whom were influenced by Enlightenment thinkers like Locke, recognized that religious freedom was essential to the new nation's identity. They sought to build a government that would protect individual rights and prevent the tyranny of a state-imposed religion.

One of the most vocal advocates for the separation of church and state was Thomas Jefferson. Jefferson, who was deeply influenced by Locke, believed that religion was a private matter and that government should play no role in promoting or endorsing any particular faith. In 1802, in a letter to the Danbury Baptist Association, Jefferson famously described the First Amendment as creating "a wall of separation between church and state." This phrase would later become a central concept in American jurisprudence, guiding the courts in their interpretation of the Establishment Clause.

James Madison, another key figure in the drafting of the Constitution, also played a pivotal role in shaping the Establishment Clause. Madison, often called the "Father of the Constitution," was deeply committed to religious freedom. He had seen the dangers of religious entanglement with government during his time in Virginia, where the Anglican Church had been the established religion, and dissenters faced fines, imprisonment, and social exclusion. In response, Madison helped to draft the Virginia Statute for Religious

Freedom in 1786, which disestablished the Anglican Church and affirmed the right of individuals to practice their faith without government interference. This statute, written by Jefferson and championed by Madison, would later serve as a model for the First Amendment's Establishment Clause.

When the Bill of Rights was drafted in 1789, the Establishment Clause was included to ensure that the new federal government would not have the power to impose or endorse a religion. The clause's simple yet profound language—"Congress shall make no law respecting an establishment of religion"—reflected the Founders' commitment to preventing religious tyranny. It was designed to create a space where people of all faiths, or no faith, could coexist without fear of government coercion.

The historical context of the Establishment Clause reveals that it was born out of a desire to protect both individual religious freedom and the integrity of government. By keeping religion and government separate, the Founding Fathers sought to create a system that would avoid the pitfalls of Europe's religious conflicts and promote a more just and equitable society. This foundational principle would go on to shape the legal and cultural landscape of the United States for centuries to come, as the country grappled with the complex relationship between religion and government in a pluralistic society.

The Establishment Clause in the U.S. Constitution and Early Interpretations

When the First Amendment was ratified in 1791, its concise wording reflected the framers' intent to establish clear boundaries between government and religion: "Congress shall make no law respecting an establishment of religion, or prohibiting the free exercise thereof." This language formed the basis of the Establishment Clause, designed to prevent the federal government from endorsing or establishing a state religion. Yet, while the text itself may seem straightforward, its interpretation and application have sparked centuries of legal debate and judicial scrutiny.

To understand the significance of the Establishment Clause, we must first consider the delicate balance the Founding Fathers sought to strike. America was a religiously diverse society, even in its infancy. Different colonies had different religious compositions, ranging from the largely Puritan Massachusetts to the more religiously pluralistic Pennsylvania, founded by Quakers. Some colonies had officially established churches, like the Anglican Church in Virginia, while others embraced religious tolerance, like Rhode Island. The framers understood that for the new nation to thrive, it was crucial to avoid religious favoritism and coercion by the federal government.

At the heart of the Establishment Clause is the idea that the government should remain neutral on matters of religion. Unlike in Europe, where national churches wielded considerable power and often enforced religious conformity, the American government would be prohibited from establishing a national religion or providing preferential treatment to one faith over another. The framers knew that religious freedom was essential to individual liberty, and by ensuring that the government could not interfere in religious matters, they hoped to protect this right for all citizens.

Despite this clear intent, the exact meaning and application of the Establishment Clause were not immediately settled. In the early years of the republic, there was little legal precedent to guide the courts on how to interpret the clause. Many of the original states still had established churches or religious tests for public office, and it wasn't until much later that the Establishment Clause would be applied to the states through the incorporation doctrine of the Fourteenth Amendment. For much of the 19th century, religious matters were primarily governed by state constitutions and laws, with little federal oversight.

The lack of early federal cases on the Establishment Clause didn't mean the issue was without controversy. In fact, debates over the role of religion in public life persisted throughout the early republic. Some politicians and religious leaders argued that Christianity should play a central role in shaping public policy, while others, like Thomas Jefferson and James Madison, remained steadfast in their belief that government should have no involvement in religious matters. Jefferson's famous 1802 letter to the Danbury Baptist Association, in which he spoke of a "wall of separation between church and state," echoed his desire to keep religion out of the political sphere. This metaphor of a wall of separation would later become a central theme in American jurisprudence regarding the Establishment Clause.

However, the Establishment Clause was not universally understood as requiring an absolute separation of church and state in the early years of the republic. Public prayer, government proclamations of days of thanksgiving, and other religious practices were still common. Even President George Washington issued proclamations calling for national days of prayer and thanksgiving, raising questions about whether such actions violated the Establishment Clause. For many early Americans, the idea of government neutrality on religion did not necessarily mean excluding religious references from public life altogether.

One of the first significant moments in the interpretation of the Establishment Clause came in 1802, with the case of *Reynolds v. United States*. Though primarily a case about the Free Exercise Clause, involving the prosecution of a Mormon man for practicing polygamy, the ruling offered early reflections on how the government should approach religion. Chief Justice Morrison Waite referenced Jefferson's wall of separation concept in the decision, reinforcing the idea that the government should not interfere with religious matters, while also setting the stage for future interpretations of the Establishment Clause.

It wasn't until the 20th century that the Establishment Clause would begin to take on its modern shape. The incorporation of the Bill of Rights to the states through the Fourteenth Amendment in the 1940s, and the landmark *Everson v. Board of Education* (1947) case, marked a turning point in the interpretation of the Establishment Clause. In *Everson*, the Supreme Court ruled that the Establishment Clause applied to the states and local governments, not just the federal government. This decision set the stage for many more rulings that would define the relationship between religion and government in modern America.

The case centered around a New Jersey law that allowed public funds to reimburse parents for transportation costs to private schools, including religious schools. While the Court upheld the law, Justice Hugo Black's majority opinion famously reiterated the principle of separation of church and state: "The First Amendment has erected a wall between church and state. That wall must be kept high and impregnable." This language reinforced the notion that government must remain neutral toward religion, even if individual citizens or groups practiced religion freely.

Everson also illustrated the complexity of interpreting the Establishment Clause in a pluralistic society. While the Court upheld the transportation reimbursement as neutral toward religion, the case sparked debates about whether such financial support for religious institutions violated the spirit of the Establishment Clause. As the Court would later demonstrate in other rulings, the challenge lay in determining where to draw the line between permissible accommodation of religion and unconstitutional government endorsement.

In the years following *Everson*, the Court continued to grapple with questions of how to apply the Establishment Clause in an increasingly diverse and religiously active society. Cases involving school prayer, religious symbols on public property, and government funding for religious activities would all force the judiciary to consider the original intent of the framers, historical practices, and contemporary challenges.

The Establishment Clause, though a simple sentence in the Constitution, has been the subject of intense scrutiny, interpretation, and re-interpretation throughout American history. What began as a safeguard against the horrors of state-imposed religion in Europe evolved into one of the most enduring principles of American democracy. It reflects the nation's commitment to religious freedom, not just for those in the majority, but for all people, regardless of their beliefs. Through its early interpretations, the Establishment Clause set the stage for the ongoing struggle to balance religious liberty with government neutrality in a rapidly changing society.

The Evolution of the Establishment Clause in the Courts

The Establishment Clause, like many constitutional provisions, has evolved over time through the decisions of the U.S. Supreme Court. While the framers of the Constitution laid the groundwork, it is the courts that have defined and refined the boundaries between church and state in America. This evolution has been marked by a series of landmark cases that have shaped the interpretation of the Establishment Clause and set important legal precedents for how the government interacts with religion.

One of the first major decisions to interpret the Establishment Clause came in 1947 with *Everson v. Board of Education*. As discussed earlier, this case involved a New Jersey law that allowed for public reimbursement of transportation costs for students attending private schools, including religious ones. The Supreme Court ultimately upheld the law, finding that it did not violate the Establishment Clause because the aid was provided to all students, regardless of the religious affiliation of the school. However, Justice Hugo Black's majority opinion reinforced the principle of separation of church and state, stating that the Establishment Clause meant that neither the state nor the federal government could "pass laws which aid one religion, aid all religions, or prefer one religion over another."

Everson was a watershed moment for the Establishment Clause, not only because it extended its application to the states through the incorporation doctrine but also because it established the idea that even indirect government support of religion must be scrutinized under the First Amendment. The decision laid the foundation for decades of legal battles over the role of religion in public life, especially in education.

The next major case to further shape the interpretation of the Establishment Clause was *Engel v. Vitale* in 1962. This case addressed the constitutionality of state-sponsored prayer in public schools. In New York, the state Board of Regents had written a prayer to be recited in public schools each morning, a practice that was challenged by a group of parents. The Supreme Court, in a 6-1 decision, ruled that the state-sponsored prayer violated the Establishment Clause, even though participation in the prayer was technically voluntary. Justice Black, writing for the majority, argued that the government's endorsement of a religious activity, even one as seemingly benign as a prayer, was unconstitutional: "It is no part of the business of government to compose official prayers for any group of the American people to recite as part of a religious program carried on by government."

Engel v. Vitale was a significant ruling that reaffirmed the government's commitment to maintaining a clear separation between church and state, particularly in public institutions like schools. The decision sparked widespread controversy and debate, with critics arguing that it removed religion from public life, while supporters saw it as a necessary step to protect religious freedom by preventing government-sponsored religious activities. The ruling was followed by a series of cases that further restricted religious practices in public schools, such as *Abington School District v. Schempp* (1963), which struck down Bible readings in public schools, and *Wallace v. Jaffree* (1985), which invalidated a state law that allowed for a moment of silence intended for prayer.

Perhaps the most famous and enduring Establishment Clause test came out of the 1971 case *Lemon v. Kurtzman*. This case arose from a challenge to laws in Pennsylvania and Rhode Island that allowed state funds to be used to support teachers in private religious schools, as long as the instruction was secular. The Court ruled that these laws violated the Establishment Clause, and in doing so, created the "Lemon Test," a three-pronged test to determine whether a government action related to religion is constitutional. According to the Lemon Test, a law or government action must:

1. Have a secular legislative purpose;
2. Neither advance nor inhibit religion as its primary effect;
3. Not foster "excessive government entanglement" with religion.

The *Lemon* decision became a cornerstone of Establishment Clause jurisprudence. The test it established provided a framework for analyzing cases where the government might be perceived as endorsing or supporting religion. If a law or action failed any of the three prongs of the Lemon Test, it was deemed unconstitutional. For decades, the *Lemon Test* served as the primary standard by which the courts evaluated government actions concerning religion, especially in education and public funding contexts.

However, the *Lemon Test* was not without its critics. Some argued that it was too rigid and did not allow for reasonable accommodation of religion in public life. Others claimed that it led to inconsistent results in the courts. Over time, the Supreme Court itself seemed to move away from strict adherence to the *Lemon Test*, particularly in cases involving religious symbols on public property.

One such case was *Lynch v. Donnelly* (1984), which dealt with a Christmas nativity scene displayed by the city of Pawtucket, Rhode Island. The plaintiffs argued that the display violated the Establishment Clause by promoting a specific religion—Christianity. The Supreme Court, in a 5-4 decision, upheld the nativity display, ruling that it had a legitimate secular purpose as part of a broader holiday display that included non-religious symbols like Santa Claus and a Christmas tree. The Court emphasized that not all religious symbols in public spaces automatically violated the Establishment Clause, especially if they were part of a larger, secular celebration. This decision marked a subtle shift away from the *Lemon Test* and towards a more flexible approach to religion in the public sphere.

Another case that demonstrated this shift was *Marsh v. Chambers* (1983), in which the Court upheld the practice of legislative prayer. The Nebraska state legislature had hired a chaplain to deliver prayers at the start of each session, a practice that was challenged as a violation of the Establishment Clause. The Court, however, ruled in favor of the legislature, citing the historical tradition of legislative prayer dating back to the Founding Fathers. This decision underscored the Court's growing reliance on historical precedent rather than the strict application of the *Lemon Test* in Establishment Clause cases.

More recently, the Supreme Court has continued to refine its interpretation of the Establishment Clause. In cases like *Town of Greece v. Galloway* (2014), the Court upheld the constitutionality of prayer at town meetings, emphasizing tradition and historical practices. In *American Legion v. American Humanist Association* (2019), the Court ruled that a cross-shaped World War I memorial on public land did not violate the Establishment Clause, arguing that longstanding symbols with religious significance could serve secular purposes, such as honoring the dead.

The evolution of the Establishment Clause in the courts reflects the tension between maintaining religious neutrality and accommodating religious expression in a diverse and pluralistic society. While early cases like *Everson* and *Engel* sought to strictly enforce the separation of church and state, later rulings have allowed for more flexibility, particularly when it comes to acknowledging the role of religion in American history and culture. As the nation continues to grapple with issues of religious freedom and government involvement in religious matters, the courts will remain a crucial battleground for defining the limits of the Establishment Clause in modern America.

School Prayer and the Battle for Religious Neutrality in Public Education

Few issues have stirred as much public debate and legal controversy around the Establishment Clause as the role of religion in public schools. While the First Amendment guarantees both freedom of religion and freedom from government-imposed religion, these freedoms have often clashed in the context of public education, where religious diversity is pronounced and government authority is most directly exercised over children. At the heart of this debate lies the question of school prayer and whether such practices violate the Establishment Clause's prohibition against government endorsement of religion.

The Supreme Court's landmark decision in *Engel v. Vitale* (1962) marked the beginning of a long and contentious battle over prayer in public schools. In this case, the New York State Board of Regents had composed a short, non-denominational prayer for public school students to recite each day: "Almighty God, we acknowledge our dependence upon Thee, and we beg Thy blessings upon us, our parents, our teachers and our country." Although students were not required to participate, the practice of officially sanctioned prayer in a public institution raised concerns about government endorsement of religion.

The Supreme Court ruled 6-1 that the prayer, despite its voluntary nature, was unconstitutional under the Establishment Clause. Justice Hugo Black, writing for the majority, emphasized that the state's involvement in drafting and promoting a prayer, no matter how neutral its language, amounted to an official endorsement of religion. Black famously wrote, "It is no part of the business of government to compose official prayers for any group of the American people to recite as part of a religious program carried on by government." The decision underscored the importance of maintaining a strict separation between church and state, particularly in the context of public education, where students are subject to state authority.

The *Engel* decision ignited a firestorm of criticism from religious groups and political leaders who argued that the ruling amounted to an attack on the nation's Christian heritage and moral foundation. To many Americans, the prohibition of school prayer seemed to symbolize a broader effort to push religion out of public life. Some even argued that the decision was contributing to a perceived moral decline in the nation. For decades following the ruling, efforts to restore prayer to public schools became a rallying cry for religious conservatives, and the debate over school prayer remained a central issue in the culture wars.

Just one year after *Engel*, the Supreme Court further solidified its position on the role of religion in public schools with *Abington School District v. Schempp* (1963). In this case, Pennsylvania had a law that required public schools to begin each day with a reading from the Bible, followed by the recitation of the Lord's Prayer. A similar case from Maryland, *Murray v. Curlett*, also challenged mandatory Bible readings in public schools. The Court combined the cases and ruled 8-1 that both practices violated the Establishment Clause.

Justice Tom Clark, writing for the majority, made clear that even if the Bible readings were technically voluntary, the government's involvement in religious exercises in public schools was unconstitutional. Clark wrote, "The place of religion in our society is an exalted one, achieved through a long tradition of reliance on the home, the church and the inviolable citadel of the individual heart and mind. We have come to recognize through bitter experience that it is not within the power of government to invade that citadel." The decision reinforced the principle that public schools must remain religiously neutral spaces, free from government-imposed religious practices.

The *Schempp* decision, like *Engel*, was met with significant opposition. Religious leaders and conservative politicians continued to argue that the absence of prayer and Bible readings in public schools undermined the moral fabric of the nation. Despite the Court's rulings, many schools across the country continued to find ways to incorporate religious elements into their daily routines, leading to further legal challenges and rulings in the years that followed.

One of the next major Establishment Clause cases involving public schools was *Wallace v. Jaffree* (1985). In this case, the state of Alabama had passed a law allowing public schools to observe a moment of silence at the beginning of each day, during which students could pray or reflect. While on the surface the law seemed to offer a neutral compromise—students could pray if they wished, but were not required to—the legislative history of the law revealed that its purpose was to encourage prayer in schools. The Supreme Court, in a 6-3 decision, struck down the law, citing its religious intent as a violation of the Establishment Clause.

Justice John Paul Stevens, writing for the majority, noted that the government could not endorse or encourage prayer, even indirectly, in public schools. He argued that the state's effort to reintroduce prayer through a moment of silence was an impermissible attempt to promote religion. Stevens wrote, "The First Amendment requires that a state must be neutral in its relations with groups of religious believers and non-believers; it does not require, and indeed forbids, the state to adopt programs or practices in its public schools or otherwise which 'aid or oppose' any religion."

The *Wallace* decision further emphasized the Court's commitment to maintaining strict religious neutrality in public schools. Yet, despite these rulings, the debate over school prayer and religious activities in public schools has persisted into the 21st century. Many school districts have faced challenges over practices such as student-led prayer at school events, religious-themed graduation ceremonies, and the display of religious symbols.

One of the more recent cases in this ongoing debate was *Santa Fe Independent School District v. Doe* (2000), which addressed the issue of student-led prayer at public school football games. In this case, the school district had a policy allowing students to vote on whether to have a prayer before football games and, if so, which student would deliver it. The policy was challenged as a violation of the Establishment Clause. The Supreme Court, in a 6-3 decision, ruled that the policy was unconstitutional because the prayers, though led by students, took place at a school-sponsored event and had the appearance of school endorsement of religion.

Justice Stevens, again writing for the majority, argued that the policy was not truly voluntary, as students who did not wish to participate would still be subjected to the prayer in a public, school-sponsored setting. He wrote, "The delivery of such a message—over the school's public address system, by a speaker representing the student body, under the supervision of school faculty, and pursuant to a school policy that explicitly and implicitly encourages public prayer—places the imprimatur of the school itself behind the religious message." The decision reinforced the principle that public schools must avoid any appearance of endorsing religious practices, even when those practices are led by students.

While the Supreme Court's rulings have consistently emphasized the need for religious neutrality in public schools, the issue of school prayer remains a deeply divisive and emotionally charged topic. For many Americans, the prohibition of prayer in public schools feels like a rejection of their religious values and traditions. For others, these rulings represent an essential protection of religious freedom, ensuring that public institutions do not impose or promote religious beliefs on students from diverse backgrounds.

The Court's Establishment Clause decisions on school prayer reflect the broader challenge of balancing religious freedom with the government's duty to remain neutral on matters of faith. As long as public schools serve as a central institution in American society, the debate over religion in schools is likely to continue, with each new generation grappling with how to interpret the First Amendment's promise of religious liberty for all.

Religious Displays, Monuments, and the Public Square

The tension between the Establishment Clause and public expressions of religion extends beyond schools and into broader public spaces. Across the United States, religious symbols and monuments can be found on government property, ranging from nativity scenes during the holidays to longstanding monuments that feature religious imagery, such as crosses. These public religious displays have become a flashpoint in the legal and cultural battle over the Establishment Clause, raising questions about whether the government, by allowing such symbols, is endorsing religion in violation of the First Amendment.

The U.S. Supreme Court has been called upon many times to resolve disputes over religious displays in public spaces, with the central issue being whether these displays constitute government endorsement of a particular faith or serve a secular purpose within a historical or cultural context. One of the most significant cases in this area was *Lynch v. Donnelly* (1984), in which the Court was asked to determine whether the city of Pawtucket, Rhode Island, could include a nativity scene in its annual Christmas display in a public park. The display also featured secular holiday symbols, such as a Christmas tree, reindeer, and Santa Claus.

In a 5-4 decision, the Supreme Court ruled that the inclusion of the nativity scene did not violate the Establishment Clause. Chief Justice Warren Burger, writing for the majority, argued that the display, taken as a whole, had a legitimate secular purpose—celebrating the holiday season—and that the presence of the nativity scene did not amount to government endorsement of Christianity. The decision marked an important shift in Establishment Clause jurisprudence, as the Court emphasized that religious symbols in public spaces could be permissible if they were part of a broader, secular context.

Justice Burger's opinion introduced what has been called the "endorsement test," which asks whether a reasonable observer would interpret a government action as endorsing religion. Under this framework, religious symbols or practices are more likely to be upheld if they are presented alongside secular symbols or serve a secular purpose. The *Lynch* decision, therefore, opened the door for religious symbols to be displayed in public spaces, provided they did not dominate or convey the message that the government was favoring one religion over others.

However, not all cases have reached the same conclusion. A decade later, in *County of Allegheny v. ACLU* (1989), the Supreme Court struck down the display of a nativity scene inside a courthouse in Pittsburgh, Pennsylvania, while upholding a nearby display of a menorah and Christmas tree outside a government building. The Court ruled that the nativity scene, which stood alone without any secular symbols, conveyed a clear endorsement of Christianity, particularly because of its prominent placement inside a government building. On the other hand, the menorah and Christmas tree, presented together, were seen as part of a secular holiday celebration and were therefore permissible.

Justice Sandra Day O'Connor, in a concurring opinion, explained the reasoning behind the endorsement test, emphasizing that government actions should not send a message to non-adherents that they are outsiders in the political community. This idea of inclusion and neutrality has become a critical element of Establishment Clause jurisprudence, as the Court seeks to balance the role of religion in public life with the need to protect religious minorities from feeling marginalized by government actions.

The debate over religious symbols in public spaces resurfaced in a more recent case, *American Legion v. American Humanist Association* (2019), which involved a large cross-shaped World War I memorial on public land in Bladensburg, Maryland. The plaintiffs argued that the cross, a distinctly Christian symbol, violated the Establishment Clause by appearing to endorse Christianity on government property. The Supreme Court, in a 7-2 decision, upheld the cross, ruling that it had become a historical symbol of war memorials and had taken on a secular meaning over time.

Justice Samuel Alito, writing for the majority, argued that while the cross is undeniably a Christian symbol, its primary purpose in this context was to honor the fallen soldiers of World War I, many of whom were Christian. Alito's opinion stressed the importance of historical context when evaluating Establishment Clause cases, noting that not all religious symbols on public property should automatically be seen as government endorsement of religion. The Court's decision reflected a growing trend toward a more lenient interpretation of the Establishment Clause when it comes to long-standing monuments with religious connotations.

The *American Legion* decision also highlighted a broader philosophical shift within the Court toward accommodating religious symbols in public spaces, especially when those symbols have acquired secular or historical significance over time. This approach, sometimes referred to as "ceremonial deism," allows for certain religious expressions in public life—such as "In God We Trust" on currency or prayers at the beginning of legislative sessions—on the grounds that they have become part of the nation's civic traditions rather than purely religious endorsements.

Nevertheless, this evolving jurisprudence has not been without its critics. Dissenting justices and civil liberties advocates argue that allowing religious symbols on government property, particularly when those symbols are overwhelmingly associated with one faith, can alienate religious minorities and blur the line between church and state. They contend that the Establishment Clause's core purpose is to ensure that government remains strictly neutral on matters of religion, and any appearance of endorsement, no matter how historical or cultural, undermines that neutrality.

These debates reflect the inherent tension within Establishment Clause cases: how to accommodate the historical and cultural significance of religion in American public life while also protecting the rights of individuals to live free from government-imposed religious messages. For many, religious symbols in public spaces, especially those funded or maintained by the government, represent an intrusion of religion into public life. For others, such symbols are a recognition of the nation's religious heritage and a way to honor traditions that have long been part of American history.

The enduring controversy over religious displays in public spaces underscores the complexities of the Establishment Clause. As American society becomes increasingly diverse, the need to balance respect for religious traditions with the protection of religious neutrality becomes ever more important. The Supreme Court's decisions in these cases have reflected shifting attitudes and interpretations, yet the fundamental question remains the same: How can the government acknowledge religion's role in public life without crossing the line into endorsement or favoritism?

As we look toward the future, the battle over religious symbols in public spaces is likely to continue. Each new case that comes before the courts will test the boundaries of the Establishment Clause and challenge our understanding of how to live together in a pluralistic society, where both religious expression and freedom from religious imposition must be equally protected.

CHAPTER 9

Chapter 7: The Free Exercise of Religion

The Free Exercise Clause – Historical Roots and Purpose
The Free Exercise Clause, enshrined in the First Amendment, holds a crucial place in American history, embodying a fundamental protection of religious liberty. To fully understand its significance, we must trace the origins of the idea itself, which was shaped by centuries of religious conflict in Europe and the unique circumstances of the American colonies. The framers of the Constitution, having seen the dangers of both religious persecution and government endorsement of specific faiths, sought to create a new system in which religious practice could thrive free from government interference.

Religious persecution in Europe played a formative role in shaping the American view of religious freedom. For centuries, European governments had enforced state-sponsored religions, often punishing dissenters. The Protestant Reformation in the 16th century, for example, led to brutal wars of religion across Europe, as Catholic and Protestant states battled for dominance. In England, the religious turmoil was particularly intense. The monarchs oscillated between Catholicism and Protestantism, with each regime imposing its religion on the populace. Those who did not conform faced fines, imprisonment, or even execution.

This history of persecution created a deep desire for religious freedom among many who sought refuge in the American colonies. The Pilgrims who landed at Plymouth Rock in 1620 were fleeing religious persecution in England. Other colonies, such as Maryland and Pennsylvania, were founded specifically as havens for religious minorities. Maryland, under Lord Baltimore, was intended as a safe place for Catholics, while Pennsylvania, under William Penn, became a refuge for Quakers and other dissenting groups. These early colonists believed that in America, they could practice their faith without fear of government intrusion.

Despite this desire for religious freedom, the colonies were far from bastions of religious tolerance. In many of the colonies, there were established churches—state-sanctioned religious institutions that wielded significant political and social power. Massachusetts, for example, had an official Puritan church, and dissenters like Baptists and Quakers faced persecution. Roger Williams, the founder of Rhode Island, was famously banished from Massachusetts for advocating the separation of church and state. In Rhode Island, Williams established the first colony with no official church, promoting the idea that government should have no role in regulating religious belief.

This idea—that government and religion should remain separate—gained traction in the decades leading up to the American Revolution. The Enlightenment, with its emphasis on reason and individual rights, influenced many American thinkers, including Thomas Jefferson and James Madison. Jefferson famously wrote about building a "wall of separation between church and state," and Madison, who is often referred to as the "Father of the Constitution," was deeply concerned with protecting religious liberty.

When the Constitutional Convention convened in 1787, there was broad agreement that the new nation must protect the freedom of religion. The debate was not over whether religious freedom should be protected, but how best to achieve that goal. Some feared that without explicit protections, the federal government could impose a national religion or infringe on individuals' rights to practice their faith. Others, like Madison, believed that the diversity of religions in the United States would naturally prevent any single faith from dominating.

Ultimately, the Bill of Rights was added to the Constitution in 1791, with the First Amendment stating, "Congress shall make no law respecting an establishment of religion, or prohibiting the free exercise thereof." These two clauses—the Establishment Clause and the Free Exercise Clause—work together to ensure that the government neither imposes a state religion nor interferes with an individual's right to practice their faith. The Free Exercise Clause, in particular, was designed to protect not just the right to believe but the right to act on those beliefs, free from government coercion.

The Free Exercise Clause was a revolutionary concept in its time. It represented a break from centuries of European practice, where governments routinely regulated religious behavior. The framers of the Constitution recognized that religious belief is deeply personal and that individuals must be free to follow their conscience, whether that led them to a traditional faith, no faith at all, or something in between.

However, the framers also understood that religious freedom could not be absolute. As Thomas Jefferson wrote, "The legitimate powers of government extend to such acts only as are injurious to others." In other words, while individuals are free to hold any religious belief they choose, their actions cannot harm others or violate public order. This distinction between belief and action would become a central issue in the interpretation of the Free Exercise Clause in the years to come.

Thus, the Free Exercise Clause was not only a product of historical necessity but a visionary commitment to individual liberty. It reflected the belief that religious diversity would strengthen the nation rather than weaken it. The clause embodied the hope that in America, people of all faiths could live together in harmony, practicing their beliefs without fear of government interference or persecution.

This foundation of religious liberty, laid by the framers of the Constitution, would shape the development of the Free Exercise Clause for centuries to come. However, as the nation grew and became more diverse, new challenges emerged. The courts would soon be called upon to interpret the boundaries of religious freedom, grappling with how to protect the rights of individuals while maintaining the government's role in ensuring public order and protecting the rights of others.

The Supreme Court's Early Interpretations of the Free Exercise Clause

The Supreme Court's initial encounters with the Free Exercise Clause of the First Amendment reflected the complexities inherent in balancing religious freedom with the state's responsibility to maintain order and enforce laws. In the earliest cases, the Court wrestled with how far the government could go in regulating religious practices, particularly when those practices conflicted with societal norms or legal obligations. The foundational cases during this period laid the groundwork for future interpretations of religious freedom, and their impact continues to resonate today.

One of the earliest and most significant cases concerning the Free Exercise Clause was *Reynolds v. United States* (1879). This case arose out of the federal government's efforts to stamp out polygamy, which was widely practiced by members of the Church of Jesus

Christ of Latter-day Saints (commonly known as Mormons) in the Utah Territory. The federal government had passed the Morrill Anti-Bigamy Act in 1862, which outlawed bigamy and polygamy in federal territories. George Reynolds, a Mormon, was convicted under the act for practicing polygamy. Reynolds argued that the law violated his constitutional right to free exercise of religion, as his faith mandated polygamy as a religious duty.

The Supreme Court, in a unanimous decision, ruled against Reynolds, upholding his conviction and establishing a critical distinction that would shape future Free Exercise cases: the difference between religious beliefs and religious practices. Chief Justice Morrison Waite, writing for the Court, explained that while the Constitution protected religious belief absolutely, religious practices that violated social order or public safety could be regulated by the government. In essence, individuals were free to believe whatever they wished, but their actions, especially if they conflicted with existing laws, could be subject to government restriction.

Chief Justice Waite famously invoked an analogy to human sacrifice, writing that to permit every religious practice would lead to chaos, allowing individuals to claim religious justification for any behavior, no matter how harmful or contrary to public order. "Laws are made for the government of actions," Waite wrote, "and while they cannot interfere with mere religious belief and opinions, they may with practices." Thus, the Court held that polygamy, though a central tenet of Mormon faith at the time, could be prohibited under federal law without violating the Free Exercise Clause.

This ruling in *Reynolds* established what became known as the "belief-action" distinction. According to this framework, while religious beliefs were inviolable, religiously motivated actions could be restricted if they conflicted with societal laws or public welfare. This distinction became a cornerstone of the Court's early interpretations of the Free Exercise Clause, and for decades it allowed the government to regulate religious practices that were deemed harmful or incompatible with legal or moral standards of the time.

The belief-action distinction became a powerful tool for the government, allowing it to regulate practices it found objectionable without infringing on religious liberty as a whole. It also reflected the Court's concern that unregulated religious practices could undermine the stability of law and order in the growing nation. Polygamy, in the eyes of the federal government, represented a threat to the social fabric of the United States, which was built on the foundation of monogamous marriage.

However, the *Reynolds* decision also raised important questions about the limits of religious freedom and the extent to which the government could intervene in religious practices. Could the state regulate all religiously motivated actions, no matter how integral they were to a person's faith? Where should the line be drawn between government authority and individual freedom of conscience? These questions would continue to surface in future cases, as religious minorities sought to challenge laws they believed violated their right to freely practice their faith.

The belief-action distinction, though influential, was not without its critics. Many argued that it failed to fully protect the religious practices of minority faiths, particularly when those practices conflicted with mainstream social norms. By allowing the government to regulate religious actions, the Court risked imposing a kind of religious conformity, privileging majority faiths and their practices while marginalizing smaller, less understood religious communities. This tension between protecting individual religious freedom and maintaining societal order would become a recurring theme in Free Exercise jurisprudence.

In addition to *Reynolds*, other early cases concerning the Free Exercise Clause similarly reflected the Court's cautious approach to balancing religious liberty with the interests of the state. In *Davis v. Beason* (1890), the Court upheld an Idaho law that required voters to swear an oath renouncing polygamy and organizations that supported it. The Court again reaffirmed that religious practices, particularly those like polygamy that conflicted with public morals, could be regulated without violating the Free Exercise Clause.

The Court's early interpretations of the Free Exercise Clause were shaped by the cultural and legal challenges of the time. The late 19th century was a period of rapid expansion for the United States, and the government was deeply concerned with ensuring social cohesion and moral order in the newly acquired western territories. Polygamy, seen as an aberration from traditional Christian monogamy, was viewed as a direct threat to these values. The Court's rulings in *Reynolds* and subsequent cases reflected the prevailing belief that certain religious practices, even if sincere, could not be tolerated if they undermined the moral or legal fabric of society.

While the early decisions of the Supreme Court may seem restrictive by modern standards, they laid the foundation for a broader conversation about the limits of religious liberty. The belief-action distinction allowed the government to regulate practices it deemed harmful, but it also opened the door to future debates about what constitutes a "harmful" practice and who gets to make that determination. As religious diversity in the United States grew, so too did the complexity of Free Exercise cases, forcing the Court to continually refine its approach to balancing religious freedom with governmental authority.

As the nation progressed into the 20th century, the Court would eventually shift its approach to Free Exercise cases, moving away from the belief-action distinction toward a more nuanced understanding of the relationship between religion and law. Yet the early cases, particularly *Reynolds*, remain a foundational part of the Free Exercise story, illustrating the Court's attempt to navigate the uncharted waters of religious freedom in a new and diverse nation.

The Rise of the Strict Scrutiny Standard and Expanding Free Exercise Rights

As the United States grew more diverse in both its population and its religious practices, the tension between protecting individual freedoms and enforcing the law became more pronounced. The early rulings of the Supreme Court, particularly the belief-action distinction established in *Reynolds v. United States* (1879), had left room for the government to regulate religious practices if they conflicted with laws deemed necessary for public welfare. However, by the mid-20th century, the Court began to reconsider its approach, particularly in cases where government actions imposed significant burdens on religious exercise. This shift led to the emergence of a new legal standard known as "strict scrutiny," which dramatically expanded the protection of religious practices.

The turning point came in 1963 with the landmark case *Sherbert v. Verner*. At the center of the case was Adell Sherbert, a member of the Seventh-day Adventist Church. Sherbert had lost her job after refusing to work on Saturdays, which her faith observed as the Sabbath. When she applied for unemployment benefits, the state of South Carolina denied her claim, citing that she was ineligible because she had refused available work. Sherbert argued that the denial of benefits violated her First Amendment rights under the Free Exercise Clause, as it effectively forced her to choose between her religious convictions and her livelihood.

In a 7-2 decision, the Supreme Court ruled in favor of Sherbert, marking a significant shift in how the Court evaluated cases involving the Free Exercise Clause. Writing for the majority, Justice

William Brennan introduced what would become known as the strict scrutiny test. Brennan argued that any law or government action that imposed a substantial burden on religious practice must meet two key criteria: it must serve a "compelling state interest," and it must be narrowly tailored to achieve that interest in the least restrictive manner possible. In Sherbert's case, the Court found that the state's denial of unemployment benefits placed an undue burden on her religious practice and that the state had not demonstrated a sufficiently compelling interest to justify this burden.

The strict scrutiny standard fundamentally altered the legal landscape for religious freedom. Under this new framework, government actions that burdened religious practices could no longer be justified by mere concerns of public welfare or social order, as had been the case in earlier rulings like *Reynolds*. Instead, the government had to show a pressing, unavoidable need for the law in question and prove that it was using the least restrictive means to achieve its goal. This placed a higher burden of proof on the government and provided much stronger protections for individuals seeking to practice their religion without interference.

The strict scrutiny test was not only a legal innovation but also a reflection of broader changes in American society during the 1960s. The civil rights movement had brought issues of individual liberty and equality to the forefront of national consciousness, and the Supreme Court's decision in *Sherbert* echoed this broader cultural shift toward protecting the rights of marginalized groups. In this case, the Court recognized that religious minorities, such as Seventh-day Adventists, could face unique challenges when their practices conflicted with prevailing societal norms, and it sought to ensure that those challenges would not be compounded by government action.

The *Sherbert* decision also set the stage for another major Free Exercise case: *Wisconsin v. Yoder* (1972). In this case, the Supreme Court once again applied the strict scrutiny standard to protect religious practices, this time for a group of Old Order Amish families who challenged Wisconsin's compulsory education law. The law required children to attend school until the age of 16, but the Amish argued that sending their children to high school violated their religious beliefs and way of life, which prioritized simple living and community-based education over formal schooling.

In a unanimous decision, the Court ruled in favor of the Amish families, holding that Wisconsin's law placed a substantial burden on their religious practices. The state had argued that compulsory education was necessary for preparing children to be responsible citizens, but the Court found that this did not constitute a compelling enough interest to justify overriding the Amish community's religious convictions. The ruling in *Yoder* reinforced the strict scrutiny standard and demonstrated the Court's growing commitment to protecting religious exercise, particularly for groups whose beliefs set them apart from mainstream society.

Together, *Sherbert* and *Yoder* signaled a new era in Free Exercise jurisprudence. The strict scrutiny standard, with its emphasis on protecting religious practices unless the government could demonstrate a compelling and narrowly tailored justification, became the dominant legal framework for Free Exercise cases. This marked a dramatic expansion of religious freedom, particularly for religious minorities who often found themselves in conflict with state laws and regulations.

However, the strict scrutiny standard was not without its critics. Some argued that it gave religious groups too much power to challenge laws that were intended to serve the public good. For example, critics pointed out that under the strict scrutiny framework, laws designed to protect public health or ensure equal treatment could be vulnerable to religious exemptions, potentially undermining those broader societal goals. The Court, in recognizing the tension between individual religious rights and the state's interest in enforcing neutral laws, had to grapple with these competing priorities in subsequent cases.

The strict scrutiny era also prompted debates about what constituted a "compelling state interest." While public safety and health were generally accepted as compelling interests, other state interests—such as economic regulation or uniform enforcement of laws—were more contentious. As religious diversity continued to increase in the United States, these debates became more complex, with courts struggling to apply the strict scrutiny test in a way that balanced religious liberty with the needs of an increasingly pluralistic society.

Despite these challenges, the rise of the strict scrutiny standard in cases like *Sherbert* and *Yoder* represented a major victory for religious freedom. By placing the burden on the government to justify its actions, the Court ensured that religious practices would receive robust protection, particularly for those outside the religious mainstream. The legacy of these cases continues to influence the Court's approach to Free Exercise issues today, even as the legal landscape continues to evolve.

In the years that followed, the strict scrutiny standard would face its own challenges, but during this period, it stood as a powerful tool for expanding and protecting the free exercise of religion, reinforcing the idea that individual conscience and religious practice are essential components of American liberty.

The Shift Away from Strict Scrutiny—*Employment Division v. Smith* and Its Aftermath

While the strict scrutiny standard provided robust protections for religious practices in the 1960s and 1970s, by the late 20th century, the Supreme Court began to move away from this approach in favor of a more restrained view of Free Exercise rights. The pivotal case that marked this shift was *Employment Division v. Smith* (1990), a ruling that dramatically altered the landscape of Free Exercise jurisprudence and set off a wave of legislative and legal responses in its wake.

The case involved two Native American men, Alfred Smith and Galen Black, who were fired from their jobs at a private drug rehabilitation center in Oregon after using peyote, a hallucinogenic drug, as part of a religious ceremony in their Native American Church. Peyote was classified as a controlled substance under Oregon law, and its use was illegal, even for religious purposes. After being terminated, Smith and Black applied for unemployment benefits, but their claims were denied on the grounds that they had been dismissed for "misconduct" related to their peyote use.

Smith and Black argued that the denial of unemployment benefits violated their rights under the Free Exercise Clause because their use of peyote was a sincere religious practice. In earlier cases, such as *Sherbert v. Verner*, the Court had ruled that the government must show a compelling interest before it could burden religious practices. However, in *Smith*, the Court took a different approach, significantly narrowing the scope of Free Exercise protections.

In a 6-3 decision written by Justice Antonin Scalia, the Court ruled against Smith and Black, holding that the state of Oregon was not required to provide a religious exemption to its drug laws. Scalia's opinion asserted that if a law is neutral and generally applicable—meaning it does not target any specific religion or religious practice—it does not need to be justified by a compelling state interest, even if it incidentally burdens religious practices. In other words, as long as the law applied to everyone equally and was not designed to single out religious groups, the state could enforce it without needing to meet the strict scrutiny standard.

This ruling marked a significant departure from the Court's earlier decisions. In cases like *Sherbert* and *Wisconsin v. Yoder*, the Court had applied strict scrutiny to laws that substantially burdened religious practices, even if those laws were neutral and generally applicable. But in *Smith*, the Court shifted the focus away from protecting religious practices against all burdens and instead emphasized the importance of enforcing generally applicable laws without granting special exemptions for religious reasons. As Justice Scalia put it, allowing individuals to opt out of generally applicable laws based on their religious beliefs would "permit every citizen to become a law unto himself."

The decision in *Smith* sent shockwaves through the legal community and religious organizations, many of which feared that the ruling would open the door for states to pass laws that could inadvertently or deliberately burden religious practices without providing sufficient protections. The ruling also raised concerns about the potential for religious minorities, in particular, to face discrimination or marginalization under laws that were nominally neutral but had disproportionate impacts on their religious practices.

Critics of the *Smith* decision argued that it represented a weakening of the Free Exercise Clause, effectively making it harder for individuals to seek exemptions from laws that conflicted with their religious beliefs. For example, under the new standard, a law prohibiting certain forms of animal slaughter could be applied to religious groups that practiced ritual animal sacrifice, as long as the law was not explicitly aimed at curbing religious practices. This concern was heightened by the recognition that, in many cases, religious minorities would be more vulnerable to the impacts of generally applicable laws that did not take their unique practices into account.

In response to the *Smith* decision, a broad coalition of religious organizations, civil rights groups, and legal scholars lobbied Congress to pass new legislation that would restore the strict scrutiny standard for Free Exercise claims. This effort led to the passage of the Religious Freedom Restoration Act (RFRA) in 1993. RFRA was designed to ensure that strict scrutiny would apply in cases where federal laws or government actions substantially burdened an individual's religious practice, even if the law in question was neutral and generally applicable.

RFRA was widely seen as a direct response to the *Smith* decision, and it received broad bipartisan support. The law stated that the federal government could not substantially burden a person's exercise of religion unless it demonstrated that doing so was in furtherance of a compelling governmental interest and was the least restrictive means of achieving that interest. In this way, RFRA sought to restore the more protective standard of Free Exercise that had been eroded by the *Smith* ruling.

However, RFRA's impact was limited by a subsequent Supreme Court decision. In *City of Boerne v. Flores* (1997), the Court struck down RFRA as it applied to state and local governments, ruling that Congress had overstepped its constitutional authority in applying the law beyond the federal government. While RFRA continued to apply to federal laws and actions, the ruling in *City of Boerne* meant that states were free to regulate religious practices under the *Smith* standard, unless they chose to adopt their own versions of RFRA or similar laws.

In the wake of *Smith* and the limitations placed on RFRA by *City of Boerne*, several states did indeed pass their own religious freedom laws, often referred to as "state RFRAs." These laws mirrored the federal RFRA by requiring state governments to demonstrate a compelling interest and use the least restrictive means when burdening religious practices. Today, many states have their own RFRAs, providing additional protections for religious exercise beyond those guaranteed by the federal government.

The legacy of *Employment Division v. Smith* remains complex and contested. On one hand, the decision affirmed the government's authority to enforce generally applicable laws, even when those laws incidentally burden religious practices. This emphasis on neutrality and equal application of the law has been praised by some as essential for maintaining social cohesion and preventing individuals from seeking exemptions from important public safety or health regulations. On the other hand, the ruling has been criticized for weakening the protections afforded to religious minorities, who may be disproportionately affected by laws that, while neutral on their face, do not take into account the specific needs of their faith communities.

In the years since *Smith*, the Court has continued to grapple with the balance between enforcing generally applicable laws and protecting religious exercise. Cases like *Hobby Lobby v. Burwell* (2014) and *Masterpiece Cakeshop v. Colorado Civil Rights Commission* (2018) have brought these issues back into the spotlight, as the Court has been asked to weigh the rights of religious individuals and businesses against the demands of public policy and anti-discrimination laws.

While *Smith* remains the controlling precedent for Free Exercise cases involving generally applicable laws, the broader debate about the limits of religious freedom in a pluralistic society continues to evolve. The strict scrutiny era, with its robust protections for religious practices, may have given way to a more limited view of Free Exercise rights, but the conversation about how to balance individual conscience with the needs of the state is far from settled. The ongoing dialogue reflects the complexity and dynamism of the First Amendment, as it continues to be interpreted and reinterpreted in light of changing social, cultural, and legal realities.

Modern Challenges and the Future of the Free Exercise Clause

In the decades following *Employment Division v. Smith* and the passage of the Religious Freedom Restoration Act (RFRA), the debate over religious freedom has continued to evolve, taking on new dimensions as American society has become more diverse and pluralistic. Today, the interpretation of the Free Exercise Clause must contend with modern challenges, including the rights of religious individuals and institutions in a secularizing society, the increasing complexity of religious accommodations, and the tension between religious freedom and other constitutional rights, such as equality and nondiscrimination. These ongoing challenges raise important questions about the future of the Free Exercise Clause and how it will shape the balance between individual conscience and the collective interests of society.

One of the central challenges in the modern era is how to reconcile religious freedom with laws aimed at protecting civil rights and promoting equality. This issue has come to the forefront in cases where religious beliefs conflict with anti-discrimination laws, particularly in the context of LGBTQ+ rights. The Supreme Court has been asked to adjudicate cases where individuals or businesses, citing religious beliefs, have sought exemptions from laws that prohibit discrimination based on sexual orientation or gender identity. Two of the most prominent examples are *Masterpiece Cakeshop v. Colorado Civil Rights Commission* (2018) and *Fulton v. City of Philadelphia* (2021), both of which highlight the ongoing tension between religious liberty and the principle of equal treatment under the law.

In *Masterpiece Cakeshop*, a Colorado baker named Jack Phillips refused to create a wedding cake for a same-sex couple, citing his religious belief that marriage is between a man and a woman. The couple filed a complaint under Colorado's anti-discrimination law, which prohibits businesses from discriminating on the basis of sexual orientation. The case reached the Supreme Court, which ruled in favor of Phillips on narrow procedural grounds, finding that the Colorado Civil Rights Commission had shown hostility toward his religious beliefs during its initial ruling. The Court did not, however, resolve the broader question of whether religious business owners have a constitutional right to refuse service based on their religious convictions. As a result, the case left many legal questions unanswered and set the stage for future conflicts over the boundaries of religious freedom.

Similarly, in *Fulton v. City of Philadelphia*, the Court addressed whether a religious foster care agency, Catholic Social Services (CSS), could refuse to place children with same-sex couples despite a city ordinance prohibiting discrimination based on sexual orientation. CSS argued that being required to place children with same-sex couples would violate its religious beliefs. In a unanimous decision, the Court ruled in favor of CSS, but it did so on narrow grounds, focusing on the fact that the city had allowed for discretionary exemptions to the nondiscrimination rule. As in *Masterpiece Cakeshop*, the Court avoided issuing a broad ruling on the larger conflict between religious freedom and anti-discrimination laws, leaving the issue open for future litigation.

These cases illustrate the delicate balance the Court must strike between protecting religious exercise and ensuring that individuals are not subject to discrimination based on their identity. The tension between these competing rights is likely to persist as American society continues to grapple with questions of religious accommodation and civil rights. Advocates for religious freedom argue that individuals and institutions should not be compelled to act in ways that violate their deeply held religious beliefs, while proponents of anti-discrimination protections maintain that granting religious exemptions to civil rights laws could undermine the rights of marginalized groups, particularly in areas like housing, employment, and public services.

Beyond the conflict between religious freedom and anti-discrimination laws, the Free Exercise Clause also faces challenges in the context of healthcare and reproductive rights. The debate over religious objections to providing certain types of healthcare, particularly contraceptive services and abortion, has intensified in recent years. In cases like *Burwell v. Hobby Lobby* (2014), the Court ruled that closely held for-profit corporations could claim religious exemptions from the Affordable Care Act's requirement that employers provide health insurance coverage for contraception. The decision, which was based on RFRA rather than the Free Exercise Clause directly, underscored the Court's willingness to protect religious exercise even when it intersects with federal mandates.

However, the ruling in *Hobby Lobby* also raised concerns about the potential for businesses to seek religious exemptions from a wide range of legal obligations, potentially limiting access to healthcare services, particularly for women. The case highlighted the broader debate over how far religious accommodations should extend in the public sphere and whether individuals or entities should be allowed to invoke religious beliefs to opt out of complying with generally applicable laws, especially when doing so could affect the rights and access of others.

The future of the Free Exercise Clause will likely be shaped by how courts address these competing claims of religious liberty and other constitutional rights. As the Court continues to adjudicate cases involving religious objections to healthcare, anti-discrimination laws, and other government regulations, it will be tasked with finding a balance between protecting the rights of religious individuals and ensuring that laws designed to protect public health, safety, and equality are enforced.

Another modern challenge is the increasing diversity of religious practices and beliefs in the United States. As the country has become more religiously pluralistic, with a growing number of non-Christian faiths and a rising population of religiously unaffiliated individuals, courts have been called upon to adjudicate Free Exercise claims from a broader array of religious traditions. This has led to questions about whether certain religious groups receive preferential treatment under the law and whether the Free Exercise Clause is being applied equitably across different faiths. For example, debates over the accommodation of Muslim religious practices in schools, prisons, and workplaces have highlighted concerns about whether religious minorities receive the same level of protection as more established or mainstream religious groups.

The role of religious institutions in the public sphere also remains a contentious issue. As religious organizations seek to expand their influence in areas such as education, healthcare, and social services, courts must determine how the Free Exercise Clause applies to religious entities that operate in the public realm. Cases involving the autonomy of religious schools, hospitals, and charities raise important questions about the extent to which religious institutions can claim exemptions from government regulations while still receiving public funding or operating in partnership with the government. The Court's decisions in cases like *Our Lady of Guadalupe School v. Morrissey-Berru* (2020), which affirmed the right of religious schools to hire and fire employees based on religious criteria, suggest that the Court may continue to favor broad protections for religious institutions, even when they intersect with secular regulations.

As the legal landscape continues to evolve, it is clear that the Free Exercise Clause will remain at the center of some of the most complex and contentious issues in American law and society. The challenges of balancing religious freedom with other constitutional rights, ensuring equitable treatment for religious minorities, and determining the scope of religious exemptions in the public sphere will require careful consideration from both the courts and policymakers. The future of the Free Exercise Clause is uncertain, but what remains clear is that it will continue to play a vital role in shaping the relationship between individual conscience and the collective values of American democracy.

CHAPTER 10

Chapter 8: The Internet Age: A New Frontier for th

The Internet and the Expansion of Public Discourse

The rise of the internet represents one of the most transformative changes in human communication since the invention of the printing press. As the internet matured into a global network, it revolutionized the way people share information, express ideas, and engage in public discourse. In the context of the First Amendment, this shift has expanded the reach of free speech, creating new opportunities—and challenges—for individuals to participate in the marketplace of ideas.

In the pre-internet era, access to mass communication was limited to those who had the resources and influence to control traditional media outlets like newspapers, radio stations, and television networks. The average citizen's ability to broadcast their thoughts to a wide audience was often constrained by these barriers. However, the advent of the internet demolished these gatekeeping mechanisms. With a simple internet connection, anyone can now share their ideas, opinions, or creative work with a potentially global audience. This democratization of speech has empowered individuals, marginalized groups, and grassroots movements to find a voice and reach communities far beyond their immediate geographic location.

Blogs, websites, and especially social media platforms have become the new town squares where people gather to debate political issues, advocate for social change, and challenge existing power structures. Whether it's a journalist sharing investigative reports, an activist promoting a cause, or an individual expressing personal opinions on current events, the internet has opened up unprecedented channels for free expression. This has fundamentally altered the relationship between citizens and the public discourse, making it more inclusive and diverse.

At the heart of this transformation is the concept of the internet as a "modern public square." In the past, public spaces like parks, streets, or town halls were crucial venues for free speech and assembly. People would gather to protest, hold rallies, or simply express their views to passersby. The First Amendment protected these activities, ensuring that citizens had access to public forums where they could exercise their rights. Today, much of this activity has shifted online. Social media platforms like Facebook, Twitter (now X), Instagram, and TikTok have become the primary venues for public expression, with millions of users engaging in debates, organizing events, and participating in movements with the click of a button.

While the internet's role in expanding public discourse is undeniable, it also presents new challenges to the First Amendment. One of the most significant is the sheer scale and speed at which information—and misinformation—can spread. In this new landscape, speech can go viral in minutes, reaching millions of people before its accuracy can be verified. This has led to widespread concerns about the role of misinformation, disinformation, and hate speech in shaping public opinion. Online platforms are now grappling with how to balance free expression with the need to regulate harmful content, and this has raised thorny legal and ethical questions about censorship, content moderation, and the limits of free speech in a digital age.

At the same time, the decentralized and often anonymous nature of online communication has amplified voices that might otherwise have been silenced. Activists in repressive regimes, for instance, have used the internet to organize protests, spread information, and expose government abuses, often at great personal risk. In this sense, the internet has not only expanded public discourse within the United States but has also become a powerful tool for advancing human rights and democratic values globally.

However, the notion of the internet as a public square is complicated by the fact that the platforms that host much of this discourse—Facebook, YouTube, X, and others—are privately owned companies, not government entities. This means that the First Amendment's protection against government censorship does not apply directly to these platforms, which have their own policies and guidelines for regulating content. The result is a complex and evolving debate over the role of private companies in shaping public discourse and how, or whether, the First Amendment should adapt to this new reality.

As we move deeper into the digital age, the internet's impact on public discourse continues to evolve. While it has undoubtedly expanded the reach of free speech and empowered individuals to participate in public life, it has also exposed the limitations and challenges of protecting free expression in an interconnected world. The questions that arise from this new frontier—about censorship, regulation, and the responsibilities of private platforms—will define the future of the First Amendment in the digital age.

Social Media, Censorship, and the First Amendment

As social media has emerged as a dominant force in public discourse, it has brought to the forefront complex questions about censorship, freedom of expression, and the role of private companies in regulating speech. Platforms like Facebook, Twitter (now X), YouTube, and Instagram have become the modern-day equivalents of public forums, where people gather to share opinions, debate political issues, and organize social movements. However, unlike traditional public spaces, these platforms are owned and operated by private corporations, which means that the First Amendment's protections do not apply in the same way. This raises significant challenges when it comes to balancing free speech with the need to regulate harmful content.

In the United States, the First Amendment protects citizens from government censorship, but it does not extend to private entities. This distinction is crucial in the context of social media, where companies have the authority to set their own terms of service and community guidelines. When users violate these rules, platforms can remove posts, suspend accounts, or permanently ban individuals from their services. Critics argue that this gives social media companies excessive control over the flow of information and the ability to silence voices they disagree with. At the same time, platforms are also under pressure to remove content that is illegal, harmful, or violates social norms, such as hate speech, incitement to violence, and disinformation.

One of the most contentious aspects of this debate is the power of platforms to moderate content. Social media companies employ vast teams of moderators, supported by artificial intelligence, to review and remove content that violates their policies. Yet, this process is far from perfect. Content moderation decisions are often inconsistent, opaque, and, in some cases, politically charged. Users on all sides of the political spectrum have accused platforms of bias—conservatives often claim that their voices are being disproportionately censored, while liberals argue that platforms do too little to combat hate speech and harmful disinformation.

The legal framework that governs social media companies in the U.S. is shaped largely by Section 230 of the Communications Decency Act, passed in 1996. This law grants internet platforms immunity from liability for content posted by their users while also allowing them to moderate content as they see fit. Section 230 has been both praised for enabling the growth of the internet and criticized for allowing platforms to evade responsibility for harmful content. Critics on both the left and the right have called for reform, though their reasons differ. Conservatives want to ensure that platforms cannot suppress their political views, while liberals push for greater accountability in removing harmful and extremist content.

One of the most high-profile cases in this debate occurred during the 2020 U.S. presidential election. Social media platforms faced enormous pressure to combat the spread of misinformation, particularly regarding the integrity of the election. Twitter, Facebook, and YouTube took unprecedented steps to label or remove false claims about voter fraud and election interference. At the same time, they faced accusations of censorship from those whose posts were flagged or removed. This situation reached its peak when several platforms, citing repeated violations of their terms of service and incitement to violence, permanently banned then-President Donald Trump in the wake of the January 6 Capitol riot.

This event ignited a fierce debate about the role of social media companies in shaping political discourse. On one hand, proponents of the ban argued that platforms had a responsibility to prevent the spread of dangerous misinformation and to limit the reach of individuals who incite violence. On the other hand, critics warned that this set a dangerous precedent, giving private companies the power to silence even the most prominent political figures. The ban of a sitting U.S. president raised profound questions about free speech in the digital age, with some calling it a necessary measure to protect democracy and others decrying it as corporate overreach.

Another area of contention is the spread of disinformation, particularly during times of crisis. The COVID-19 pandemic saw an explosion of false information about the virus, vaccines, and public health measures. Social media companies faced the difficult task of balancing the need to promote accurate information with the risk of infringing on free speech. Platforms implemented new policies to remove COVID-19-related misinformation, but the rapid spread of false information highlighted the limitations of content moderation. Once again, the question arose: Where is the line between responsible regulation and censorship?

The complexity of these issues is compounded by the global nature of social media platforms. U.S.-based companies operate in countries with vastly different legal and cultural standards for free speech. While the First Amendment provides robust protections in the U.S., many other nations impose stricter limits on speech, particularly when it comes to issues like hate speech, defamation, and national security. Social media companies must navigate these different legal landscapes while attempting to apply a uniform set of rules across their platforms. This has led to accusations that companies apply double standards, censoring content more aggressively in some regions than in others.

Despite these challenges, social media has undeniably expanded the reach of free expression. It has empowered individuals, especially those in marginalized or repressed communities, to speak out and organize in ways that were previously unimaginable. Activists have used social media to bring attention to injustices, challenge authoritarian regimes, and build global movements for change. Yet, as these platforms have grown in influence, the questions surrounding their role in moderating speech have become more urgent.

As the debate over censorship and free speech on social media continues, the courts, Congress, and the public will need to grapple with fundamental questions about the future of the First Amendment in the digital age. Should social media companies be treated like public utilities, subject to greater regulation to ensure fair and equal access? Or should they continue to operate as private entities with the freedom to enforce their own rules? How can society protect free speech while also addressing the real harms that can arise from unchecked online expression? These questions remain unresolved, but their answers will shape the future of public discourse in the internet era.

Privacy, Surveillance, and Free Speech Online

As the internet has become an integral part of daily life, it has also raised critical concerns about privacy, surveillance, and how these issues intersect with free speech. The digital age offers unprecedented opportunities for communication, but it also exposes individuals to new forms of monitoring—both by governments and private companies. This constant surveillance threatens to chill free expression, as individuals become more aware that their online activities can be tracked, recorded, and analyzed. Understanding the delicate balance between privacy and free speech is essential for protecting First Amendment rights in the internet era.

One of the most pressing issues is government surveillance. In the years following the 9/11 attacks, the U.S. government dramatically expanded its surveillance capabilities in the name of national security. Programs run by the National Security Agency (NSA), such as the bulk collection of phone metadata, have raised concerns about the erosion of privacy rights. Whistleblower Edward Snowden's revelations in 2013 exposed the extent to which the government was monitoring not just foreign targets but also U.S. citizens. The disclosures revealed that the NSA was collecting vast amounts of data on Americans' phone calls, emails, and internet activities, often without individualized warrants.

This widespread surveillance has serious implications for free speech. When people know they are being watched, they may self-censor, refraining from expressing controversial or unpopular opinions out of fear that their words could be used against them. This chilling effect undermines the core purpose of the First Amendment, which is to foster a vibrant, open marketplace of ideas where citizens can freely debate and challenge government actions without fear of reprisal. For activists, journalists, and dissidents, the knowledge that their communications might be monitored can be especially stifling, as it raises the stakes for speaking out against injustice or governmental abuses.

The legal protections for privacy in the digital age are murky. While the Fourth Amendment offers protection against unreasonable searches and seizures, it has not been fully adapted to the realities of modern technology. The courts have grappled with questions about what constitutes a reasonable expectation of privacy in the digital world. In *Carpenter v. United States* (2018), the U.S. Supreme Court ruled that the government must obtain a warrant to access historical cellphone location data, recognizing that tracking individuals' movements over time through their phones constitutes a serious intrusion into privacy. This decision was a victory for privacy advocates, but it also highlighted the gaps in legal protections for online privacy, which remain incomplete and subject to interpretation.

On the private sector side, corporations collect vast amounts of data about their users—often more than the government does. Every time individuals browse the web, post on social media, or use mobile apps, they leave behind a trail of personal information. This data is harvested, analyzed, and sold to advertisers, but it can also be shared with law enforcement agencies or hacked by malicious actors. Companies like Google, Facebook, and Amazon hold detailed profiles of billions of users, including their search history, location data, purchasing habits, and social connections. While these companies argue that data collection helps improve services and provide more personalized experiences, the sheer scale of their surveillance raises concerns about how this information could be misused.

The growing awareness of data collection practices has led to calls for greater transparency and control over personal information. The European Union's General Data Protection Regulation (GDPR), implemented in 2018, is one of the most comprehensive efforts to address these concerns. The GDPR gives users the right to know what data is being collected about them, the right to request that this data be deleted, and the right to opt out of data collection entirely. In the U.S., similar efforts are gaining momentum, though privacy protections remain fragmented across states. California's Consumer Privacy Act (CCPA), for instance, grants users some of these rights, but there is no national standard for data privacy.

The tension between privacy and free speech also plays out in the context of online anonymity. The internet allows individuals to express themselves without revealing their true identities, which can be crucial for those living under authoritarian regimes or those participating in controversial or sensitive discussions. Anonymity enables whistleblowers to expose corruption, activists to organize protests, and everyday citizens to speak truth to power without fear of retribution. However, it also allows for the rise of harmful behaviors like cyberbullying, harassment, and the spread of extremist content. Platforms must balance the need to protect free speech with the responsibility to prevent their services from being used to harm others.

For example, in repressive countries, anonymity is often the only shield citizens have against government surveillance and punishment for dissent. The use of encrypted messaging apps like Signal and Telegram has become a vital tool for organizing protests and sharing information in countries like Iran, Russia, and China. These apps provide an essential layer of security, allowing users to communicate without fear of government snooping. However, governments around the world have increasingly sought to weaken encryption standards or gain backdoor access to private communications, claiming that such measures are necessary to combat terrorism and crime. These efforts, if successful, would further erode the privacy protections that underpin free speech.

At the same time, the ability to post anonymously online has led to an explosion of harmful and abusive behavior, particularly on social media. Trolls, hate groups, and cyberbullies often hide behind anonymous accounts to target individuals with threats, harassment, and defamatory statements. This has sparked debates over whether anonymity should be limited or regulated to protect individuals from online abuse. Some have called for stricter verification processes to ensure that users are accountable for their actions, while others argue that such measures would disproportionately impact marginalized groups who rely on anonymity for protection.

As society continues to navigate these challenges, the balance between privacy, surveillance, and free speech will remain a critical issue in the digital age. While technology has empowered individuals to communicate more freely than ever before, it has also made them more vulnerable to surveillance and data exploitation. Ensuring that privacy protections keep pace with technological advancements is essential for safeguarding the free expression that the First Amendment guarantees. The future of free speech online depends not only on protecting individuals' right to speak but also on their ability to do so without constant monitoring and fear of retaliation.

The Rise of Online Hate Speech and Extremism

As the internet has expanded the possibilities for free expression, it has also become a breeding ground for hate speech and extremist ideologies. While the First Amendment robustly protects most forms of speech, including offensive or unpopular opinions, the proliferation of online platforms has created new challenges in addressing content that incites violence, spreads hatred, and fuels radicalization. The tension between preserving free speech and curbing harmful rhetoric is one of the defining dilemmas of the digital age.

Hate speech, while not explicitly defined by U.S. law, generally refers to speech that attacks or demeans individuals or groups based on attributes such as race, religion, ethnicity, gender, sexual orientation, or disability. Under the First Amendment, hate speech is protected unless it crosses the line into direct threats, incitement to imminent violence, or harassment. However, the global nature of the internet means that content that is legally protected in the United States can easily cross borders and inflame tensions in regions with stricter hate speech laws. This has led to growing pressure on tech companies to police the content on their platforms and find ways to reduce the spread of harmful rhetoric.

The problem of online hate speech and extremism became particularly visible during the 2010s with the rise of various extremist groups that leveraged social media platforms to spread their ideologies. Groups promoting white supremacy, anti-Semitism, misogyny, and other forms of extremism found fertile ground online, using platforms like YouTube, Twitter, Reddit, and fringe message boards to recruit followers and spread their messages. These platforms allowed hate groups to reach a global audience, radicalizing individuals and, in some cases, inspiring acts of violence.

One of the most notorious examples of this was the rise of ISIS (the Islamic State) in the early 2010s, which used social media to recruit fighters, spread propaganda, and encourage lone-wolf attacks in Western countries. The group's sophisticated use of social media platforms to glorify violence and radicalize individuals underscored the power of the internet to amplify extremist ideologies. In response, platforms like Twitter and Facebook began to crack down on ISIS-affiliated accounts, removing content and suspending users who promoted terrorism. These efforts were largely successful in reducing the group's online presence, but they also raised important questions about how to balance the removal of extremist content with the need to protect free speech.

Domestic extremism in the United States has also been fueled by the spread of online hate speech. The rise of the alt-right movement, a loose collection of far-right extremists, was closely linked to online spaces like 4chan, 8chan, and Reddit, where users could share racist, xenophobic, and anti-Semitic content with little oversight. The 2017 Charlottesville "Unite the Right" rally, which resulted in the death of a counter-protester, highlighted how online hate could spill over into real-world violence. In the aftermath of the rally, major platforms like Facebook, Twitter, and YouTube took stronger measures to ban users and groups associated with white supremacy and other forms of extremism. However, these bans also sparked debates about censorship, with some arguing that the platforms were infringing on free speech.

The algorithms that power social media platforms have also come under scrutiny for their role in amplifying hate speech and extremist content. Many platforms use algorithms to prioritize content that generates high engagement, such as likes, shares, and comments. Unfortunately, inflammatory and sensational content often drives more engagement than measured or moderate viewpoints. This creates a perverse incentive for platforms to promote content that stokes outrage and division, even if that content includes hate speech or extremist rhetoric. Critics argue that these algorithms have contributed to the radicalization of individuals by pushing them down "rabbit holes" of increasingly extreme content.

The role of online communities in radicalizing individuals has been highlighted in a series of mass shootings, many of which have been linked to online forums where extremists gather. For instance, the gunmen in the 2019 Christchurch mosque shootings in New Zealand, the 2018 Tree of Life synagogue shooting in Pittsburgh, and the 2019 El Paso Walmart shooting all had ties to online spaces where white supremacist ideologies were promoted. These tragedies underscored the real-world consequences of allowing hate speech and extremism to proliferate unchecked online.

In response to growing public outcry, social media platforms have implemented stricter policies to combat hate speech and extremism. Facebook, for example, banned white nationalist and white separatist content in 2019, while Twitter introduced new rules against dehumanizing speech. YouTube, too, began removing videos that glorify violence or promote hate groups. These efforts have had some success in curbing the spread of extremist content, but enforcement remains inconsistent, and hate speech continues to flourish on many platforms, particularly those with less stringent moderation policies.

One of the ongoing challenges in addressing online hate speech is defining its boundaries. While many people agree that incitement to violence should be banned, there is less consensus on where to draw the line for other forms of hateful content. Some argue that banning hate speech infringes on free speech rights and creates a slippery slope that could lead to the suppression of legitimate political or social viewpoints. Others contend that allowing hate speech to go unchecked poses a direct threat to vulnerable communities and undermines the principles of equality and justice.

The U.S. legal framework offers limited recourse for individuals targeted by online hate speech. While victims of online harassment and threats can sometimes seek legal remedies, hate speech that does not rise to the level of direct threats is generally protected under the First Amendment. This has led to calls for reform, particularly as hate speech has become a weapon used to silence marginalized voices and undermine civil discourse. However, any changes to existing laws would need to be carefully balanced to ensure that they do not unduly infringe on free speech rights.

As society grapples with the rise of online hate speech and extremism, it is clear that there are no easy solutions. The internet has opened up new avenues for free expression, but it has also made it easier for hate groups and extremists to spread their messages and recruit followers. Social media platforms will need to continue refining their policies and moderation practices to address these issues, while policymakers, courts, and civil society must engage in ongoing debates about the best ways to balance free speech with the need to protect individuals and communities from harm.

In the broader context of the First Amendment, the rise of online hate speech represents a new frontier in the struggle to protect free speech while ensuring that the internet remains a safe and inclusive space for all. The challenge moving forward will be finding ways to address the spread of hateful ideologies without sacrificing the freedoms that the First Amendment was designed to protect.

The Role of Social Media Companies: Moderators or Censors?

The rise of social media platforms has transformed how people communicate, share ideas, and engage in public debate. At the heart of this transformation lies a critical question: what responsibility do these platforms have in moderating content, and where is the line between moderation and censorship? As private companies, social media giants like Facebook, Twitter, YouTube, and others are not bound by the First Amendment in the same way government entities are. This distinction allows them to establish their own rules about what speech is allowed or prohibited on their platforms. Yet, their influence is so vast that their decisions can significantly shape the landscape of public discourse, making them de facto gatekeepers of free expression in the digital age.

The debate over content moderation versus censorship came to the forefront in recent years as social media companies faced increasing pressure to address issues like misinformation, hate speech, harassment, and extremism. In response to high-profile incidents—such as the role of Facebook in the spread of false information during the 2016 U.S. election or the use of YouTube by extremist groups to recruit followers—platforms began to tighten their rules and increase the use of content moderation practices. Algorithms were tweaked to identify and remove harmful content, and human moderators were employed to enforce platform policies more effectively. While these efforts were designed to protect users and the broader public from harmful content, they also raised concerns about overreach and the potential for stifling legitimate speech.

One of the main criticisms of social media companies' content moderation practices is the lack of transparency in how decisions are made. Users often have little visibility into why their posts are removed, accounts suspended, or content demoted in visibility. This lack of transparency has fueled accusations of political bias, with individuals on both the right and the left claiming that their voices are being unfairly silenced. For instance, conservative groups in the U.S. have alleged that platforms like Twitter and Facebook disproportionately censor right-wing viewpoints, a claim bolstered by several high-profile account suspensions of conservative figures. On the other hand, progressive activists have argued that social media companies have failed to take sufficient action against hate speech, misogyny, and racism that disproportionately affect marginalized communities.

The issue of political bias in content moderation became particularly contentious in the wake of the January 6th Capitol riot in 2021, when platforms like Twitter and Facebook permanently banned then-President Donald Trump for violating their rules against incitement to violence. While some praised the decision as a necessary step to prevent further unrest, others decried it as an unprecedented act of censorship against a sitting U.S. president. The move ignited fierce debates over the power of social media companies and their ability to shape political discourse. Some argued that platforms had become too powerful and should be treated as public utilities subject to stricter regulation, while others warned that such regulation could lead to government overreach and the erosion of free speech online.

In response to these concerns, some policymakers have proposed changes to Section 230 of the Communications Decency Act, a 1996 law that shields online platforms from liability for content posted by their users while allowing them to moderate content in good faith. Section 230 has been described as the law that "created the internet" by enabling platforms to host user-generated content without fear of constant lawsuits. However, critics argue that the law gives tech companies too much power without sufficient accountability. Proposals to amend or repeal Section 230 range from increasing transparency around content moderation decisions to holding platforms liable for hosting illegal or harmful content. These proposals have sparked intense debates about the future of free speech online and the role of platforms in regulating content.

At the same time, social media companies have struggled to navigate the challenge of moderating content on a global scale. Platforms operate in numerous countries with vastly different legal standards and cultural norms regarding free speech. In the European Union, for example, hate speech laws are much stricter than in the United States, and companies can face hefty fines for failing to remove illegal content within specific timeframes. In countries like China, platforms must comply with stringent government censorship requirements or risk being banned altogether. These global pressures force companies to adapt their moderation practices to comply with local laws while maintaining a consistent approach to free speech principles across their platforms. This balancing act often leads to difficult trade-offs, where platforms must decide between adhering to free speech values and complying with authoritarian regimes that demand censorship of political dissent.

Another important aspect of this debate is the rise of alternative platforms that promise less moderation and more free speech. In response to perceived censorship by mainstream platforms, new platforms like Parler, Gab, and others have emerged, promoting themselves as free-speech havens. However, these platforms have often become home to extremist content, conspiracy theories, and violent rhetoric, raising questions about whether unrestricted speech truly fosters healthy public discourse. After the January 6th Capitol riot, Parler was temporarily removed from app stores for failing to adequately police violent content, underscoring the challenges faced by platforms that seek to limit moderation in the name of free speech.

The ongoing evolution of content moderation practices has led some to call for the creation of independent oversight bodies to review platform decisions and ensure accountability. Facebook, for instance, launched its Oversight Board in 2020, a quasi-independent body tasked with reviewing the company's most controversial content moderation decisions. The Oversight Board, often referred to as Facebook's "Supreme Court," reviews cases submitted by users and makes binding decisions on whether specific content should be restored or removed. While the creation of the Oversight Board represents a step toward greater accountability, it is only one part of the broader conversation about how to balance free speech with the need for content moderation.

The tension between moderation and censorship will likely continue to shape the future of free expression online. As social media companies refine their policies and governments weigh new regulations, the question remains: how can we ensure that the internet remains a forum for free speech while protecting users from harm? Striking this balance is no easy task, but it is essential for preserving the integrity of the First Amendment in the digital age.

Ultimately, the role of social media companies as moderators of speech presents both opportunities and challenges. While platforms have the potential to foster inclusive, respectful dialogue, they also have the power to shape public opinion and restrict speech in ways that may undermine democratic principles. Navigating this complex landscape requires careful consideration of both the rights and responsibilities of platforms, users, and governments. Only by engaging in thoughtful, informed debates can society develop the policies and practices needed to protect free speech while addressing the unique challenges of the internet age.

CHAPTER 11

Chapter 9: The Global Perspective on Free Speech a

Comparative Approaches to Free Speech Around the World

Free speech, while universally recognized as a fundamental human right, is interpreted and protected in vastly different ways around the globe. In the United States, the First Amendment offers broad protections, making it one of the most robust legal frameworks for free expression in the world. In contrast, many other democracies place more emphasis on balancing free speech with other social goods like the prevention of hate speech, protection of public order, and the safeguarding of individuals from harm.

At the core of the U.S. approach is a deep commitment to free speech absolutism, where the right to express oneself, even in controversial or offensive ways, is fiercely protected. American courts have long upheld this broad interpretation, allowing everything from flag-burning and hate speech to demonstrations by extremist groups. The logic behind this approach is that the marketplace of ideas—the free and open exchange of differing opinions—should decide which ideas flourish and which falter. The belief is that suppressing speech, even speech we may find deeply offensive, can set a dangerous precedent that could lead to greater censorship and the erosion of democratic values.

However, this form of free speech absolutism is not shared by many other democratic nations, which place more restrictions on expression in the interest of protecting societal harmony and individual dignity. In Germany, for instance, the legal framework emphasizes the protection of human dignity and historical responsibility, particularly in light of its Nazi past. The country has strict laws against Holocaust denial, hate speech, and the public display of Nazi symbols. These laws reflect a societal commitment to prevent the resurgence of harmful ideologies that once led to catastrophic violence and oppression.

Similarly, in the United Kingdom, the legal system strikes a balance between free expression and other rights, such as the right to privacy and protection from defamation. British libel laws, for example, are much stricter than those in the U.S., often placing the burden of proof on the defendant rather than the plaintiff. This means that journalists, authors, and individuals in the UK must be particularly cautious about accusations they make in public, as they can be sued for defamation more easily than in the U.S. While this legal framework is designed to protect individuals from false or harmful statements, critics argue that it can also stifle important investigative journalism or discourage public scrutiny of powerful figures.

In France, the legal concept of *laïcité*, or secularism, governs much of the public sphere. This principle emphasizes a strict separation of religion from government, which manifests in laws that sometimes restrict religious expression in the name of public order. For instance, France's ban on religious symbols in public schools, including Muslim headscarves, has been a source of controversy both domestically and internationally. Proponents of *laïcité* argue that it protects the secular nature of the state and promotes equality by preventing any single religion from dominating public life. Critics, however, view these policies as restrictive and discriminatory, particularly against religious minorities.

Even within the European Union, member states exhibit a wide range of approaches to free speech. The European Convention on Human Rights guarantees the right to free expression but also allows for restrictions "in the interests of national security, territorial integrity, or public safety." European countries are generally more comfortable than the U.S. with placing limits on speech to prevent incitement to violence, the spread of extremist ideologies, or harm to vulnerable communities. In Denmark, for example, the infamous 2005 publication of cartoons depicting the Prophet Muhammad sparked a global debate about the boundaries of free speech. While Denmark upheld the newspaper's right to publish the cartoons, the controversy underscored the delicate balance between free expression and respect for religious sensitivities.

International human rights law, particularly through instruments like the Universal Declaration of Human Rights (UDHR) and the International Covenant on Civil and Political Rights (ICCPR), also shapes how countries interpret free speech. Article 19 of the UDHR guarantees the right to freedom of expression, but it leaves room for restrictions "for respect of the rights or reputations of others" and "for the protection of national security or of public order." As such, even countries that are signatories to international human rights treaties often implement different policies based on their historical, cultural, and political contexts.

A key element in the comparative study of free speech is understanding how different legal frameworks reflect varying priorities within societies. While the U.S. prioritizes individual liberty and the free marketplace of ideas, many other democracies are more willing to sacrifice certain expressions of speech in favor of protecting social cohesion and preventing harm. These distinctions offer insight into how free speech is not a monolithic concept but a flexible one that adapts to the values and needs of each society.

In recent years, global debates about free speech have intensified, particularly in light of growing concerns over hate speech, misinformation, and the role of social media platforms in shaping public discourse. Countries like Germany and the UK have passed laws requiring tech companies to remove harmful content or face penalties, a trend that contrasts sharply with the more hands-off approach in the U.S., where tech platforms are granted wide latitude under Section 230 of the Communications Decency Act. This divergence raises important questions about the future of free expression in an increasingly interconnected world and whether countries will continue to adhere to their traditional free speech models or adapt to the changing digital landscape.

In the end, comparing approaches to free speech across different cultures and legal systems offers valuable insights into the diverse ways that societies protect and regulate this fundamental right. It highlights how free speech, far from being a universally understood concept, is shaped by historical experiences, legal traditions, and social values unique to each nation.

Free Speech in Authoritarian and Restrictive Regimes

While democracies worldwide debate the balance between free expression and societal well-being, authoritarian regimes take a starkly different approach. In countries where power is tightly centralized, free speech is often viewed not as a right, but as a threat. In these nations, the suppression of dissent is a fundamental tool of governance, used to maintain control over the population and silence opposition. Countries like China, North Korea, and Iran serve as key examples of how authoritarian governments use censorship, propaganda, and punishment to stifle free speech, turning the marketplace of ideas into a tightly regulated space where only state-approved narratives are permitted.

China is perhaps the most notable example of this controlled environment, wielding one of the most sophisticated censorship systems in the world. Dubbed "The Great Firewall," China's internet censorship regime is designed to prevent citizens from accessing information the government deems harmful to its interests. Major platforms like Facebook, Twitter, and Google are blocked, while domestic alternatives like WeChat and Weibo are heavily monitored. The government employs a massive network of censors and algorithms to scrub the internet of any dissenting viewpoints, including criticism of the Chinese Communist Party (CCP), discussions about human rights abuses, or pro-democracy movements. In recent years, the crackdown has extended to seemingly mundane activities like sharing jokes or memes that are deemed politically sensitive. This constant surveillance and censorship create a chilling effect, where citizens are acutely aware that their words—online or offline—are being watched, and the consequences of dissent can be severe.

Punishment for challenging the state is swift and harsh. Dissidents, journalists, and activists in China who speak out against the government are often arrested, detained, or even disappeared. One high-profile case was that of the Nobel laureate Liu Xiaobo, a prominent Chinese writer and human rights activist who was imprisoned for advocating for democratic reforms. He died in custody in 2017 after years of imprisonment, a stark reminder of the personal cost of free speech in authoritarian regimes. The CCP also tightly controls the media, ensuring that news coverage aligns with state narratives. Independent journalism is virtually nonexistent, and foreign journalists are often harassed or expelled if their reporting is seen as too critical of the government.

North Korea takes the suppression of free speech to an even more extreme level. The Hermit Kingdom, under the iron-fisted rule of the Kim dynasty, is one of the most isolated and repressive regimes in the world. The state controls every aspect of information, with all media outlets serving as mouthpieces for government propaganda. Citizens are inundated with stories praising the Kim family and portraying North Korea as a utopia, while the outside world is painted as a hostile, poverty-stricken wasteland. Access to foreign media is strictly prohibited, and even the possession of a smuggled foreign movie or song can lead to severe punishment, including labor camps or execution. This total control over information has created an Orwellian society where the state dictates reality, and citizens have little to no concept of free speech as understood in democratic nations.

Iran, too, offers a striking example of a regime that uses the suppression of free speech as a means of maintaining its theocratic rule. The Iranian government tightly controls the media and frequently censors content it deems contrary to Islamic values or the interests of the state. Social media platforms like Twitter and Facebook are banned, and websites that promote liberal ideologies, secularism, or criticism of the regime are blocked. However, unlike China or North Korea, Iran has a vibrant and persistent opposition, with activists and ordinary citizens frequently using social media and encrypted messaging apps to share dissenting views. Despite the risk of arrest, imprisonment, or even death, Iranians continue to fight for their right to free expression, as seen in the widespread protests following the 2009 Green Movement and, more recently, the 2022 protests sparked by the death of Mahsa Amini, a young woman who died in police custody after being arrested for violating the country's strict hijab laws. These movements illustrate that even in the most repressive environments, the desire for free speech and human rights remains a powerful force.

Technology, which has often been heralded as a tool for democratizing information, also serves as a double-edged sword in authoritarian regimes. While the internet and social media have provided new avenues for activism and dissent, they have also become tools for state surveillance and repression. In countries like Russia and Turkey, where authoritarian tendencies have been on the rise, governments have ramped up their efforts to control online spaces. Russia, under President Vladimir Putin, has passed laws requiring social media companies to store data on Russian servers, making it easier for the state to monitor online activity and suppress dissent. Opposition figures like Alexei Navalny have used social media platforms to expose corruption and rally supporters, but they have also faced arrest and censorship. Similarly, in Turkey, President Recep Tayyip Erdoğan's government has repeatedly shut down social media platforms during times of political unrest, arrested journalists, and prosecuted individuals for "insulting the president" online.

Authoritarian regimes often use these measures to maintain a façade of public support. Through censorship and propaganda, they craft a narrative of unity and strength, portraying dissent as a fringe element or the work of foreign agitators. By controlling the flow of information, they prevent citizens from organizing against the government and ensure that alternative viewpoints remain marginalized or invisible. The punishment for those who challenge the state is not just imprisonment or harassment but also social isolation, as friends and family members often distance themselves from dissenters to avoid guilt by association.

Despite these oppressive tactics, dissent continues to bubble beneath the surface in many of these regimes. Social media, even in its censored form, provides a lifeline for activists, journalists, and ordinary citizens to connect with the outside world and each other. In places like China and Iran, digital tools such as VPNs, encrypted messaging apps, and satellite television offer citizens ways to circumvent state censorship, allowing them to access uncensored information and share their voices. The rise of decentralized networks and platforms like blockchain-based social media is also providing new opportunities for free expression in restrictive environments, although these technologies remain in their early stages.

In conclusion, free speech is often seen as a threat by authoritarian regimes, which rely on the suppression of dissent to maintain their power. Through censorship, propaganda, and harsh punishment, these governments control the flow of information and ensure that alternative viewpoints are silenced. However, the desire for free expression is a powerful force that continues to inspire resistance, even in the most repressive environments. In today's interconnected world, the struggle for free speech in authoritarian regimes is not just a local issue but a global one, as activists and citizens use technology to amplify their voices and seek solidarity from the international community. The ongoing battle between state control and individual expression highlights the enduring importance of free speech as a cornerstone of human dignity and democratic governance.

International Human Rights Law and the Universal Right to Free Speech

In the wake of World War II, as the world sought to prevent the atrocities and authoritarianism that had led to such global devastation, international human rights law began to take shape. The creation of the United Nations (UN) and the adoption of key human rights treaties marked the beginning of an era where the protection of fundamental rights, including free speech, became a global priority. One of the most significant developments during this time was the adoption of the Universal Declaration of Human Rights (UDHR) in 1948, a landmark document that articulated the rights and freedoms to which all human beings are inherently entitled.

Article 19 of the UDHR specifically guarantees the right to freedom of opinion and expression. It states: "Everyone has the right to freedom of opinion and expression; this right includes freedom to hold opinions without interference and to seek, receive, and impart information and ideas through any media and regardless of frontiers." This declaration underscored the belief that free expression is a cornerstone of human dignity and democracy. The UDHR, though not legally binding, set the stage for subsequent treaties and covenants that would enforce these rights internationally.

The International Covenant on Civil and Political Rights (ICCPR), adopted in 1966 and ratified by over 170 countries, is one of the most important binding international treaties regarding free speech. Article 19 of the ICCPR echoes the language of the UDHR but goes further by outlining specific conditions under which free speech can be limited. These limitations must be provided by law and necessary for the respect of the rights or reputations of others, or for the protection of national security, public order, or public health and morals. The ICCPR thus provides a framework that recognizes the importance of free speech while acknowledging that it is not an absolute right.

This recognition of both the importance and limitations of free speech has led to varying interpretations and implementations of Article 19 across different countries. The ICCPR encourages states to respect the principle of free expression while also allowing them to enact laws that restrict certain forms of speech, such as hate speech, incitement to violence, or speech that threatens national security. Countries like the United States tend to emphasize the broad protection of free speech, while others, particularly in Europe, have adopted more balanced approaches that prioritize public order and the protection of vulnerable groups.

International human rights law, particularly as embodied by the ICCPR, also mandates that any restrictions on speech must meet a three-part test: they must be provided by law, pursue a legitimate aim, and be necessary and proportionate. This test ensures that limitations on speech are not arbitrary and that they serve a clear purpose, such as protecting individuals from defamation or ensuring public safety. The principle of proportionality is particularly important, as it ensures that any restrictions are no broader than necessary to achieve the legitimate aim in question. For example, while a country might restrict hate speech to protect individuals from harm, it cannot use this as a pretext to silence all dissenting voices or curtail legitimate political discourse.

International courts and bodies, such as the European Court of Human Rights (ECHR) and the UN Human Rights Committee, play a crucial role in interpreting and enforcing these principles. The ECHR, which oversees the European Convention on Human Rights (ECHR), has been especially influential in shaping global norms around free speech. While the ECHR recognizes the right to free expression under Article 10 of the Convention, it also allows for restrictions in certain circumstances, such as when speech incites hatred or violence. This approach, while more restrictive than the U.S. First Amendment, reflects a broader European commitment to balancing individual rights with the protection of democratic society and the prevention of social harm.

A pivotal case that illustrates the complexities of balancing free speech and other rights is *Handyside v. United Kingdom* (1976), where the ECHR upheld the UK government's decision to seize and destroy a book that was deemed obscene under British law. The Court reasoned that, while free speech is essential, it is not absolute and can be limited to protect public morality. This case set an important precedent in European human rights law, emphasizing that while free expression is a vital democratic right, it must coexist with other societal values, such as protecting minors from harmful content or safeguarding public decency.

At the same time, the UN Human Rights Committee has taken a slightly different stance, often leaning more toward the protection of free expression. In *Kimel v. Argentina* (2008), the Committee ruled that a law used to convict a journalist for defamation violated Article 19 of the ICCPR. The Committee emphasized that public figures, including politicians and state officials, must tolerate more criticism than ordinary citizens, as open debate and scrutiny are essential to democracy. This decision reinforced the idea that free speech, particularly political speech, must be robustly protected, even in the face of potential harm to an individual's reputation.

Despite these global frameworks, enforcement remains a challenge. Many countries that have ratified the ICCPR or are members of the Council of Europe regularly violate the free speech rights outlined in these treaties. Authoritarian regimes, as discussed in Point 2, often ignore international human rights obligations in favor of maintaining control over their populations. Even some democratic nations struggle with the tension between national laws and international human rights obligations. In countries like Turkey and Hungary, where crackdowns on free speech have become more common, the principles enshrined in the ICCPR and the ECHR are often sidelined in favor of political expediency or national security concerns.

Another challenge to international human rights law is the evolving nature of technology and communication. The rise of the internet and social media has created new opportunities for free speech but has also led to new threats. Misinformation, cyberbullying, and extremist content now proliferate online, creating difficult questions for international bodies. How do you balance the right to free expression with the need to prevent harm in a digital age? These questions have prompted renewed debates within the UN and other international organizations about how to apply existing human rights laws to the internet, with some advocating for stronger regulations to combat online hate speech and disinformation.

In conclusion, international human rights law provides a crucial framework for understanding and protecting free speech on a global scale. Through documents like the UDHR and ICCPR, the international community has established free expression as a fundamental human right. However, the interpretation and enforcement of this right vary widely, with some countries embracing broad protections and others imposing more restrictive measures in the name of public order or national security. As the world continues to grapple with the challenges of free speech in an increasingly digital and interconnected age, the principles of international human rights law will remain a vital guide for ensuring that this essential freedom is upheld while balancing the rights and safety of all individuals.

The Challenges of Balancing Free Speech and Hate Speech in Democracies

In democratic societies, the question of how to balance free speech with the need to protect individuals and groups from harm has been a persistent challenge. While the right to free expression is a core democratic value, the spread of hate speech—speech that incites hatred, violence, or discrimination against individuals based on race, religion, ethnicity, gender, or other characteristics—forces governments to consider whether, and how, speech should be limited. The tension between protecting freedom of expression and preventing harm is at the heart of debates over hate speech laws in many democratic nations.

The United States provides a unique and often extreme example of how this balance is struck. Under the First Amendment, free speech is given broad protection, with very few exceptions. The U.S. Supreme Court has repeatedly upheld the notion that even offensive, hateful, or unpopular speech must be protected to ensure a free and open marketplace of ideas. The landmark case *Brandenburg v. Ohio* (1969) set the standard for what constitutes unlawful speech, ruling that speech can only be restricted if it incites "imminent lawless action." This means that even hate speech is generally protected under U.S. law unless it directly calls for violence or unlawful behavior.

This approach stems from the belief that the best way to combat harmful ideas is not to suppress them, but to allow more speech—particularly counter-speech—to flourish. The marketplace of ideas theory suggests that in a free and open exchange, the truth will eventually prevail over falsehoods and hate. This philosophy has led to significant legal protection for speech that many other democracies would consider dangerous or harmful. For example, neo-Nazi rallies, white supremacist marches, and the spread of racist or homophobic propaganda are typically allowed under U.S. law, as long as they do not cross the line into incitement to violence. One of the most famous cases exemplifying this is the 1977 Skokie controversy, where the American Civil Liberties Union (ACLU) defended the right of a neo-Nazi group to march through a predominantly Jewish town, home to many Holocaust survivors. While the content of the speech was deeply offensive to many, the U.S. courts ruled that the group had the right to express their views, no matter how distasteful, under the First Amendment.

However, this near-absolute protection of free speech has its critics. Some argue that allowing hate speech to flourish unchecked creates a climate of fear and intimidation, particularly for marginalized groups. They point to the rise of online hate speech, harassment, and doxxing (the public release of private information) as examples of how harmful speech can have real-world consequences, including threats to physical safety, mental health, and social cohesion. While the U.S. courts have largely held the line in favor of free speech, the ongoing national debate reflects the deep discomfort many feel with protecting speech that seems intended to cause harm.

In contrast, many European democracies have adopted a more cautious approach to free speech, particularly when it comes to hate speech. Countries like Germany, France, and the United Kingdom have passed laws that criminalize speech that incites hatred, violence, or discrimination against certain groups. These laws are rooted in the belief that free speech, while essential, should not be used as a weapon to promote intolerance or social division. For example, in Germany, where the legacy of the Holocaust continues to influence legal and political thought, laws against Holocaust denial, Nazi propaganda, and hate speech targeting ethnic and religious minorities are strictly enforced. These laws reflect a commitment to preventing the kind of extreme hate that fueled the atrocities of World War II.

France, too, has strict laws against hate speech, particularly regarding racist, anti-Semitic, and homophobic speech. In recent years, the country has faced increasing tension between its commitment to free expression and its efforts to combat hate speech, especially in the wake of high-profile terrorist attacks and the rise of far-right political movements. The Charlie Hebdo massacre in 2015, in which Islamic extremists killed 12 people at the satirical newspaper known for publishing controversial cartoons of the Prophet Muhammad, reignited the debate over the limits of free speech. While many in France rallied in support of the paper's right to offend, others argued that speech that deliberately insults religious groups, particularly vulnerable minorities, should be curtailed to prevent violence and social unrest.

The United Kingdom has also implemented hate speech laws that prohibit the use of threatening, abusive, or insulting words or behavior intended to stir up hatred on the grounds of race, religion, or sexual orientation. The 2006 Racial and Religious Hatred Act, for example, makes it a criminal offense to incite hatred against people based on their religion. However, the UK's approach, like those of other European countries, attempts to strike a balance between protecting individuals from harm and preserving free speech. Critics argue that the broad wording of hate speech laws can lead to overreach, stifling legitimate political debate or the discussion of controversial topics, particularly around issues of immigration, national identity, and religion.

The European Court of Human Rights (ECHR) has played a significant role in shaping the legal landscape around hate speech in Europe. In several cases, the court has upheld the right of governments to impose restrictions on speech that incites hatred or violence, while also maintaining that these restrictions must be narrowly tailored and proportionate. For instance, in the case of *Garaudy v. France* (2003), the ECHR upheld the conviction of a Holocaust denier, ruling that denying the Holocaust did not fall under the protection of free speech because it undermined the values of democracy and human rights. This ruling reflects the broader European commitment to balancing the right to free expression with the responsibility to prevent harm, particularly to vulnerable groups.

One of the key debates in this area is whether hate speech laws actually achieve their intended goals. Proponents argue that these laws are necessary to protect marginalized communities and to prevent the spread of harmful ideologies that can lead to violence, as seen in cases of far-right terrorism and religious extremism. They contend that allowing hate speech to go unchecked creates a toxic environment in which prejudice and discrimination can flourish, eroding social cohesion and equality. In this view, hate speech laws are not a threat to free speech, but a necessary safeguard against the abuse of that freedom.

Opponents, however, caution that hate speech laws can be used to stifle legitimate debate and dissent, particularly when governments wield them to silence political opponents or unpopular viewpoints. They warn that the subjective nature of what constitutes "hate speech" can lead to overreach, where individuals are punished not for inciting violence or discrimination, but simply for expressing controversial or unpopular opinions. This concern has been raised in countries like Hungary and Poland, where hate speech laws have been used to target LGBTQ+ activists, feminist groups, and journalists critical of the government. In these cases, the very laws intended to protect free speech have been turned into tools of repression.

In conclusion, the challenge of balancing free speech and hate speech remains one of the most contentious issues in democratic societies. While the United States prioritizes broad protections for free expression, even for offensive or hateful speech, many European nations have taken a more cautious approach, enacting laws that aim to prevent the harm caused by speech that incites hatred or violence. The ongoing debates reflect deeper philosophical differences about the role of free speech in democracy and the responsibilities that come with it. As hate speech continues to evolve in the digital age, particularly on social media platforms, societies will need to grapple with new questions about how to protect both free expression and the safety and dignity of individuals.

The Role of Social Media in Shaping Global Free Speech Norms

As the world becomes increasingly interconnected through the rise of the internet and social media, the dynamics of free speech have undergone a profound transformation. Platforms like Twitter,

Facebook, Instagram, and YouTube have created unprecedented opportunities for individuals to share their voices, connect with global audiences, and engage in public discourse. These platforms have democratized speech in ways previously unimaginable, allowing anyone with internet access to participate in discussions that were once limited to traditional media outlets. However, with this transformation has come a new set of challenges, particularly concerning the regulation of harmful speech and the role that private companies play in determining the boundaries of free expression.

Social media platforms have, in many ways, become the modern-day public square—a place where political debates, social movements, and cultural exchanges unfold in real-time. From the Arab Spring to the #MeToo movement, social media has played a pivotal role in amplifying marginalized voices, organizing protests, and holding those in power accountable. Activists and dissidents have used platforms like Twitter and Facebook to bypass state-controlled media, spread awareness about human rights abuses, and rally support for democratic reforms. In this sense, social media has emerged as a powerful tool for free speech, providing a global platform for ideas to flourish and for individuals to challenge injustice.

However, the decentralized and unregulated nature of these platforms has also given rise to significant challenges, particularly when it comes to hate speech, disinformation, and online harassment. Social media companies are now at the forefront of a global debate over the limits of free speech, as they grapple with how to balance the right to express unpopular or controversial opinions with the need to protect users from harm. This tension is exacerbated by the fact that these companies are not bound by the same legal standards that apply to governments. Instead, they operate according to their own terms of service and community guidelines, which can vary widely in their interpretation and enforcement.

The debate over content moderation on social media reflects broader tensions between free speech and accountability. On one hand, advocates of free expression argue that platforms should remain as open as possible, allowing for a diversity of viewpoints, even those that may be offensive or controversial. They point out that heavy-handed censorship by private companies can stifle legitimate debate and disproportionately affect marginalized groups who rely on social media to make their voices heard. For example, during the 2020 Black Lives Matter protests, many activists accused social media platforms of disproportionately removing or flagging content related to police brutality, while allowing inflammatory rhetoric from right-wing groups to remain unchecked.

On the other hand, critics argue that the unfettered flow of information on social media can lead to serious harm, particularly when it comes to the spread of hate speech, extremism, and disinformation. In the wake of high-profile incidents, such as the Capitol insurrection in the United States and the spread of false information about COVID-19, there has been growing pressure on social media companies to take a more active role in policing harmful content. Many governments, particularly in Europe, have passed or are considering legislation that would impose stricter regulations on platforms to prevent the spread of hate speech, terrorism-related content, and harmful disinformation.

Germany's Network Enforcement Act (NetzDG), passed in 2017, is one of the most prominent examples of government regulation aimed at holding social media companies accountable for the content on their platforms. Under this law, social media companies are required to remove "obviously illegal" content, including hate speech and defamation, within 24 hours of receiving a complaint or face heavy fines. While proponents of the law argue that it is necessary to combat the rise of online hate and extremism, critics warn that it could lead to over-censorship, as platforms may remove legitimate content out of fear of financial penalties.

In the United States, where the First Amendment's protections are among the strongest in the world, the role of social media platforms has sparked intense political debate. Section 230 of the Communications Decency Act, which provides immunity to platforms for content posted by third parties, has been both praised and criticized. Advocates argue that Section 230 is essential for maintaining the open nature of the internet, allowing platforms to operate without being held liable for every post or comment made by users. Critics, however, contend that it gives social media companies too much leeway, allowing them to avoid responsibility for the harmful content they host.

Recent debates over "de-platforming" — the practice of removing users or groups from social media — have highlighted the complexities of balancing free speech with corporate responsibility. The permanent suspension of former President Donald Trump from Twitter and Facebook following the January 6, 2021 Capitol riots was a watershed moment in the regulation of online speech. Supporters of the decision argued that Trump's rhetoric had incited violence and posed a clear danger to public safety, justifying the platform's actions. Opponents, however, warned that the decision set a dangerous precedent, allowing private companies to silence political figures and influence public discourse in ways that could undermine democracy.

Beyond the issue of political speech, social media platforms have also faced criticism for their role in amplifying harmful content related to public health. The COVID-19 pandemic brought this issue into sharp focus, as misinformation about the virus, vaccines, and treatments spread rapidly across social media. In response, platforms like Facebook, YouTube, and Twitter implemented new policies aimed at curbing the spread of false information, including labeling or removing posts that contradicted established public health guidelines. While these efforts were widely praised by health experts, they also sparked a backlash from those who viewed the policies as censorship, particularly in countries where trust in government institutions and the media is low.

The global nature of social media complicates efforts to regulate speech, as platforms must navigate different legal standards and cultural norms in the countries where they operate. For example, what constitutes hate speech or offensive content in one country may be protected under free speech laws in another. In India, where Facebook and WhatsApp are used by hundreds of millions of people, the government has clashed with social media companies over the regulation of political speech, with authorities accusing platforms of bias and interference in domestic affairs. Similarly, in countries like Turkey and Russia, where authoritarian regimes tightly control the media, social media has become a battleground for free speech, with governments passing laws that require platforms to comply with local censorship rules or face restrictions.

In this global context, social media companies are not just gatekeepers of free speech; they are also powerful players in shaping public discourse. Their algorithms determine what content is promoted or suppressed, often with little transparency or accountability. Critics argue that these algorithms can create echo chambers, amplifying extreme views and reinforcing users' preexisting beliefs, while filtering out opposing perspectives. This "filter bubble" effect has been blamed for deepening political polarization and fueling the rise of populist movements around the world.

In conclusion, the rise of social media has transformed the landscape of free speech, offering new opportunities for expression while also creating new challenges for regulation and accountability. As platforms continue to navigate the complex terrain of free speech, hate speech, and disinformation, the global debate over the limits of online expression will undoubtedly intensify. Ultimately, the role that social media platforms play in shaping public discourse and enforcing the boundaries of free speech will have far-reaching implications for democracy, human rights, and the future of global communication.

CHAPTER 12

Chapter 10: The Ongoing Battle for First Amendment

The Evolution of First Amendment Challenges in Modern Times

The First Amendment of the U.S. Constitution has been a living, breathing document, constantly evolving as society changes. From the time it was adopted in 1791, its interpretation has been shaped by the courts, particularly the U.S. Supreme Court, in response to the shifting tides of American life. The broad freedoms guaranteed—speech, press, religion, assembly, and petition—are not static rights but dynamic ones that must be re-examined in the context of modern challenges.

In the early days of the Republic, First Amendment protections were narrow in scope. Many states had their own restrictions on speech, press, and religious expression. It wasn't until the 20th century, through the process of incorporation, that the First Amendment's protections were applied to state governments through the Fourteenth Amendment. This period marked the beginning of the modern era of First Amendment jurisprudence. Landmark cases such as *Gitlow v. New York* (1925) established that states could not infringe on free speech rights, setting the stage for a century of legal battles that would define the limits of the First Amendment.

One of the most significant shifts in the interpretation of the First Amendment occurred during the civil rights movement of the 1960s. Activists fighting for racial equality relied heavily on their right to free speech, assembly, and petition. The movement produced landmark Supreme Court cases, such as *New York Times Co. v. Sullivan* (1964), which established the "actual malice" standard for defamation cases involving public figures. This ruling protected the press's ability to criticize public officials, bolstering both free speech and freedom of the press.

During this era, the courts were also forced to grapple with the concept of "symbolic speech"—nonverbal expressions of ideas, such as protests, demonstrations, and sit-ins. The case of *Tinker v. Des Moines Independent Community School District* (1969) underscored this, when the Supreme Court ruled that students did not lose their First Amendment rights when they entered school, so long as their expression did not cause substantial disruption. The Tinker case cemented the notion that freedom of expression was not limited to spoken or written words, opening the door to a broader interpretation of what constitutes protected speech.

The Vietnam War era brought another wave of First Amendment challenges, as protesters clashed with government restrictions on speech and assembly. In *Cohen v. California* (1971), the Court ruled that the First Amendment protected a man's right to wear a jacket bearing the words "F*** the Draft" in a public courthouse, as it was a form of political expression. The Court concluded that the government could not prohibit the use of offensive language simply because it was distasteful or provocative. This case was a landmark victory for free speech, affirming that even unpopular or controversial speech deserves protection under the First Amendment.

As the 20th century progressed, new technologies began to complicate traditional understandings of free speech and the press. The advent of television, radio, and, later, the internet introduced new mediums for expression, raising questions about how far First Amendment protections could stretch. The Supreme Court's rulings continued to adapt to these changes. In *Reno v. ACLU* (1997), the Court struck down anti-indecency provisions of the Communications Decency Act, which sought to restrict online speech, marking a significant victory for free expression in the digital age. The ruling established that the internet deserved the same robust First Amendment protections as print media.

More recently, the rise of social media platforms like Facebook, Twitter, and YouTube has further complicated the landscape. These platforms have become central arenas for public discourse, yet they are controlled by private companies that are not subject to the same First Amendment constraints as the government. This has led to a new wave of challenges as courts, activists, and lawmakers grapple with issues of online censorship, misinformation, and the extent to which social media companies can regulate speech on their platforms. Cases involving de-platforming and content moderation have sparked heated debates about the role of private entities in shaping the public square, especially when government officials use these platforms to communicate with constituents.

The modern evolution of First Amendment challenges shows that the fight to define the boundaries of free expression is ongoing. New technologies, political climates, and social movements will continue to push the limits of what the First Amendment protects. As history has demonstrated, the courts will play a crucial role in shaping these boundaries. Whether it's symbolic speech in the form of protest or new forms of communication in the digital age, the First Amendment remains a flexible and evolving cornerstone of American democracy. Its protections are not a given, and the continued re-examination of its scope is essential to ensure that the foundational rights it guarantees remain vibrant and relevant in a changing world.

The Role of Activists and Social Movements in Defending the First Amendment

Throughout American history, activists and social movements have been at the forefront of defending and expanding the scope of First Amendment rights. These movements, from civil rights to LGBTQ+ advocacy, have used free speech, assembly, and petition as their most powerful tools to challenge the status quo, expose injustice, and demand change. The First Amendment has served as both a shield and a sword for these movements, enabling them to express dissent, challenge authority, and engage in the democratic process.

One of the earliest examples of a social movement leveraging the First Amendment was the abolitionist movement in the 19th century. Anti-slavery activists like Frederick Douglass and William Lloyd Garrison used their right to free speech and press to challenge the institution of slavery and call for its abolition. Despite facing violent opposition and attempts to silence them, these activists used pamphlets, speeches, and newspapers like *The Liberator* to spread their message. Garrison, in particular, believed that free speech was a necessary weapon in the fight for human rights. The First Amendment allowed abolitionists to expose the horrors of slavery and galvanize public opinion, even as their opponents sought to censor them.

The civil rights movement of the 1950s and 1960s represents another powerful example of how social movements have used the First Amendment to advance justice. Leaders like Martin Luther King Jr., Rosa Parks, and John Lewis organized peaceful protests, boycotts, and marches that relied on the freedoms of speech, assembly, and petition. The 1963 March on Washington for Jobs and Freedom, where King delivered his famous "I Have a Dream" speech, is one of the most iconic demonstrations of the First Amendment in action. It was a peaceful assembly that called attention to racial inequality and demanded action from the federal government. The fact that these protests were nonviolent, yet forceful in their demands, exemplified the power of protected speech and assembly in enacting social change.

However, the civil rights movement also faced significant opposition from the government, which sought to limit its activities. State and local officials used everything from restrictive permits for protests to police violence to suppress these demonstrations. Activists were arrested, jailed, and sometimes beaten for exercising their rights, yet the First Amendment provided them with a legal framework to challenge these abuses. Landmark cases such as *Edwards v. South Carolina* (1963) reaffirmed the right of individuals to peacefully assemble and protest, even when their message was unpopular. The Supreme Court ruled in favor of African American students who were arrested for protesting racial segregation, declaring that their First Amendment rights had been violated.

Social movements have also expanded the scope of the First Amendment in less traditional ways. For example, LGBTQ+ activists have used symbolic speech—like the display of the rainbow flag or same-sex couples marching in pride parades—to assert their right to equal treatment under the law. In cases such as *Hurley v. Irish-American Gay, Lesbian, and Bisexual Group of Boston* (1995), the Supreme Court ruled that the First Amendment protected the right of parade organizers to exclude LGBTQ+ groups, but it also sparked a broader conversation about how marginalized communities could use free speech and symbolic expression to advocate for their rights. Over time, this struggle helped lead to greater acceptance of LGBTQ+ rights and same-sex marriage.

In recent years, a new wave of activists—First Amendment auditors—has emerged, pushing the boundaries of free speech in public spaces. These activists, often armed with cameras, conduct audits of public buildings, law enforcement, and government institutions to ensure that citizens' constitutional rights, especially free speech and the right to film in public spaces, are being respected. By doing so, they test the limits of First Amendment protections and challenge the government's attempts to restrict or control speech in the public square. While controversial, these auditors are part of a long tradition of activists who use their constitutional rights to hold authorities accountable.

Another significant modern example is the Black Lives Matter movement, which was founded in response to police violence against African Americans. Like the civil rights movement before it, Black Lives Matter has relied on the First Amendment to organize protests, marches, and social media campaigns. The 2020 protests following the murder of George Floyd, which took place in cities across the United States, are among the largest demonstrations in U.S. history. The movement's use of social media, a relatively new platform for free speech, enabled it to mobilize millions of people and bring global attention to issues of racial injustice. Although many of these protests were peaceful, they faced heavy-handed government responses, including police violence, curfews, and the use of tear gas to disperse crowds. Once again, activists turned to the courts to assert their First Amendment rights and challenge these restrictions.

Throughout history, the First Amendment has proven to be an indispensable tool for activists and social movements. Whether fighting against slavery, segregation, police violence, or discrimination based on sexual orientation, these groups have used free speech, assembly, and petition to challenge unjust laws and practices. They have forced America to confront its contradictions and strive to live up to its ideals of liberty and equality. As new social movements continue to emerge, the First Amendment will remain a vital part of their arsenal, ensuring that the voices of dissent are heard and that democracy continues to evolve. The ongoing battle for civil rights and social justice demonstrates that the First Amendment is not only about protecting individual freedoms but also about empowering people to demand a more just and equitable society.

Government and Corporate Responses to First Amendment Rights

The tension between the government's duty to protect First Amendment rights and its attempts to limit these rights for the sake of security, order, and public welfare is a recurring theme throughout American history. While the Constitution prohibits Congress from making laws that infringe upon free speech, freedom of the press, or the right to assemble and petition, the government has often sought to place restrictions on these rights in the name of public safety or national security. In more recent years, corporations, particularly those in the technology sector, have emerged as powerful gatekeepers of free expression, raising new questions about the balance between private authority and public rights.

One of the most well-known examples of government restrictions on First Amendment rights occurred during World War I. The Espionage Act of 1917 and the Sedition Act of 1918 were passed to suppress dissent and criticism of the war effort. Under these laws, thousands of people were prosecuted for making antiwar statements, distributing pamphlets critical of the government, or participating in protests. One such case, *Schenck v. United States* (1919), led to the Supreme Court upholding the Espionage Act, stating that the government could restrict speech that posed a "clear and present danger." The ruling introduced the famous analogy of "shouting fire in a crowded theater," which argued that certain forms of speech that incite panic or violence are not protected by the First Amendment.

However, in the decades that followed, the courts began to take a more expansive view of free speech rights, even in cases where the speech was unpopular or controversial. For instance, during the Vietnam War, the Supreme Court struck down attempts by the government to silence anti-war protesters. In *Brandenburg v. Ohio* (1969), the Court established a new standard for limiting speech, ruling that the government could only restrict speech that is "directed to inciting or producing imminent lawless action" and is "likely to incite or produce such action." This decision significantly narrowed the government's ability to curtail free speech and reaffirmed the principle that even inflammatory or offensive speech is protected under the First Amendment.

Despite these legal precedents, government efforts to curtail First Amendment rights persist, especially in the context of national security and public safety. Following the 9/11 attacks, the Patriot Act was passed, which gave the government broad surveillance powers in the name of combating terrorism. This raised serious concerns about privacy and the freedom of speech. Activists, journalists, and ordinary citizens feared that their communications were being monitored, and that the mere act of criticizing the government could lead to surveillance or worse. The case of whistleblower Edward Snowden, who exposed the National Security Agency's mass surveillance programs, highlighted the delicate balance between national security and the protection of civil liberties, including the right to free speech.

Beyond government actions, private corporations, particularly tech companies, have become key players in regulating speech. Social media platforms like Facebook, Twitter, and YouTube now serve as the primary public squares where people express their opinions, share information, and engage in debates. However, these platforms are not subject to the same First Amendment constraints as the government because they are private entities. As a result, they have the power to regulate speech on their platforms, often in ways that spark controversy.

One of the most contentious issues surrounding corporate regulation of speech is content moderation. Social media companies have policies in place to remove content that violates their terms of service, which often include prohibitions on hate speech, misinformation, and incitements to violence. While these policies are designed to create safe and respectful online environments, they have been criticized for being overly broad or inconsistently applied. For instance, many users argue that platforms disproportionately target certain political viewpoints or censor controversial but important discussions. The banning of former President Donald Trump from Twitter and Facebook following the January 6th, 2021, Capitol riot ignited a nationwide debate about the role of private companies in regulating public discourse. While some applauded the decision as necessary to prevent further violence, others argued that it represented a dangerous precedent for corporate censorship.

In addition to social media companies, traditional media corporations have also been implicated in the debate over free speech. The consolidation of media ownership has led to concerns about a lack of diversity in viewpoints and the suppression of dissenting opinions. With a handful of corporations controlling most of the news outlets in the U.S., critics argue that the freedom of the press is under threat. Journalists face increasing pressure from their corporate owners to toe certain editorial lines, and investigative reporting that challenges powerful interests is becoming more difficult to publish. This raises questions about how freedom of the press can be preserved in an era where profit-driven corporations control much of the information that reaches the public.

The rise of tech companies as gatekeepers of speech, coupled with the government's ongoing efforts to regulate speech for the sake of security and public order, complicates the traditional understanding of First Amendment rights. While the Constitution explicitly restricts the government from infringing upon these rights, it does not account for the immense power that private corporations now wield over public discourse. As social media becomes increasingly integral to democratic participation, new legal and ethical frameworks may be necessary to ensure that the fundamental principles of free expression are preserved.

The evolving relationship between government, corporations, and the First Amendment underscores the importance of vigilance in protecting free speech and other rights guaranteed by the Constitution. In an age of digital communication, the lines between public and private control of speech are blurring, and the consequences of these shifts are still being understood. What remains clear, however, is that the fight to defend and define the scope of First Amendment rights is far from over. Both the government and private corporations have significant roles to play, and their actions will continue to shape the future of free expression in America.

The Role of the Courts in Shaping First Amendment Rights

The judiciary, particularly the U.S. Supreme Court, has played a crucial role in interpreting and shaping the scope of First Amendment rights. While the text of the First Amendment is relatively simple—"Congress shall make no law... abridging the freedom of speech, or of the press; or the right of the people peaceably to assemble, and to petition the Government for a redress of grievances"—its application to real-world situations has been anything but straightforward. Over the centuries, the courts have been tasked with deciding what kinds of speech, press, assembly, and petition are protected, and when the government can lawfully intervene. Through landmark rulings, the courts have expanded, clarified, and, at times, limited the protections offered under the First Amendment.

One of the most significant judicial developments in the realm of free speech came during the early 20th century with the introduction of the "clear and present danger" test in *Schenck v. United States* (1919). This case revolved around Charles Schenck, a socialist who was arrested for distributing leaflets opposing the draft during World War I. The Supreme Court upheld his conviction, reasoning that Schenck's speech presented a clear and present danger to national security during wartime. Justice Oliver Wendell Holmes, in his famous opinion, wrote that "the most stringent protection of free speech would not protect a man in falsely shouting fire in a theatre and causing a panic." This established the idea that not all speech is absolute—speech that threatens public safety can be restricted by the government.

The "clear and present danger" standard was a starting point, but the Court would continue to refine its stance on free speech in the years that followed. In *Brandenburg v. Ohio* (1969), the Court set a new precedent by ruling that speech could only be restricted if it was "directed to inciting or producing imminent lawless action" and was "likely to incite or produce such action." This marked a significant expansion of free speech protections, as it allowed for the expression of controversial, even offensive, ideas as long as they did not incite immediate violence or illegal activity. In this case, Clarence Brandenburg, a Ku Klux Klan leader, had given a speech advocating violence, but the Court ruled that his speech was protected because it did not pose an imminent threat of lawless action. The *Brandenburg* ruling remains a cornerstone of First Amendment jurisprudence, protecting a wide range of speech, including inflammatory and extremist speech, so long as it does not directly lead to violence.

The judiciary has also had to navigate complex questions about the freedom of the press. One of the most important cases in this area is *New York Times Co. v. United States* (1971), commonly referred to as the "Pentagon Papers" case. The Nixon administration attempted to prevent the *New York Times* and *Washington Post* from publishing classified documents detailing the U.S. government's conduct during the Vietnam War, citing national security concerns. The Supreme Court, in a 6-3 decision, ruled against the government, holding that the First Amendment's protection of a free press outweighed the government's claims of national security in this instance. Justice Hugo Black wrote in his concurring opinion that "the press was to serve the governed, not the governors." The *Pentagon Papers* case established that prior restraint—government censorship before publication—is highly disfavored under the First Amendment, and that the press has a vital role in holding the government accountable, even in matters of national security.

Assembly and petition, though less frequently discussed than speech and press, have also been shaped by the courts. One of the key cases regarding the right to assembly is *NAACP v. Alabama* (1958). In this case, the state of Alabama sought to compel the NAACP to turn over its membership lists, arguing that the organization was engaging in illegal activities. The Supreme Court ruled in favor of the NAACP, holding that the forced disclosure of membership lists would infringe on the right to free association, which is an essential component of the right to assemble. The Court reasoned that compelling disclosure would likely deter individuals from joining the organization and participating in civil rights activities due to fear of harassment or retribution. This case expanded the understanding of the right to assemble, protecting not only physical gatherings but also organizational affiliations from government interference.

The courts have also played a role in defining the limits of free speech in special contexts, such as schools and the workplace. In *Tinker v. Des Moines Independent Community School District* (1969), the Supreme Court ruled that students do not "shed their constitutional rights to freedom of speech or expression at the schoolhouse gate." This case involved students who wore black armbands to protest the Vietnam War, and the Court ruled that their symbolic speech was protected under the First Amendment. However, this right is not unlimited. The Court clarified that schools can restrict speech if it materially disrupts the learning environment. The *Tinker* decision marked a significant victory for student rights and has since been cited in numerous cases involving free speech in educational settings.

In more recent years, the courts have been faced with challenges involving new technologies and forms of communication, particularly in the digital age. The rise of social media has prompted debates over what constitutes protected speech online, especially in cases of hate speech, harassment, and misinformation. In *Packingham v. North Carolina* (2017), the Supreme Court struck down a North Carolina law that prohibited registered sex offenders from using social media, ruling that access to social media platforms is a vital part of free speech in the modern era. Justice Anthony Kennedy, writing for the majority, declared that "cyberspace... is one of the most important places for the exchange of views." This decision highlights the evolving nature of First Amendment rights as society continues to shift toward digital communication.

The judiciary's role in interpreting the First Amendment has been indispensable in defining its practical application. Through its decisions, the courts have expanded protections for speech, press, assembly, and petition while also establishing important boundaries. The Supreme Court's rulings have not only protected individual rights but have also reinforced the First Amendment's central role in maintaining a vibrant democracy. As new challenges continue to arise, particularly in the digital age, the courts will remain key players in the ongoing battle to preserve and protect First Amendment freedoms.

Grassroots Movements and the Citizen's Role in Defending First Amendment Rights

While the courts have played a significant role in interpreting and safeguarding First Amendment rights, the true power of these freedoms lies with ordinary citizens. Throughout American history, grassroots movements have been instrumental in shaping the understanding and application of the First Amendment. From civil rights activists to modern-day First Amendment auditors, these movements demonstrate the vital role that everyday people play in defending and exercising their constitutional rights. Citizens, empowered by the First Amendment, have continually challenged authority, sought justice, and ensured that the freedoms enshrined in the Constitution are not mere words on paper but living principles that shape the nation.

One of the most profound examples of grassroots activism is the civil rights movement of the 1950s and 1960s. African Americans, facing systemic racism and oppression, used the freedoms of speech, assembly, and petition to push for social change. Leaders like Martin Luther King Jr., Rosa Parks, and countless unnamed activists organized marches, sit-ins, and boycotts that relied heavily on the right to assemble and petition the government. The iconic March on Washington for Jobs and Freedom in 1963, where King delivered his famous "I Have a Dream" speech, exemplifies the power of peaceful assembly to challenge the status quo and demand justice.

Civil rights activists understood that the First Amendment was not just a legal protection but a tool for empowerment. By using their voices and their collective presence, they brought national attention to the injustices of segregation, voter suppression, and police brutality. This grassroots activism, often met with violent resistance, forced the courts and the government to confront the contradiction between the nation's ideals of freedom and equality and its realities of discrimination. The passage of the Civil Rights Act of 1964 and the Voting Rights Act of 1965 are testaments to the power of citizen-led movements in pushing for legal and societal change. The legacy of the civil rights movement continues to influence modern activism, reminding Americans that the fight for First Amendment rights is often led by those on the ground.

In more recent years, the rise of First Amendment auditors has highlighted a new form of citizen activism aimed at ensuring government accountability. These individuals, often armed with cameras, exercise their right to free speech and assembly by filming public officials, particularly law enforcement, in the performance of their duties. The premise behind First Amendment auditing is simple: public servants, especially those in law enforcement, should be held accountable to the people, and the right to film in public spaces is a critical tool in achieving that accountability. These auditors challenge the overreach of government power by asserting their rights to record and document public activities, often leading to confrontations with officials unfamiliar with or hostile to this practice.

First Amendment auditors have drawn both praise and criticism. Supporters argue that they are exercising a fundamental right and shedding light on government transparency and the limits of official authority. By documenting interactions with police officers, security personnel, and other public officials, these auditors have exposed abuses of power and helped spark debates about the balance between security and civil liberties. Critics, however, claim that some auditors provoke confrontations or engage in reckless behavior, using the First Amendment as a shield for disruptive or even antagonistic actions. Regardless of the controversy, First Amendment auditors represent a broader trend of citizen engagement with constitutional rights, demonstrating that ordinary individuals can play a crucial role in upholding the principles of freedom.

The modern-day protest movements, such as the Black Lives Matter (BLM) and Women's March movements, further illustrate the continued relevance of grassroots activism in defending First Amendment rights. The BLM movement, sparked by the deaths of unarmed African Americans at the hands of police, has organized mass protests around the country to call for police reform, racial justice, and an end to systemic racism. These protests, protected by the First Amendment, have drawn millions of people into the streets to peacefully demonstrate. Despite facing opposition from law enforcement and political leaders, BLM activists have used their right to free speech and assembly to shape public discourse and influence policy debates on police accountability and racial equity.

Similarly, the Women's March, which began as a response to the 2016 election, has mobilized millions of people to advocate for women's rights, reproductive freedom, and gender equality. These movements showcase how the right to assemble and petition the government remains a vital part of American democracy. By organizing mass protests and rallies, citizens have the power to voice their concerns, push for legislative changes, and hold elected officials accountable. These movements not only exercise First Amendment rights but also expand public understanding of what these rights entail, particularly when it comes to issues of justice and equality.

In the digital age, grassroots activism has taken on new forms, with social media becoming a powerful tool for organizing and amplifying First Amendment rights. Movements like #MeToo, which exposed widespread sexual harassment and assault, grew rapidly online, demonstrating the capacity of digital platforms to bring about real-world change. Through the use of hashtags, viral videos, and online petitions, activists have harnessed the power of the internet to reach a global audience, raising awareness and advocating for policy reforms. This new form of activism blurs the lines between traditional and digital organizing, but at its core, it remains rooted in the First Amendment principles of free speech and the right to assemble and petition for change.

These examples underscore the critical role that grassroots movements and ordinary citizens play in shaping the ongoing battle for First Amendment rights. While the courts and the government are key players in defining the scope of these rights, it is ultimately the people who bring these rights to life. From the civil rights movement to modern protests, citizens have continually pushed the boundaries of the First Amendment, challenging authority, demanding justice, and expanding the scope of freedom for all.

The First Amendment's promise is not static; it is dynamic, evolving in response to the needs and actions of the people. Every protest, every petition, every video filmed by a First Amendment auditor serves as a reminder that these rights belong to the people and are most powerful when exercised by them. As new challenges to free speech, press, assembly, and petition arise, it will be the citizens—armed with the protections of the First Amendment—who continue to defend and define these freedoms for future generations.

CHAPTER 13

Chapter 11: Case Studies of First Amendment Heroes

The Legacy of James Madison: Father of the First Amendment

James Madison, often called the "Father of the Constitution," was also the architect of the First Amendment. His legacy as a staunch defender of individual liberty, and as the principal drafter of the Bill of Rights, stands as a cornerstone in American constitutional history. Madison's contribution to the First Amendment, which guarantees freedom of speech, religion, press, assembly, and petition, cannot be overstated. His vision for a government that both empowered and restrained itself through law laid the foundation for a democratic society that continues to evolve today.

Madison's belief in the need for a Bill of Rights was not initially shared by all of his contemporaries. During the Constitutional Convention of 1787, there was debate about whether such protections were necessary. Many believed that the Constitution, as written, already limited the government enough. However, Madison recognized the potential for government overreach and the necessity of explicitly safeguarding individual freedoms. His advocacy for the inclusion of a Bill of Rights was driven by his deep understanding of human nature and his fears of unchecked governmental power. Madison believed that without these explicit protections, the liberties of the people could be eroded over time.

To understand Madison's motivations, it is essential to look at the philosophical influences that shaped him. He was deeply influenced by Enlightenment thinkers such as John Locke, whose writings on natural rights and the separation of church and state had a profound impact on Madison's thinking. Locke's concept of government as a social contract—whereby the power of the government is derived from the consent of the governed—resonated with Madison. He believed that the primary role of government was to protect the inherent rights of individuals, including freedom of conscience and expression.

Madison's personal experiences during the American Revolution also shaped his views on liberty. Having witnessed British censorship and restrictions on colonial assemblies and speech, he understood the dangers of government suppression. These experiences, combined with his philosophical grounding, convinced him that a new government, while stronger than the loose confederation of states that existed after the revolution, must not trample on the rights of individuals.

The fight for the First Amendment took center stage during the debates over the ratification of the Constitution. The Anti-Federalists, those opposed to the Constitution's ratification, feared that a strong central government would infringe on individual liberties. They demanded a Bill of Rights as a condition for their support. Although Madison was initially skeptical of the need for these amendments—believing that the structure of the new government would prevent tyranny—he eventually conceded that it was essential to calm the fears of the opposition and to enshrine these rights as fundamental protections.

In 1789, as a member of the newly formed U.S. House of Representatives, Madison introduced a series of amendments to the Constitution that would eventually become the Bill of Rights. His First Amendment proposal was groundbreaking in its scope. It protected not only freedom of speech and press but also the right to religious liberty, the right to assemble peaceably, and the right to petition the government. These were revolutionary ideas at the time, as most governments in the world did not recognize such extensive personal freedoms.

Madison's drafting of the First Amendment was not merely a political move; it was a deeply held belief in the necessity of these freedoms for the survival of a democratic society. He argued that without the ability to express dissent, criticize the government, or worship freely, a republic could not truly represent the will of the people. He recognized that power, if unchecked, would inevitably lead to tyranny. For Madison, the First Amendment was the key to preserving the democratic experiment.

The passage of the First Amendment in 1791 marked the beginning of a new era in the United States. It became the foundation for the country's commitment to free expression and personal liberty. Madison's vision, though tested over time, has endured. His insistence on protecting these essential rights laid the groundwork for the many legal battles that would follow, as individuals and groups sought to define and expand the scope of First Amendment protections.

In modern times, James Madison's legacy continues to be invoked in courtrooms, legislatures, and public discourse. His work has influenced countless Supreme Court decisions, from those protecting free speech during wartime to those defending the press from government censorship. Madison's insistence that a democracy could not survive without the free exchange of ideas remains a central tenet of American law and society.

Madison's First Amendment was not a static document; it was intended to evolve with the needs of the people it protected. Over the centuries, the amendment has been interpreted to cover a wide range of issues, from political protests to artistic expression, from religious practices to the right to criticize public officials. Madison's genius lay in his understanding that freedom, to be meaningful, must be flexible enough to encompass the changing landscape of society.

James Madison's legacy as the father of the First Amendment lives on in the freedoms Americans enjoy today. His foresight in recognizing the importance of these protections—and his persistence in ensuring their inclusion in the Constitution—has left an indelible mark on the nation. The rights enshrined in the First Amendment continue to inspire movements for justice, challenge government authority, and protect the voice of the individual against the power of the state. In this way, Madison's vision for a free and open society endures, reminding Americans of the ongoing need to defend these freedoms for future generations.

Elijah Lovejoy: The Martyr for Press Freedom

Elijah Lovejoy's story is one of courage, conviction, and ultimate sacrifice in defense of a free press. His life and tragic death serve as a powerful reminder of the cost of standing up for one's principles in the face of mob violence and government inaction. Lovejoy's legacy is that of a martyr for press freedom, and his name became a rallying cry for abolitionists and advocates of free speech in the turbulent decades leading up to the Civil War.

Born in Maine in 1802, Elijah Lovejoy was raised in a deeply religious family that instilled in him a strong sense of morality and justice. After completing his education, Lovejoy became a Presbyterian minister and eventually moved to St. Louis, Missouri, where he transitioned into journalism. His passion for the written word, coupled with his strong religious convictions, led him to take up the cause of abolitionism—a stance that would soon place him in direct conflict with pro-slavery forces in the region.

In 1833, Lovejoy became the editor of the *St. Louis Observer*, a religious newspaper through which he began to express his growing opposition to slavery. At first, his criticisms were measured, but as he witnessed the brutal realities of slavery in Missouri—a slave state—his tone became increasingly uncompromising. Lovejoy's articles denounced slavery as a moral evil and called for its immediate abolition. His bold stance earned him the ire of pro-slavery factions, who saw his words as a threat to their way of life.

Tensions quickly escalated. Lovejoy's office and printing press were attacked multiple times by pro-slavery mobs who sought to silence his voice. Undeterred, Lovejoy continued to publish articles condemning both slavery and the violence being used to suppress the abolitionist movement. The attacks on his press only strengthened his resolve, as he believed deeply in the right to speak and publish freely, regardless of the personal consequences.

In 1836, fearing for his safety and under intense pressure, Lovejoy moved his newspaper operations across the Mississippi River to Alton, Illinois, a free state. He hoped that the laws in Illinois would offer him greater protection from the violence he had experienced in Missouri. However, his presence in Alton was no less controversial. His outspoken abolitionist views made him a target once again, and local pro-slavery sympathizers began plotting to destroy his press.

On three separate occasions, mobs in Alton attacked Lovejoy's printing press, each time attempting to destroy his ability to publish. Yet each time, Lovejoy found a way to continue his work, replacing the damaged presses and reaffirming his commitment to free expression. He understood that a free press was essential not only for the abolitionist cause but also for the preservation of a democratic society in which individuals could challenge injustice without fear of reprisal.

The turning point came on November 7, 1837. Lovejoy had just received a new printing press after the latest attack, and rumors spread that another mob was planning to destroy it. Determined to protect his right to publish, Lovejoy and a group of supporters armed themselves and guarded the warehouse where the press was stored. That night, a violent mob of pro-slavery men surrounded the building. What began as a standoff soon escalated into a deadly confrontation. The mob set fire to the warehouse and, in the chaos that followed, Elijah Lovejoy was shot and killed as he attempted to flee.

Lovejoy's death sent shockwaves throughout the country. For abolitionists, he became a martyr, his murder symbolizing the violent lengths to which pro-slavery forces would go to silence dissent. But for advocates of a free press, Lovejoy's death underscored the dangers faced by journalists who dared to challenge the status quo. His refusal to be intimidated, even in the face of repeated attacks and the threat of death, highlighted the vital role that the press plays in holding power accountable and fostering public debate.

In the aftermath of Lovejoy's murder, many Americans began to grapple with the broader implications of his death. It was not just an attack on an individual or even the abolitionist movement—it was an attack on the fundamental right to free expression. Lovejoy's courage and sacrifice became a catalyst for a renewed national conversation about the importance of press freedom and the dangers of allowing mob violence to dictate the limits of public discourse.

Among those deeply affected by Lovejoy's death was a young Illinois lawyer named Abraham Lincoln. Lovejoy's martyrdom, and the broader struggle for press freedom, would influence Lincoln's own views on the importance of protecting civil liberties, even in the face of intense opposition. Decades later, as President, Lincoln would confront similar questions about the limits of free speech and the role of the press during the Civil War.

Lovejoy's legacy lives on as a symbol of the enduring struggle for press freedom. His story reminds us that the right to publish and disseminate ideas, particularly controversial ones, is not guaranteed without sacrifice. Throughout American history, the press has often found itself at odds with powerful interests—whether political, economic, or social—and those in power have frequently sought to stifle critical voices. Lovejoy's defiance in the face of such efforts is a testament to the importance of an independent press in a free society.

Today, as journalists around the world continue to face threats of violence, censorship, and repression, the story of Elijah Lovejoy is more relevant than ever. His unwavering commitment to truth and justice, even at the cost of his life, serves as a powerful reminder of the essential role the press plays in the fight for human rights and democracy. In standing up for what he believed in, Elijah Lovejoy did more than simply defend his own right to speak—he championed the cause of free expression for all. His legacy challenges us to continue the fight for a free and fearless press, recognizing that without it, the very foundation of democracy is at risk.

Frederick Douglass: A Voice for Liberty and Justice

Frederick Douglass, one of the most prominent voices of the 19th century, stands as a towering figure in the fight for civil liberties, human rights, and the abolition of slavery. Born into slavery in 1818, Douglass's life was defined by his unyielding pursuit of freedom—both for himself and for the millions of African Americans held in bondage. As an orator, writer, and activist, Douglass understood the transformative power of speech and the press, using both as weapons in his battle against the institution of slavery and for the broader struggle for freedom and equality.

Douglass's own story is a testament to the power of education and free expression. He was born on a Maryland plantation and spent his early years witnessing the brutal realities of slavery. But unlike many others, Douglass refused to be intellectually shackled. He secretly taught himself to read and write, an act of defiance that would later prove pivotal in his role as a leader in the abolitionist movement. His early understanding of literacy as a form of empowerment highlights a fundamental principle of the First Amendment: knowledge and the free exchange of ideas are crucial to the pursuit of justice.

After escaping slavery in 1838, Douglass settled in the North, where he quickly became involved in the abolitionist movement. His powerful oratory and commanding presence made him a sought-after speaker. Douglass was a living example of the horrors of slavery, but also a symbol of the potential for African Americans to thrive as free individuals. His speeches were not just calls to end slavery; they were profound critiques of a nation that professed liberty and justice for all while holding millions in bondage. In his speeches, Douglass wielded the First Amendment like a sword, attacking the hypocrisies of the American government and society.

Douglass's most famous speech, "What to the Slave is the Fourth of July?" delivered on July 5, 1852, remains a searing indictment of the nation's moral contradictions. In this speech, Douglass exposed the absurdity of celebrating freedom in a country that denied freedom to an entire race of people. He challenged his audience, asking how they could celebrate liberty when millions were still enslaved. The speech was a masterclass in rhetoric and moral clarity, as Douglass balanced his fierce condemnation of slavery with a hopeful vision for America's future. He did not reject the ideals of the Declaration of Independence or the Constitution; instead, he called upon America to live up to those ideals by extending liberty and justice to all its people.

Douglass's use of the press was equally important in his fight for abolition and civil rights. In 1847, he founded *The North Star*, an abolitionist newspaper that became one of the most influential publications in the movement to end slavery. Through *The North Star*, Douglass provided a platform for black voices, publishing articles that condemned slavery, argued for equal rights, and celebrated the achievements of African Americans. His newspaper was not merely a tool for spreading information; it was a beacon of hope and empowerment for a disenfranchised community.

In founding *The North Star*, Douglass was exercising the very freedom of the press that the First Amendment guarantees, a right he knew was essential for the advancement of the abolitionist cause. He used the paper to challenge pro-slavery propaganda and to rebut the widespread racist notions that justified slavery. Douglass's editorial voice was sharp, eloquent, and unafraid to confront both the institution of slavery and the broader social systems that supported racial oppression. His belief in the power of the written word to inspire action and change was rooted in his personal journey from illiteracy to intellectual leadership.

Douglass's work as a journalist and public speaker was not without its challenges. Like many abolitionists, he faced threats, harassment, and violence from those who sought to silence his message. Despite these dangers, Douglass remained steadfast, knowing that the struggle for freedom required the full exercise of his rights to speak, write, and publish. His defiance in the face of these threats is a reminder that the freedoms protected by the First Amendment are often hard-won and require constant vigilance.

Beyond his role in the abolitionist movement, Douglass was a tireless advocate for the rights of all oppressed groups. After the Civil War and the abolition of slavery, Douglass continued to fight for civil rights, including women's suffrage and the rights of free African Americans. He understood that freedom of speech, freedom of the press, and the right to petition the government were essential tools in the fight for equality. His vision for America was one in which these rights were not only protected but were used as vehicles for social change.

Frederick Douglass's legacy is deeply intertwined with the First Amendment. His life's work exemplified the belief that speech and the press are not just personal liberties but are foundational to the struggle for justice. Douglass's speeches and writings did more than just expose the evils of slavery—they called the nation to account for its failure to live up to its own ideals. In doing so, Douglass demonstrated the transformative power of free expression, inspiring generations of activists to continue the fight for civil rights and social justice.

Today, Douglass's legacy continues to resonate in movements for racial equality, social justice, and freedom of expression. His belief in the power of words to challenge injustice remains as relevant as ever in an era where marginalized voices still fight to be heard. Frederick Douglass's life is a testament to the enduring importance of the First Amendment in the ongoing battle for human dignity and equality, a reminder that freedom of expression is not only a right but a responsibility—to speak out against oppression and to demand a more just and inclusive society.

Douglass's unwavering commitment to liberty, equality, and justice makes him one of the great heroes of the First Amendment, and his example continues to inspire those who seek to use their voices to make the world a better, fairer place for all.

Lillian Hellman: Courage in the Face of McCarthyism

Lillian Hellman, the acclaimed playwright and screenwriter, was a fearless defender of free speech and civil liberties during one of the most repressive periods in American history: the McCarthy era. Her unwavering stance against the House Un-American Activities Committee (HUAC) and her refusal to name names at the height of the Red Scare are emblematic of the courage required to defend the First Amendment, even when the cost is personal and professional destruction.

The Red Scare, which reached its zenith in the late 1940s and early 1950s, was a time of national paranoia over the perceived threat of communism infiltrating American institutions. In an effort to root out suspected communists, the U.S. government initiated a series of investigations led by Senator Joseph McCarthy and HUAC. These hearings targeted intellectuals, entertainers, and political activists, many of whom were accused—often without evidence—of communist sympathies. Those who were called before the committee were pressured to confess their political affiliations and to inform on colleagues, leading to widespread fear, blacklisting, and the destruction of countless careers.

In this climate of fear and coercion, Lillian Hellman's decision to stand up for her principles was nothing short of heroic. Born in 1905, Hellman rose to prominence as one of the most influential American playwrights of the 20th century. Her works, including *The Children's Hour* and *The Little Foxes*, tackled themes of moral corruption, greed, and the abuse of power—issues that would later resonate in her own life when she faced the might of the U.S. government.

Hellman was first subpoenaed to testify before HUAC in 1952. Like many others in the entertainment industry, she was suspected of having communist affiliations due to her political activism and leftist sympathies. The committee's intention was clear: they wanted her to name others who were involved in leftist political activities, particularly those in the Hollywood community. For many, the pressure to comply with HUAC's demands was overwhelming. Refusing to name names could lead to professional ruin, as those who defied the committee were blacklisted from working in their respective industries. Nonetheless, Hellman refused to bow to this pressure.

In a letter to the committee, Hellman made her stance clear: "I cannot and will not cut my conscience to fit this year's fashions." Her words, now legendary, exemplify her determination to hold true to her moral convictions, no matter the personal cost. Hellman's refusal to cooperate with HUAC was not just an act of personal defiance—it was a principled stand against what she saw as an assault on the very freedoms enshrined in the First Amendment. To name others, she argued, would be to participate in a witch hunt that sought to silence dissent and suppress free expression.

Her testimony before HUAC remains one of the most memorable moments of the McCarthy era. Hellman appeared before the committee and invoked her Fifth Amendment right against self-incrimination but did so in a way that was both bold and defiant. She refused to answer questions about her political affiliations or to name others, knowing full well the consequences of her actions. As a result, she was blacklisted from Hollywood, and her career suffered greatly. Studios, fearing reprisals from the government, refused to work with her, and for many years, Hellman was unable to produce films or plays.

Despite the personal and professional toll, Hellman never wavered in her commitment to free speech and civil liberties. In her later years, she continued to be an outspoken critic of McCarthyism and a staunch advocate for civil rights. Her autobiography, *Scoundrel*

Time, published in 1976, offers a scathing critique of the McCarthy era and the individuals who participated in the persecution of their fellow citizens. In the book, Hellman reflects on the cowardice of those who betrayed their colleagues to save themselves, contrasting their actions with the bravery of those who, like her, chose to stand up for their principles.

Hellman's refusal to cooperate with HUAC had far-reaching implications beyond her personal experience. Her courageous stand helped to expose the moral bankruptcy of the McCarthy-era witch hunts, showing that the fight for free speech and expression often requires great personal sacrifice. She was part of a larger movement of intellectuals and artists who stood up to the government's repressive tactics, and her defiance contributed to the eventual decline of McCarthy's influence.

In the broader context of First Amendment history, Hellman's story is a powerful example of the importance of protecting free speech, even in times of national crisis. The Red Scare was a period in which the fear of communism was used to justify the erosion of civil liberties, and the government's actions during this time stand as a stark reminder of how easily freedoms can be stripped away when fear and hysteria take hold. Hellman's bravery in the face of these pressures is a testament to the resilience of those who recognize that the right to free expression is not something that can be compromised, no matter how great the threat.

Today, Lillian Hellman's legacy lives on as a symbol of resistance to government overreach and the suppression of free thought. Her refusal to betray her colleagues, even when faced with personal ruin, underscores the fundamental importance of the First Amendment's protections. In standing up to HUAC, Hellman demonstrated that the true strength of a democracy lies in its citizens' ability to speak their minds without fear of retribution.

Lillian Hellman's story, like those of many others who fought against the injustices of the McCarthy era, is a reminder that the freedoms guaranteed by the First Amendment must be vigilantly protected. Her courage in the face of overwhelming pressure serves as an enduring example of the power of conscience and the critical role that free expression plays in preserving democracy.

The Westboro Baptist Church: A Case Study in Protecting Unpopular Speech

The Westboro Baptist Church, infamous for its virulently anti-LGBTQ rhetoric and provocative public demonstrations, represents one of the most extreme and controversial cases of protected speech in modern America. While their messages are deeply offensive to many, their case stands as a stark reminder of the broad scope of the First Amendment's protection of free speech—even when that speech is hateful, divisive, and harmful to the public conscience.

Founded by Fred Phelps in 1955, the Westboro Baptist Church is a small congregation based in Topeka, Kansas, but its reach and notoriety are far greater. The church gained widespread attention in the early 1990s for picketing the funerals of AIDS victims, but it is perhaps best known for its protests at the funerals of U.S. soldiers. Holding signs with slogans such as "God Hates Fags" and "Thank God for Dead Soldiers," Westboro members claim that the deaths of soldiers are divine punishment for America's tolerance of homosexuality. Their protests have shocked and outraged communities across the country, leading to widespread calls for their suppression.

Despite the offensive nature of their message, the Westboro Baptist Church's actions are protected under the First Amendment. This was solidified in the landmark 2011 Supreme Court case *Snyder v. Phelps*, which revolved around Westboro's picketing of the funeral of Marine Lance Corporal Matthew Snyder, who had died in Iraq. The Snyder family sued Westboro for emotional distress, arguing that the church's protests at their son's funeral were a targeted attack on their grief and dignity.

The case made its way to the Supreme Court, where the central question was whether Westboro's speech, offensive as it was, could be restricted under the First Amendment. In an 8-1 decision, the Court ruled in favor of Westboro Baptist Church, holding that their speech was indeed protected, as it addressed matters of public concern on public property. Writing for the majority, Chief Justice John Roberts emphasized that speech cannot be prohibited simply because it is offensive or disturbing. The First Amendment, Roberts argued, protects even speech that "inflicts great pain," as long as it pertains to public issues and does not directly incite violence or lawlessness.

The ruling in *Snyder v. Phelps* is a profound affirmation of the First Amendment's broad protections. The case makes clear that the government cannot regulate speech based on its content or because it is offensive to the majority. Even when speech is hateful and aimed at vulnerable individuals during moments of profound personal loss, the Court held that it must be protected if it touches on matters of public concern. In the case of Westboro Baptist Church, their protests were deemed a commentary on issues like military policy, homosexuality, and America's moral direction—topics that fall squarely within the realm of public debate, however distasteful the language used may be.

This ruling was met with significant public backlash, as many Americans found it difficult to reconcile the idea that such hate-filled speech could be constitutionally protected. The emotional weight of the case—the grief of a family mourning their son and the callousness of Westboro's message—made the decision all the more controversial. However, the Supreme Court's decision underscores a key principle of the First Amendment: protecting free speech requires the defense of even the most unpopular or offensive expressions. The alternative—allowing the government to decide which views are acceptable and which are not—poses a far greater danger to democracy.

While the *Snyder v. Phelps* case affirms Westboro's right to protest, it also highlights the limits of the First Amendment. The ruling does not grant the church unrestricted freedom to harass or target individuals. Laws that impose reasonable time, place, and manner restrictions on protests, such as buffer zones around funerals, have been upheld as constitutional. These laws are designed to protect the rights of grieving families and others from undue harassment while preserving the right to free speech in public spaces. The balance struck in such cases is a delicate one, aimed at ensuring that both free expression and personal dignity are respected.

The Westboro Baptist Church case raises difficult questions about the nature of free speech in a democratic society. How do we reconcile the protection of offensive speech with the harm it may cause to individuals and communities? Where do we draw the line between public discourse and personal attacks? These are not easy questions, but the *Snyder v. Phelps* ruling demonstrates that, for the most part, the Court will err on the side of protecting speech, even when it is deeply unpopular.

The case also illustrates the essential role of the First Amendment in safeguarding minority viewpoints, no matter how repugnant they may seem to the majority. Free speech is not about protecting the views we agree with; it is about protecting the right to express ideas that challenge, discomfort, or even offend us. Without this protection, any dissenting voice could be silenced by those in power, leading to a society where only sanctioned opinions can be expressed.

The Westboro Baptist Church continues to protest and provoke, but their influence remains marginal. While their speech is protected, it has not gained widespread acceptance, a reminder that the marketplace of ideas is not dictated solely by legal protection but also by public discourse and the power of reason. The church's actions have galvanized communities across the country to respond not with censorship but with counter-protests, acts of solidarity, and expressions of support for the very groups Westboro seeks to demean.

In the broader narrative of First Amendment heroes, the Westboro Baptist Church does not fit the traditional mold. They are not celebrated activists or defenders of noble causes. Yet, their case represents an essential chapter in the history of free speech jurisprudence. It forces us to confront the uncomfortable reality that, in a free society, the right to express unpopular and even hateful views must be protected if we are to ensure that all voices can be heard.

In the end, the story of Westboro Baptist Church is less about their message and more about the resilience of the First Amendment. It serves as a stark reminder that the true test of our commitment to free speech lies in our willingness to defend the rights of those whose views we abhor. Only by safeguarding the speech we find most offensive can we preserve the right to speak freely ourselves.

CHAPTER 14

Chapter 12: The Future of the First Amendment

The Challenges of Digital Speech

The dawn of the digital age has revolutionized how we communicate, but it has also introduced new and complex challenges for the First Amendment. While the principles of free speech remain the same, the platforms on which people now exercise this right—social media, online forums, and other digital spaces—present unique obstacles that were unimaginable when the First Amendment was drafted. As the internet becomes the primary venue for speech, questions arise about how the First Amendment should apply in this new frontier, particularly when private companies, rather than the government, hold the power to regulate content.

Social media platforms such as Facebook, Twitter (now X), YouTube, and Instagram have become central to public discourse. These platforms host billions of users and act as de facto public squares, where individuals share opinions, engage in debate, and disseminate information at an unprecedented scale. However, unlike the traditional public square, these platforms are not government entities—they are private corporations. As such, they have the legal right to set their own rules regarding what speech is allowed or disallowed on their sites. This creates a tension between users' expectations of free expression and the companies' responsibility to moderate harmful content.

One of the most significant challenges facing digital speech is the spread of misinformation and disinformation. The internet provides a platform where false information can spread rapidly, often with devastating consequences. Whether it's false claims about elections, vaccine conspiracies, or manipulated media, misinformation undermines the public's ability to make informed decisions. In response, tech companies have implemented various strategies to curb the spread of false information, such as fact-checking, labeling misleading posts, and, in some cases, removing content entirely.

However, these efforts have sparked heated debates about the boundaries of free speech. Critics argue that platforms are overstepping by censoring content and disproportionately silencing certain political or ideological viewpoints. For instance, when Twitter permanently banned former President Donald Trump following the January 6th Capitol riots, it ignited a national conversation about whether social media companies should have the power to silence even the most influential voices. Many conservative voices felt targeted by what they perceived as selective enforcement of content moderation policies, while others argued that Trump's speech had incited violence and posed a genuine threat to public safety.

The question of whether social media platforms should be considered public forums—where First Amendment protections would apply more robustly—remains unresolved. Some have suggested that platforms should be regulated like utilities or public services, given their role in facilitating public discourse. Under this model, platforms would be subject to stricter rules about content moderation, ensuring that no viewpoint could be arbitrarily silenced.

Others, however, caution against government regulation of digital platforms, arguing that it could stifle innovation and free enterprise, and ultimately lead to government overreach in dictating what content is permissible.

Another pressing issue is the rise of hate speech online. Social media has given voice to extremists who use the internet to promote hate, recruit followers, and organize violent movements. Platforms have increasingly adopted stricter policies against hate speech, banning users who engage in racist, sexist, or violent rhetoric. Yet, hate speech often falls into a gray area of free speech jurisprudence. In the United States, hateful speech is largely protected under the First Amendment unless it directly incites violence. This has led to platforms like Facebook and YouTube facing criticism from both sides—being accused of censoring legitimate speech in some instances while allowing harmful ideologies to flourish in others.

These challenges point to a larger question: Who should control speech in the digital age? Should tech companies be the gatekeepers of online discourse, or should the government step in to enforce regulations? The current model, in which private companies have broad discretion to moderate content, has led to a patchwork of policies that vary widely from platform to platform. While some see this as a necessary form of self-regulation, others view it as a threat to the free exchange of ideas.

In the absence of clear legal precedents governing online speech, courts and lawmakers are grappling with how to apply First Amendment principles to the digital realm. The Supreme Court has yet to rule definitively on the role of social media companies as public forums, leaving the issue in a state of flux. Meanwhile, legislative efforts such as Section 230 of the Communications Decency Act, which shields platforms from liability for user-generated content, have come under increasing scrutiny. Some argue that Section 230 should be reformed to hold platforms more accountable for the content they host, while others fear that changing the law could lead to increased censorship and stifle innovation.

As digital speech continues to evolve, the First Amendment faces its greatest test in the internet age. The challenge will be striking the right balance between protecting free expression and addressing the harms that can arise in the vast, unregulated spaces of the internet. Just as the Founders could not have predicted the rise of the internet, today's policymakers must navigate uncharted territory as they seek to uphold the timeless principles of free speech in a rapidly changing world.

In this new frontier, the future of the First Amendment will depend not only on how courts and lawmakers address these issues but also on how society as a whole chooses to engage with digital speech. The internet offers unparalleled opportunities for communication and connection, but it also demands a collective responsibility to safeguard the values of open discourse, critical thinking, and respect for diverse perspectives.

The Tension Between National Security and Free Speech

In times of crisis, the delicate balance between national security and the protection of civil liberties often comes under intense scrutiny. Throughout American history, the First Amendment's guarantee of free speech has been tested against the government's responsibility to maintain national security, especially during wars, terrorism threats, and periods of social unrest. The 21st century, with its complex geopolitical challenges and evolving nature of warfare, has heightened these tensions, raising critical questions about how much speech should be protected when it appears to undermine national security interests.

The terrorist attacks of September 11, 2001, represent a pivotal moment when the balance between free speech and national security shifted dramatically. In the wake of the attacks, the U.S. government enacted the Patriot Act, a sweeping piece of legislation designed to enhance surveillance capabilities and prevent future attacks. While many Americans initially supported the Act as a necessary measure to combat terrorism, it soon became a flashpoint for debates over the erosion of civil liberties, particularly free speech and privacy rights.

One of the key criticisms of post-9/11 national security measures is the expansion of government surveillance programs. Whistleblowers such as Edward Snowden revealed the extent to which agencies like the National Security Agency (NSA) were monitoring the communications of millions of Americans, often without their knowledge. While the government defended these programs as essential tools for identifying and preventing terrorist threats, civil liberties advocates argued that they posed a significant threat to free speech. The fear of being monitored, they contended, could lead people to self-censor or avoid discussing politically sensitive topics, undermining the very essence of the First Amendment.

The challenge lies in defining the line between legitimate national security concerns and the overreach of governmental powers that stifle free expression. History provides numerous examples of governments exploiting national crises to clamp down on dissent. During World War I, for instance, the U.S. government passed the Espionage Act of 1917, which made it a crime to interfere with military operations or support the nation's enemies. This law was used to prosecute individuals who spoke out against the war, including socialist leader Eugene V. Debs, who was sentenced to ten years in prison for delivering an anti-war speech. The case, *Schenck v. United States*, led to the famous ruling by Justice Oliver Wendell Holmes Jr., who declared that speech creating a "clear and present danger" was not protected by the First Amendment.

The question of what constitutes a "clear and present danger" continues to evolve, especially in an era where national security threats are more diffuse and difficult to pinpoint. For example, the rise of "lone wolf" terrorists, radicalized through online propaganda, has prompted governments to scrutinize the role of speech in inciting violence. In the digital age, speech that advocates terrorism or extremist ideologies can be disseminated widely and rapidly, leading governments to seek legal mechanisms to prevent such speech from inciting violence or recruiting new followers.

However, the government's attempts to restrict certain forms of speech in the name of national security are not without controversy. For instance, laws that criminalize "material support" for terrorism have been criticized for being overly broad, sometimes ensnaring individuals who are not directly involved in terrorist activities. In the 2010 case of *Holder v. Humanitarian Law Project*, the Supreme Court upheld a law that prohibited providing legal advice to designated terrorist organizations, even if the advice was intended to help the group engage in peaceful negotiations or human rights work. Critics argued that this ruling infringed on free speech and the right to advocate for peaceful solutions to conflicts, demonstrating how national security concerns can sometimes stifle legitimate expression.

The war on terror has also seen the rise of debates over censorship, particularly in regard to leaks of classified information. Journalists who report on government activities often walk a fine line between informing the public and facing prosecution under laws like the Espionage Act. One of the most high-profile cases in recent years was the prosecution of WikiLeaks founder Julian Assange, who was charged under the Espionage Act for publishing classified documents related to U.S. military activities in Iraq and Afghanistan. Supporters of Assange argue that his actions are protected under the First Amendment's guarantee of a free press, while critics claim that the release of sensitive government information posed a serious threat to national security.

As the U.S. continues to navigate threats from cyberattacks, domestic terrorism, and global instability, the tension between national security and free speech is unlikely to diminish. In the digital age, where information flows across borders instantly and anonymously, the government's efforts to monitor and control dangerous speech will likely become more aggressive, further complicating the boundaries of First Amendment protections.

However, it is crucial to remember that the First Amendment was designed not only to protect popular speech but also to safeguard dissent and criticism, especially in times of crisis. Throughout history, the most significant advances in civil liberties have often come from those who dared to speak out against government overreach, even in the face of threats to national security. As the courts continue to grapple with cases that pit national security against free speech, they must be guided by the principle that a robust defense of free expression is essential to maintaining a healthy democracy, even in times of peril.

In the coming years, the challenge will be to develop a legal framework that allows the government to respond effectively to threats without eroding the foundational freedoms that define the United States. Striking this balance will require constant vigilance, thoughtful jurisprudence, and a commitment to protecting both national security and the core values enshrined in the First Amendment.

Free Speech in Academia and the Battle Over "Safe Spaces"

One of the most heated debates in recent years surrounding free speech has taken place on college campuses, where the tension between freedom of expression and the desire for "safe spaces" has sparked national conversation. Universities, long regarded as bastions of open inquiry and debate, have increasingly become the focal point for clashes over what constitutes protected speech versus speech that is considered harmful, offensive, or even dangerous. As the future of the First Amendment is debated, college campuses serve as a microcosm of the broader cultural and legal battles over the limits of free expression.

Historically, universities have been at the forefront of social and political change. From the Free Speech Movement at Berkeley in the 1960s to protests against the Vietnam War, students and faculty have used academic spaces to challenge the status quo and engage in bold, sometimes controversial, forms of speech. This tradition of free expression is rooted in the belief that the university should be a place where ideas, no matter how unpopular or unsettling, can be explored and debated without fear of censorship or retribution. However, in recent years, this ideal has come under strain as student groups, faculty, and administrators have grappled with the boundaries of acceptable speech in an increasingly polarized environment.

The rise of "safe spaces" on college campuses has been one of the key issues in this debate. Safe spaces are environments where individuals, particularly those from marginalized or historically oppressed groups, can feel protected from speech or ideas that they find harmful or triggering. These spaces are intended to provide a refuge from the emotional and psychological impact of hate speech, harassment, or even deeply offensive but legally protected speech. Supporters of safe spaces argue that they are necessary for the mental and emotional well-being of students who face discrimination or hostility in other areas of their lives. They contend that universities have a responsibility to foster inclusive environments where all students can feel secure and supported.

However, critics of safe spaces argue that they can have a chilling effect on free speech. They assert that creating zones where certain ideas or expressions are off-limits runs counter to the very purpose of higher education, which is to challenge assumptions, test ideas, and engage in difficult but necessary conversations. By shielding students from uncomfortable or opposing viewpoints, critics argue, universities risk stifling intellectual growth and fostering a culture of intolerance toward dissent. In this view, universities should be places where all speech—even speech that some might find offensive—can be heard, debated, and ultimately evaluated on its merits.

One of the most visible manifestations of this tension has been the controversy over campus speakers. In recent years, numerous high-profile incidents have occurred where speakers—often those with conservative or controversial viewpoints—were either disinvited from speaking engagements or met with protests, sometimes resulting in the cancellation of events. These instances have raised questions about whether universities are truly upholding the principles of free speech or whether they are bowing to pressure from vocal student groups who seek to silence certain voices.

For example, in 2017, violent protests erupted at the University of California, Berkeley, in response to a scheduled speech by rightwing provocateur Milo Yiannopoulos. The event was ultimately canceled due to safety concerns, but the incident ignited a national debate over whether universities are obligated to host controversial speakers, even if their views are considered offensive or inflammatory. Yiannopoulos's opponents argued that his speech constituted hate speech and posed a genuine threat to marginalized students. His supporters, on the other hand, claimed that the university had caved to mob rule and failed to defend the principle of free expression.

This debate over free speech and the limits of acceptable discourse is not confined to conservative speakers. Progressives and social justice activists have also found themselves at odds with university policies regarding speech, particularly when their activism is met with administrative pushback. In some cases, student protesters advocating for racial justice or LGBTQ+ rights have been accused of disrupting campus activities or creating a hostile environment for others, leading to disciplinary action or legal challenges. This raises important questions about how universities can balance the need to protect free expression with the imperative to maintain a safe and inclusive learning environment for all students.

Adding complexity to the debate is the issue of academic freedom. Faculty members, in particular, face challenges when their research, teaching, or public statements are deemed controversial. In recent years, professors have been fired, censured, or faced calls for their resignation over comments made on social media, in the classroom, or in academic publications. While academic freedom is a cornerstone of university life, allowing professors to pursue lines of inquiry without fear of retribution, it is increasingly being tested as universities face pressure from donors, students, and the public to take action against faculty whose speech is viewed as offensive or inappropriate.

A notable example of this tension occurred in 2020, when a professor at the University of California, Los Angeles, was placed on leave after refusing to change his grading policy in response to student demands for leniency in light of the Black Lives Matter protests. The professor's decision, and his subsequent public defense of it, led to accusations of racism and calls for his dismissal. Supporters of the professor argued that his academic freedom was being violated, while critics contended that his refusal to accommodate students during a period of social unrest demonstrated a lack of empathy and understanding of their lived experiences.

Ultimately, the debate over free speech in academia is a reflection of broader societal trends. As political polarization deepens and conversations about identity, power, and privilege take center stage, universities are being forced to confront difficult questions about whose voices should be amplified and whose should be restrained. The future of free speech on college campuses may well determine the future of the First Amendment itself, as the next generation of leaders, thinkers, and citizens shapes its understanding of what free expression means in a diverse and increasingly interconnected world.

What remains clear is that universities must continue to grapple with the challenges of balancing free speech with the need for inclusive, respectful environments. As legal battles and cultural debates continue to unfold, the way universities navigate these issues will set important precedents for how society as a whole approaches the complex relationship between speech, power, and responsibility.

Hate Speech and the Limits of Tolerance

The debate over hate speech is one of the most contentious issues in the realm of free expression, posing the question of whether all speech, even that which promotes hatred or discrimination, deserves protection under the First Amendment. In recent years, hate speech has come under increasing scrutiny, as societies wrestle with the balance between protecting free speech and preventing harm to vulnerable communities. While the First Amendment of the U.S. Constitution offers broad protection for speech, it does not explicitly outlaw hate speech, leaving the courts and public debate to grapple with its boundaries.

Hate speech is generally understood to be speech that expresses hatred, bigotry, or discrimination against individuals or groups based on characteristics such as race, religion, gender, sexual orientation, or ethnicity. In some countries, hate speech is criminalized, and penalties are imposed on individuals who incite violence, discrimination, or hatred. However, the U.S. takes a different approach, with courts consistently ruling that the First Amendment protects even the most offensive forms of speech, so long as they do not directly incite violence or constitute "fighting words."

The landmark Supreme Court case *Brandenburg v. Ohio* (1969) is frequently cited as the legal standard for determining the limits of free speech when it comes to hate speech. In this case, Clarence Brandenburg, a Ku Klux Klan leader, was convicted under Ohio law for advocating violence during a rally. The Supreme Court overturned his conviction, ruling that speech advocating illegal action is protected under the First Amendment unless it is directed at inciting "imminent lawless action" and is likely to produce such action. This decision established a high threshold for restricting speech, ensuring that even inflammatory or hateful rhetoric is protected unless it directly leads to violence.

This legal precedent has shaped the way American society approaches hate speech, often leading to heated debates over what should be tolerated in the public sphere. For many, the idea of defending the rights of hate groups like the Ku Klux Klan, neo-Nazis, or white supremacists is deeply unsettling. They argue that such speech not only spreads harmful ideologies but also contributes to an environment of fear and intimidation, particularly for marginalized communities. In their view, hate speech can be just as dangerous as direct incitement to violence, as it perpetuates societal inequalities and reinforces systems of oppression.

On the other hand, free speech advocates argue that suppressing hate speech sets a dangerous precedent. They contend that once the government begins to censor certain forms of speech, it becomes difficult to draw clear lines about what constitutes acceptable and unacceptable expression. Who gets to decide what is considered hate speech? They caution that empowering the government to police speech could lead to abuses, where speech critical of those in power or challenging the status quo might be suppressed under the guise of combating hate.

This tension came to the forefront in the aftermath of the 2017 "Unite the Right" rally in Charlottesville, Virginia, where white supremacists, neo-Nazis, and other far-right groups gathered to protest the removal of Confederate statues. The rally turned violent, culminating in the tragic death of Heather Heyer, a counter-protester, who was killed when a white supremacist drove his car into a crowd. In the wake of Charlottesville, calls to limit hate speech intensified, with many questioning how far the First Amendment should go in protecting groups that advocate for racial violence and supremacy.

Critics of unrestricted free speech argue that allowing hate groups to organize and express their views publicly legitimizes their dangerous ideologies and emboldens their followers. They point to the fact that the internet and social media have provided a platform for the rapid spread of extremist content, making it easier for hate groups to recruit new members and incite violence. In the digital age, the consequences of hate speech can be far-reaching and devastating, as online radicalization can quickly translate into real-world acts of violence and terror.

However, free speech defenders maintain that the answer to hate speech is not suppression, but more speech. This principle, often referred to as the "marketplace of ideas," suggests that the best way to counter hateful or false speech is through open debate and the presentation of opposing viewpoints. They argue that by allowing all ideas—even repugnant ones—to be aired, society can more effectively challenge and discredit harmful ideologies. This approach, they contend, is more in line with the democratic values of the First Amendment, which seeks to protect dissenting and minority views, no matter how unpopular.

Indeed, some of the most important advances in civil rights have come as a result of allowing free speech to flourish, even when it was controversial or unpopular. The civil rights movement of the 1960s, for instance, was initially met with widespread hostility and censorship from government authorities who sought to suppress its message. Activists like Martin Luther King Jr. faced legal and extralegal consequences for their efforts to challenge racial segregation and discrimination. However, the power of their ideas, communicated through free speech, ultimately prevailed in reshaping the legal and moral landscape of the country.

The question of how to deal with hate speech in the future will continue to challenge lawmakers, courts, and society as a whole. As incidents of hate crimes and extremism rise, there is a growing sense that the First Amendment may need to be reinterpreted to address the realities of a more connected and diverse world. At the same time, any attempts to regulate hate speech must be approached with caution, as the potential for government overreach and the suppression of legitimate dissent remains a serious concern.

Ultimately, the debate over hate speech and the limits of tolerance forces society to confront some of its deepest values. It challenges Americans to think critically about what kind of speech should be protected and what the cost of protecting it might be. As the nation moves forward, it will have to find ways to reconcile its commitment to free expression with the need to protect individuals and communities from the harm that hateful ideologies can cause. Whether through legal reforms, cultural change, or grassroots activism, the future of the First Amendment will be shaped by how society navigates this complex and emotionally charged issue.

The Role of Social Media in Shaping Modern Free Speech

The rise of social media has transformed the way we communicate, organize, and engage with the world around us. Platforms like

Twitter, Facebook, YouTube, and Instagram have given individuals an unprecedented ability to broadcast their thoughts, ideas, and opinions to global audiences. In many ways, social media has become the new public square, a space where free speech plays out in real time, allowing anyone with an internet connection to participate in conversations that once would have been restricted to traditional media or local forums. However, the democratization of speech online has brought new challenges to the First Amendment, forcing society to reevaluate the meaning and boundaries of free expression in the digital age.

Social media platforms have revolutionized communication by removing the traditional gatekeepers of information. Before the internet, newspapers, television, and radio stations had significant control over the flow of information and could decide which voices were amplified and which were silenced. Now, anyone with a smartphone or computer can bypass these traditional outlets and speak directly to the public. This has been a powerful tool for activists, marginalized communities, and everyday citizens to share their perspectives and organize movements that can rapidly gain traction. Movements like #MeToo, Black Lives Matter, and the Arab Spring were all fueled by the power of social media to disseminate information and mobilize action, often challenging entrenched power structures and forcing important social changes.

However, the same qualities that make social media a force for good can also lead to significant problems. The decentralized nature of these platforms has allowed misinformation, hate speech, and extremist content to spread with alarming speed. Unlike traditional media, which is bound by journalistic standards and editorial oversight, social media content is largely unregulated, relying on users to flag inappropriate material and platforms to moderate content. This raises questions about the responsibility of social media companies in curating speech, as well as the limits of free expression in the digital space.

One of the most contentious issues surrounding social media is the question of content moderation. Major platforms like Facebook, Twitter, and YouTube have adopted policies to regulate certain types of speech, such as hate speech, harassment, and misinformation. These companies often use a combination of algorithms and human moderators to remove content that violates their terms of service. However, the decisions about what to remove or allow have been met with significant controversy. Critics from across the political spectrum have accused social media companies of bias—either for not doing enough to remove harmful content or for overstepping by censoring legitimate speech.

Conservative voices, in particular, have often argued that social media companies disproportionately target right-leaning users, removing posts or suspending accounts for expressing controversial but legally protected views. High-profile bans, such as those of former President Donald Trump from Twitter and Facebook following the January 6, 2021, Capitol riot, have sparked intense debate about whether social media platforms are infringing on free speech rights by de-platforming individuals or groups based on political content. These concerns have led some to argue that social media platforms should be regulated like public utilities, ensuring that all viewpoints are treated equally and that companies cannot act as private censors.

On the other hand, others argue that social media platforms are private companies with the right to enforce their own rules. They point out that the First Amendment protects individuals from government censorship, not from actions taken by private entities. In this view, social media platforms are not obligated to provide a platform for every kind of speech, particularly speech that violates their community standards or promotes violence, harassment, or hate.

Furthermore, they contend that the proliferation of harmful content—such as conspiracy theories, disinformation, and hate speech—necessitates some form of moderation to protect the public and prevent real-world harm.

The debate over content moderation reached a boiling point during the COVID-19 pandemic, when social media platforms became major battlegrounds for misinformation about the virus, vaccines, and public health measures. Companies like Facebook and YouTube introduced stricter policies to combat misinformation, removing posts that spread false claims about the pandemic. While many applauded these efforts to stem the tide of dangerous misinformation, others saw them as a slippery slope toward increased censorship. The question of how to balance the need for accurate information with the principles of free speech remains a difficult one, and it is likely to shape the future of online communication for years to come.

Another issue complicating the free speech debate on social media is the rise of algorithms that determine which content users see. These algorithms are designed to keep users engaged by showing them content that aligns with their interests, often leading to the creation of echo chambers where individuals are exposed only to information that reinforces their existing beliefs. This phenomenon has been linked to increased political polarization, as users become more entrenched in their views and less likely to engage with opposing perspectives. The role of algorithms in shaping public discourse raises concerns about how free speech functions in an environment where speech is curated by unseen forces and tailored to individual preferences.

The global nature of social media also adds layers of complexity to the free speech debate. Unlike traditional media, which is often localized to specific countries or regions, social media platforms operate on a global scale, subject to varying laws and cultural norms. In some countries, governments have exerted pressure on social media companies to restrict certain types of content, often using national security or hate speech laws to justify censorship. In other cases, platforms have voluntarily complied with local laws, leading to the suppression of speech that would be protected under the U.S. First Amendment. The international dimensions of social media governance highlight the difficulties of applying consistent free speech standards across different political and legal systems.

As society continues to grapple with the challenges posed by social media, the future of free speech may depend on how these platforms evolve. Will social media companies be held accountable for the content they host, or will they remain largely unregulated, allowing harmful speech to flourish? Will governments step in to regulate these platforms, potentially curbing free expression in the process, or will the marketplace of ideas thrive online, with users self-regulating what they consume and share?

One possible solution lies in greater transparency and accountability from social media companies. By clearly articulating their content moderation policies and making their decision-making processes more transparent, platforms could help restore trust in the system. Additionally, users themselves may play a critical role in shaping the future of free speech online. As digital citizens, individuals have the power to demand changes from platforms, hold them accountable, and engage in responsible speech practices. In the end, the future of free speech on social media will likely be determined by a combination of legal frameworks, corporate policies, and public pressure.

In conclusion, social media has revolutionized the way we engage with free speech, creating new opportunities for expression while raising profound questions about its limits. As these platforms continue to shape modern discourse, society must navigate the delicate balance between protecting free speech and mitigating the harms that can arise in an unregulated digital environment. The future of the First Amendment in the internet age will depend on how these issues are addressed, and whether we can adapt our legal and cultural frameworks to meet the challenges of a rapidly evolving digital landscape.

CHAPTER 15

Chapter 13: First Amendment Auditors: Guardians of

The Rise of First Amendment Auditors

The First Amendment, which protects freedoms of speech, press, assembly, and the right to petition the government, has long been a cornerstone of American democracy. In recent years, a grassroots movement has emerged, known as First Amendment auditors. These individuals, often equipped with little more than a smartphone or camera, set out to test the boundaries of these rights by filming public officials and government employees in the course of their duties. Their mission is simple but powerful: to ensure that government actors respect the constitutional rights of citizens, particularly the right to film in public spaces without interference.

The rise of First Amendment auditors coincides with the rapid advancement of technology, particularly the widespread availability of high-quality cameras on smartphones. This technological development has made it possible for anyone to document their interactions with public officials in real-time, whether it be at a post office, a police station, or a city hall. The footage is often uploaded to social media platforms like YouTube, where it can reach a global audience within hours. As a result, these audits have not only served as a check on government power but also as a form of public education, reminding people of their rights and responsibilities under the Constitution.

The auditing movement gained significant traction in the early 2010s, as a handful of high-profile auditors began to attract widespread attention online. One of the most notable early figures in the movement was Phillip Turner, known online as The Battousai, whose audits of police stations and government buildings helped solidify the practice. His calm and collected demeanor in the face of confrontation set the tone for what many auditors strive to achieve—an unwavering commitment to exercising their rights while maintaining a peaceful and non-confrontational stance. Turner's interactions with law enforcement highlighted the gaps in public officials' understanding of citizens' First Amendment rights, particularly the right to film in public places.

The popularity of auditing videos exploded in part because they tap into a deep-seated desire for accountability, particularly in an era when public trust in government institutions is waning. For many viewers, these videos offer a form of empowerment, showing that ordinary citizens can stand up to authority and demand that their rights be respected. The appeal of these audits also lies in their simplicity: they demonstrate that one does not need to be a lawyer, journalist, or activist to hold the government accountable. Instead, any citizen with knowledge of their rights and a willingness to assert them can play a role in preserving the freedoms enshrined in the Constitution.

Moreover, social media has played a critical role in amplifying the impact of First Amendment audits. Platforms like YouTube, Instagram, and Facebook provide auditors with a global stage, allowing them to share their experiences and educate others about their rights. Many auditors have amassed large followings, with some garnering hundreds of thousands of subscribers who tune in regularly to watch new audits. These platforms have also created a sense of community among auditors, who often collaborate on audits or share tips and strategies for engaging with public officials.

However, the rise of First Amendment auditors has not been without controversy. While many view their actions as a necessary and noble exercise of constitutional rights, others see them as provocateurs, intentionally creating confrontations to gain attention or views. Critics argue that some auditors engage in behavior that borders on harassment, using their cameras to antagonize public employees or disrupt government operations. This tension between the auditors' mission and the reactions they provoke is a recurring theme in the movement, raising important questions about the limits of free speech and the responsibilities that come with it.

Despite the controversy, the growth of the First Amendment auditing movement signals a broader shift in the relationship between citizens and their government. At its core, the movement is a reflection of the American ideal that government should be transparent, accountable, and always answerable to the people. By exercising their rights in public spaces and documenting their interactions with public officials, auditors serve as a reminder that the freedoms guaranteed by the First Amendment are not just abstract principles but practical tools that citizens can use to safeguard democracy.

Legal Framework and Constitutional Protections

At the heart of the First Amendment auditing movement lies the bedrock principle that public officials are accountable to the people they serve. This accountability is ensured in part through the First Amendment's guarantee of the right to free speech and a free press, which has been interpreted by courts to include the right to record public officials in the performance of their duties. The legal foundation for this right is robust, though its application in practice is sometimes met with resistance or confusion, particularly by law enforcement and government employees who may not be fully aware of the extent of citizens' rights under the Constitution.

The First Amendment explicitly protects several fundamental freedoms: speech, press, assembly, petition, and religion. In the context of First Amendment audits, the key provisions are the freedoms of speech and press. Recording interactions with public officials is not only an exercise of the right to free speech—since the act of documenting and disseminating those recordings can be considered a form of expression—but also an exercise of press freedom. In the modern digital era, the distinction between traditional journalism and citizen journalism has blurred. Today, anyone with a smartphone can serve as a journalist, shining a light on government conduct and ensuring transparency. This reality is central to the auditors' mission: the power to hold government officials accountable is no longer reserved for established media outlets; it belongs to everyone.

One of the most significant legal precedents supporting the right to record public officials is the 2011 federal court ruling in *Glik v. Cunniffe*. In this case, Simon Glik, a private citizen, used his cell phone to record police officers making an arrest in Boston Common. Glik was arrested and charged with violating the state's wiretapping law, but he sued the officers, claiming that his arrest violated his First and Fourth Amendment rights. The U.S. Court of Appeals for the First Circuit ruled in Glik's favor, establishing a critical precedent: the act of recording public officials in public spaces is protected by the First Amendment.

The *Glik* ruling clarified that individuals have a right to record matters of public interest, particularly when they involve government officials performing their duties in public. The court noted that "gathering information about government officials in a form that can readily be disseminated to others serves a cardinal First Amendment interest in protecting and promoting the free discussion of governmental affairs." This case became a cornerstone for First Amendment auditors, affirming that their actions are not only legal but constitutionally protected, provided they remain within the bounds of the law—i.e., recording in public spaces where there is no reasonable expectation of privacy and not obstructing the duties of public officials.

Other federal circuit courts have followed suit, reinforcing the right to record public officials in public settings. For instance, in *Fields v. City of Philadelphia* (2017), the Third Circuit Court of Appeals ruled that "recording police officers in the public discharge of their duties is protected by the First Amendment." Similar rulings from the Fifth, Seventh, and Ninth Circuits have strengthened this interpretation, creating a body of case law that supports the rights of auditors to film interactions with public officials.

Despite these legal protections, challenges remain. Some government employees and law enforcement officers, either out of ignorance or defiance, may still attempt to prevent auditors from recording, citing privacy concerns or claiming that filming constitutes interference with official duties. In many cases, these encounters end with auditors being asked to leave or even arrested for trespassing, disorderly conduct, or obstruction. However, the vast majority of these cases are dismissed once the legal protections for filming in public spaces are brought to light.

Moreover, First Amendment auditors often invoke the legal concept of a "limited public forum" when conducting their audits. Public buildings such as libraries, post offices, and government offices are often classified as limited public forums, meaning they are open to public use for certain purposes, though reasonable restrictions may apply. Auditors argue that as long as they are not causing a disruption, their right to record in these spaces is protected. While there have been cases where courts ruled in favor of limiting access to specific areas of government buildings, the general principle remains that public spaces—especially those paid for and maintained by taxpayers—are open to public scrutiny.

It is worth noting that while the right to record is generally upheld, it is not absolute. Certain restrictions can be legally imposed, particularly when filming in secure or sensitive locations, such as military bases, hospitals, or courtrooms, where privacy concerns or security risks are heightened. However, in most cases involving public officials performing public duties in public spaces, the courts have consistently ruled in favor of auditors, reinforcing the idea that transparency and accountability are essential to a functioning democracy.

In summary, the legal framework that supports First Amendment auditing is both clear and powerful: the right to record public officials in the performance of their duties is constitutionally protected, with few exceptions. By documenting these interactions, auditors not only exercise their own rights but also play a crucial role in ensuring that government officials remain accountable to the people. The courts have affirmed this right repeatedly, establishing a firm legal foundation for the auditing movement and its role in promoting transparency and civic engagement.

The Impact of Audits on Public Accountability

First Amendment audits have had a profound impact on public accountability in the United States, particularly when it comes to the actions of government employees and law enforcement officers. By filming their encounters and making these recordings publicly available, auditors hold public officials to a higher standard of transparency and behavior. The mere presence of a camera can act as a powerful deterrent against misconduct, as officials are made acutely aware that their actions are being documented and could be subject to public scrutiny. This dynamic has made audits an effective tool for promoting accountability, especially in cases where citizens feel powerless in the face of government authority.

The concept of public accountability is central to any democratic society. Citizens delegate authority to public officials with the expectation that they will serve the public interest in a transparent and responsible manner. However, when this trust is broken—whether through abuse of power, corruption, or negligence—the very foundation of democracy is undermined. First Amendment auditors, by documenting their interactions with public officials, play a vital role in reinforcing this accountability. They remind officials that their actions are not conducted in a vacuum but are subject to public oversight. The visibility created by auditing serves as a check on power, reinforcing the notion that government officials work for the people and must be answerable to them.

One of the key impacts of First Amendment audits is their role in exposing instances of government overreach or misconduct. Auditors have captured footage of public officials who, either out of ignorance or disregard for constitutional rights, attempt to shut down legal recordings, detain auditors unlawfully, or otherwise overstep their authority. These incidents, when shared online, often go viral, sparking outrage and prompting further investigation by the media, legal professionals, or watchdog organizations. By bringing these encounters to light, auditors help to foster a culture of accountability and ensure that officials are held responsible for their actions.

For example, there have been numerous cases where audits have led to significant legal and policy changes. In some cities, footage from audits has prompted local governments to retrain law enforcement officers on citizens' rights to record in public spaces. Some police departments, in response to viral audit videos, have implemented reforms to ensure that officers are better informed about the boundaries of First Amendment rights. This not only protects citizens but also benefits law enforcement by reducing unnecessary confrontations and potential legal liabilities.

One notable instance of an audit prompting institutional change occurred when an auditor in Texas filmed police officers attempting to prevent him from recording inside a public building. The video quickly went viral, attracting millions of views and sparking a public debate about the officers' conduct. In response, the police department issued a public apology and initiated a comprehensive review of their training procedures regarding First Amendment rights. The case also resulted in a lawsuit, which was ultimately settled in favor of the auditor, reinforcing the legal protections that support the movement. This case illustrates the ripple effect that audits can have: not only do they expose individual incidents of overreach, but they can also lead to broader systemic changes.

Beyond law enforcement, First Amendment audits have also shed light on issues of government transparency in other public sectors. Auditors frequently conduct their work in places like city halls, post offices, and public libraries, testing the willingness of government employees to respect citizens' rights. In many cases, auditors have revealed that employees in these settings are unaware of the laws surrounding public recording, leading to unnecessary confrontations or attempts to block filming. As a result, audits have raised public awareness about the importance of government employees being educated on the rights of citizens and the limitations of their authority.

These audits have an educational impact as well. For the viewing public, audit videos serve as real-time lessons in civics and constitutional rights. Many people are unaware of their right to record in public or the legal parameters that govern public interactions with law enforcement and government employees. Watching auditors calmly assert their rights in the face of opposition provides viewers with practical examples of how to stand up for their constitutional freedoms. This educational component has contributed to the growth of the auditing movement, as more citizens feel empowered to hold public officials accountable.

However, the impact of First Amendment audits is not solely limited to exposing misconduct. Many audits also highlight positive interactions between auditors and public officials. In these cases, government employees and law enforcement officers are seen respecting citizens' rights, engaging in courteous dialogue, and demonstrating a clear understanding of the law. These videos often go viral as well, reinforcing the idea that transparency and accountability do not need to be adversarial. When public officials conduct themselves professionally and respect the rights of citizens, it creates a positive feedback loop of trust and cooperation.

The presence of auditors has also encouraged some public institutions to take a proactive approach to transparency. Aware that their actions might be recorded and shared online, some government offices and police departments have adopted policies aimed at improving their interactions with the public. For example, some police departments have introduced body cameras to create their own record of interactions, ensuring that they have evidence to counter any allegations of misconduct. Similarly, public offices have begun training employees on how to handle interactions with auditors, emphasizing the importance of respecting citizens' rights while maintaining professional standards.

In conclusion, First Amendment audits have had a significant impact on promoting public accountability. By recording their interactions with government officials and sharing these videos with a broad audience, auditors not only expose instances of misconduct but also highlight positive examples of public service. Their work serves as a powerful reminder that government officials are ultimately accountable to the people, and that transparency is essential to maintaining the public's trust in its institutions. Through their efforts, auditors have brought about both legal and institutional changes, strengthening the democratic fabric of society.

The Challenges Faced by First Amendment Auditors

While First Amendment auditors play a critical role in upholding public accountability, their efforts are not without significant challenges. Auditors frequently find themselves in contentious situations where public officials—often unfamiliar with the scope of constitutional rights—respond to their presence with hostility or attempts to curtail their activities. This tension can lead to confrontations, arrests, and sometimes legal battles, making the role of a First Amendment auditor both rewarding and perilous. The challenges faced by auditors highlight the ongoing struggle to ensure that constitutional rights are respected in practice, not just in theory.

One of the most common challenges auditors face is the lack of understanding or awareness among public officials regarding citizens' rights to record in public spaces. Despite the legal precedents that firmly establish this right, many government employees, including law enforcement officers, react to audits with suspicion or hostility. This can lead to confrontations where auditors are told to stop recording, leave public property, or face arrest. Often, these officials cite vague justifications such as "privacy concerns" or "security threats," despite the fact that public spaces and the actions of public officials in those spaces are generally not subject to privacy protections.

These misunderstandings can escalate quickly, especially when law enforcement is involved. In many cases, auditors find themselves detained or even arrested for actions that are well within their constitutional rights. Charges such as trespassing, disorderly conduct, or obstruction of justice are commonly used against auditors, even though these charges are often dropped once the legal facts are reviewed. However, the immediate consequences of such confrontations—being handcuffed, placed in jail, or having equipment confiscated—can be distressing and intimidating. For some auditors, the fear of legal reprisals or physical confrontations is a constant concern, though it rarely deters them from their mission.

A significant challenge comes from the public perception of auditors and the auditing movement. While many view auditors as defenders of constitutional rights and public accountability, others—particularly those who are unfamiliar with the movement—may see them as provocateurs or troublemakers. Some critics argue that auditors deliberately seek confrontations with public officials to create dramatic footage for their online platforms, which can then be monetized through ads or donations. This perception is fueled by the confrontational nature of some audits, where auditors challenge officials' knowledge of the law or refuse to comply with orders that they know to be unlawful. As a result, auditors are often portrayed in a negative light by those who see their actions as antagonistic rather than educational or civic-minded.

This criticism can also be found within the media, where coverage of First Amendment audits sometimes frames auditors as disruptive or opportunistic. While many mainstream news outlets highlight the importance of government transparency, they may also emphasize the more contentious aspects of auditing, such as heated exchanges with law enforcement or public officials. This focus on conflict can overshadow the broader goals of the auditing movement, skewing public perception and making it more difficult for auditors to be seen as legitimate champions of constitutional rights.

Another challenge faced by First Amendment auditors is the legal grey areas in which they sometimes operate. Although courts have consistently ruled that recording public officials in public spaces is protected by the First Amendment, the exact boundaries of this right can be murky. For example, auditors frequently test the limits of their rights by recording in "limited public forums" such as post offices or government buildings, where certain restrictions may be imposed. While these spaces are generally open to the public, they may have specific rules governing behavior or the use of recording devices. In these situations, auditors often find themselves navigating a fine line between exercising their rights and being accused of causing a disruption or violating local ordinances.

Additionally, auditors sometimes face challenges related to the public's misunderstanding of their rights. Members of the general public who are unaware of the legal framework surrounding audits may view the act of recording as invasive or threatening. In some cases, bystanders have called the police on auditors, believing that their presence or filming is suspicious or unlawful. These misunderstandings can lead to unnecessary escalations, further complicating the auditors' interactions with law enforcement. The auditors' mission to educate public officials about the law is sometimes extended to educating the public as well, adding another layer of complexity to their work.

The risks auditors face also extend beyond legal consequences. In some cases, auditors have been threatened with violence, either by public officials or by private individuals angered by the presence of a camera. Some auditors have reported being physically assaulted or having their equipment damaged while conducting audits, making personal safety a major concern. The confrontational nature of some audits, particularly those involving police officers, increases the risk of such encounters turning violent. While most auditors take steps to de-escalate situations and remain calm, the unpredictable nature of human interactions means that danger is always a possibility.

In response to these challenges, many auditors have developed strategies to protect themselves and ensure their rights are upheld. Some auditors work in pairs or groups to increase safety and provide witnesses in case of an unlawful arrest. Others livestream their audits, ensuring that any misconduct is immediately broadcast to a wide audience and creating a real-time record of the event. Legal support networks have also sprung up around the auditing community, with some auditors collaborating with civil rights attorneys who specialize in First Amendment cases. This support is crucial, as legal battles can be lengthy and costly, and the threat of lawsuits can serve as a deterrent to officials who might otherwise act unlawfully.

Despite the obstacles they face, First Amendment auditors remain committed to their cause. The challenges they encounter—whether legal, social, or physical—serve to underscore the importance of their work. In a democratic society, the protection of constitutional rights is not automatic; it requires vigilance and, often, personal sacrifice. Auditors understand this better than most, and their willingness to face these challenges head-on is a testament to the strength of their convictions. Through their efforts, they shine a light on the areas where constitutional rights are not fully respected, reminding public officials and citizens alike that the fight for liberty is ongoing.

In conclusion, the challenges faced by First Amendment auditors are numerous and multifaceted. From confrontations with public officials and law enforcement to legal uncertainties and negative public perceptions, auditors must navigate a complex landscape in their efforts to promote accountability and transparency. However, these challenges also highlight the importance of their work and the enduring need to protect and exercise constitutional rights. Auditors serve as a crucial check on government power, ensuring that the freedoms guaranteed by the First Amendment are respected and upheld in everyday practice.

The Impact of First Amendment Auditors on Government Transparency

The influence of First Amendment auditors on government transparency has been profound, though often underappreciated. Through their direct engagements with public officials and their persistent efforts to hold government institutions accountable, auditors have shone a spotlight on both the strengths and weaknesses of American democracy. By documenting interactions in real time, they have created a powerful and accessible record that allows the public to see, often for the first time, how their government operates at a very granular level. This transparency is central to the First Amendment's core principles, emphasizing the importance of an informed and empowered citizenry.

At the heart of the auditing movement is the belief that government transparency is not just a right but a requirement for a functioning democracy. Without an informed public, it becomes easier for government officials to act outside the bounds of law, shielded from scrutiny. Auditors provide a critical layer of oversight that supplements the work of formal watchdog organizations and the press. By going into public spaces—city halls, post offices, police stations—auditors make visible the everyday workings of government, from how bureaucracies function to how public servants treat citizens. These interactions offer a lens into the quality of government service and the respect for constitutional rights.

A significant contribution of First Amendment auditors has been their exposure of instances where government officials overstep their authority. Through video footage, auditors have documented unlawful detentions, wrongful arrests, and instances where public employees have tried to restrict free speech or press rights. These documented violations have not only led to increased public awareness but have, in some cases, resulted in legal reforms or policy changes. Government agencies have been prompted to revise internal procedures, conduct training sessions on the public's right to record, and, in some instances, discipline or terminate employees who acted unlawfully during these interactions.

A notable impact of the auditing movement is the heightened awareness among public officials regarding their legal obligations to citizens. While confrontational situations still arise, auditors have contributed to a growing recognition that government spaces are subject to public oversight. In response to the presence of auditors, many law enforcement agencies and other public offices have implemented changes in how they train their personnel to interact with the public, especially concerning the right to record. Training programs that once focused narrowly on internal procedures now often include sections on First Amendment rights, especially after public controversies sparked by auditing videos.

For example, many police departments have developed updated guidelines on how officers should interact with auditors, recognizing that transparency is integral to building public trust. These guidelines often emphasize the need for restraint, clear communication, and respect for constitutional rights. By adhering to these principles, public agencies can avoid confrontations that could escalate and lead to legal challenges. The long-term impact of this heightened awareness has led to a more accountable government, where public officials are increasingly mindful that their actions are being observed, recorded, and potentially broadcast to millions.

In addition to influencing public officials, First Amendment auditors have also played a crucial role in educating the broader public about their rights. Through their recorded interactions and subsequent discussions, auditors have sparked conversations about civil liberties, government accountability, and the importance of transparency. The videos posted online serve as educational tools, teaching viewers about their own rights and how to assert them. Many people who watch these videos gain a clearer understanding of the First Amendment, learning how they can lawfully record in public spaces and what to expect when dealing with government officials.

The accessibility of auditing videos has helped democratize the conversation around civil rights. Unlike courtroom battles or formal policy debates, which can feel distant or opaque, the footage captured by auditors brings these issues into homes and smartphones across the country. Viewers witness, in real-time, how quickly a peaceful recording of a public space can escalate into a confrontation over rights. These first-hand accounts resonate deeply with audiences, many of whom may have experienced similar misunderstandings or tensions with public officials. The immediacy and transparency of these recordings make constitutional rights feel more real and relatable to everyday people.

Further, the videos serve as a form of documentation that can be used in both legal and political advocacy. Lawyers, civil rights organizations, and policymakers often draw upon these videos to support cases of civil rights violations, using the footage as irrefutable evidence of misconduct. In some instances, this documentation has led to lawsuits that challenge unlawful detentions or policies, pushing courts to reaffirm and expand First Amendment protections. The impact of auditors on the legal system cannot be overstated; their videos provide a vital record that can lead to systemic change when brought before a court of law.

Beyond the legal and educational impacts, First Amendment auditors have contributed to a broader cultural shift regarding the importance of government transparency. The auditing movement encourages citizens to see themselves not just as passive recipients of government services but as active participants in holding public officials accountable. This shift in perspective can lead to a more engaged, vigilant public that understands the importance of civic responsibility. By witnessing the actions of auditors, many people are inspired to become more involved in their own communities, whether through auditing, attending local government meetings, or simply paying closer attention to how their tax dollars are spent.

Auditors also demonstrate that the First Amendment is not merely an abstract legal concept but a living, breathing set of principles that must be exercised to be preserved. By taking the First Amendment into public spaces, auditors remind both public officials and private citizens that democracy requires constant participation and oversight. Their efforts to safeguard civil liberties serve as a reminder that rights, if not actively protected, can be easily eroded.

In conclusion, the impact of First Amendment auditors extends far beyond the confrontations and controversies captured in their videos. Through their work, they have made government operations more transparent, held public officials accountable, and educated the public about their constitutional rights. By acting as a visible, active force for government oversight, auditors ensure that the First Amendment remains robust and relevant in contemporary society. Their contributions to government transparency and public accountability cannot be ignored, as they represent a crucial defense against the erosion of civil liberties in the modern age.

CHAPTER 16

Conclusion: Liberty in Action

The Enduring Significance of the First Amendment

The First Amendment to the United States Constitution stands as a cornerstone of American democracy, enshrining freedoms that are essential to the health and vitality of the nation. It is a living testament to the founders' vision of a society where individuals could freely express their thoughts, challenge authority, worship as they please, assemble in protest, and demand change from their government. These five freedoms—speech, press, religion, assembly, and petition—are not just legal protections; they form the foundation of civic life, empowering individuals to participate fully in the democratic process.

At its core, the First Amendment is a reflection of the belief that a healthy democracy depends on the free exchange of ideas. Freedom of speech allows citizens to express their thoughts, whether popular or controversial, without fear of government censorship. This marketplace of ideas is essential to the evolution of society, enabling new concepts to emerge, be debated, and shape the course of public policy. The right to speech not only protects the speaker but also the listener, ensuring that people can hear diverse viewpoints and make informed decisions about their government and society.

The freedom of the press is equally important, serving as a check on government power and a safeguard against tyranny. The founders understood that a free press would be the watchdog of democracy, holding public officials accountable and exposing corruption, abuses of power, and violations of public trust. Without the press's ability to investigate and report without fear of reprisal, the public would be left in the dark, unable to fully participate in the democratic process. Throughout history, the press has played a pivotal role in shaping public opinion and influencing government action, from exposing the Watergate scandal to shedding light on civil rights abuses.

Religious freedom, as guaranteed by the First Amendment, was a radical concept when the Constitution was written. In a time when state-sponsored religion was the norm around the world, the idea that individuals could choose their own faith—or none at all—was groundbreaking. This freedom has allowed the United States to become one of the most religiously diverse nations in the world, where people of all faiths and beliefs can coexist. The First Amendment ensures that the government cannot favor one religion over another, nor can it interfere in the private practice of an individual's faith. This protection has fostered a culture of tolerance and respect for diverse religious practices, even in the face of disagreement.

The right to assemble and the right to petition the government are also crucial to the functioning of a democracy. The ability to gather in protest or support of a cause allows citizens to express their collective will, demand change, and hold their leaders accountable. Throughout American history, the right to assemble has been used by various movements, from civil rights activists marching for equality to environmentalists advocating for climate action. The right to petition the government ensures that citizens have a direct line of communication with their elected representatives, allowing for grievances to be addressed and policy changes to be made in response to public demand.

Together, these five freedoms form the bedrock of the American democratic experiment. They provide the tools for citizens to shape their society, challenge injustices, and protect their individual liberties. The First Amendment is not static; it has evolved with the nation, adapting to new challenges and technologies while remaining steadfast in its protection of these core freedoms. It serves as a reminder that democracy is not guaranteed—it must be actively maintained and defended by each generation.

The enduring significance of the First Amendment lies in its universality and its power to inspire. It is a promise to every American that their voice matters, that their beliefs are protected, and that their government is accountable to them. In a world where authoritarianism and censorship continue to rise, the First Amendment stands as a beacon of liberty, ensuring that the principles of democracy are preserved for future generations. It reminds us that the strength of a democracy is measured by how well it protects the rights of its people to think, speak, and act freely.

Challenges to First Amendment Rights in the Modern Era

While the First Amendment has been a powerful safeguard of individual liberties throughout American history, it faces new and complex challenges in the modern era. The evolution of technology, the rise of disinformation, and increasing political polarization have created tensions that test the boundaries of free speech, press, religion, assembly, and petition. These challenges highlight the delicate balance between maintaining a free society and addressing the legitimate concerns of safety, security, and public order.

One of the most pressing challenges to First Amendment rights today is the tension between national security and personal freedom. Since the events of September 11, 2001, there has been an ongoing debate over the extent to which the government should be allowed to curtail certain freedoms in the name of security. Laws such as the USA PATRIOT Act expanded the government's ability to monitor communications and restrict access to certain information, raising concerns about government overreach and the erosion of privacy rights. While protecting national security is undoubtedly important, it is essential to ensure that these measures do not infringe on the very freedoms that the government is tasked with defending.

The rise of the digital age has further complicated the issue of free speech. The internet, and particularly social media platforms, have transformed how people communicate, providing unprecedented opportunities for expression while also presenting new risks. On one hand, these platforms democratize information, giving a voice to those who might otherwise be silenced. On the other hand, they have become breeding grounds for disinformation, hate speech, and online harassment. The question of whether social media companies, as private entities, should regulate speech on their platforms has sparked heated debates. While these companies are not bound by the First Amendment in the same way that the government is, their decisions about what content to allow or remove can have significant implications for public discourse.

Disinformation, in particular, poses a serious challenge to the principles of free speech. While the First Amendment protects the right to express controversial or even unpopular opinions, it does not protect speech that deliberately spreads falsehoods designed to deceive or harm. The spread of misinformation about elections, public health, and other critical issues has led to real-world consequences, undermining trust in democratic institutions and threatening public safety. Policymakers are grappling with how to address this issue without infringing on the fundamental right to free expression. Striking the right balance between combating disinformation and preserving the open exchange of ideas is a difficult but necessary task for the modern era.

Political polarization has also heightened tensions surrounding the limits of free speech. In recent years, the concept of "cancel culture" has emerged as a flashpoint in debates over speech and accountability. Some argue that holding individuals or institutions accountable for harmful speech is necessary to protect vulnerable communities from hate and discrimination. Others believe that cancel culture stifles free expression by punishing people for expressing dissenting or unpopular opinions. This divide reflects a broader societal struggle over how to reconcile the protection of free speech with the need to create inclusive, respectful public spaces.

Another area where First Amendment rights are being tested is in the context of religious freedom. As society becomes more diverse, questions arise about the extent to which religious beliefs should be accommodated in public life. Recent legal battles, such as those over the rights of businesses to refuse services based on religious convictions or the role of religion in public schools, highlight the ongoing tension between individual religious freedoms and the rights of others. The Supreme Court has faced difficult decisions in determining where to draw the line between the free exercise of religion and the need to protect against discrimination and ensure equal treatment under the law.

In light of these challenges, it is clear that the First Amendment is not immune to the pressures of modern society. However, its resilience lies in its ability to adapt to new circumstances while maintaining its core principles. As new threats to free expression and civil liberties emerge, it is crucial that the public remains engaged and vigilant in defending the First Amendment. This means not only standing up against government overreach but also navigating the complex ethical questions that arise in a rapidly changing world.

Ultimately, the challenges to the First Amendment in the modern era serve as a reminder that freedom is not static. The rights enshrined in the Constitution must be continually reassessed and reaffirmed in light of new developments and changing societal norms. While the First Amendment has withstood the test of time, its future depends on the willingness of citizens, courts, and policymakers to strike a careful balance between protecting freedom and addressing the legitimate concerns that arise in an interconnected, digital world. The ongoing defense of these freedoms is critical to ensuring that the First Amendment remains a vibrant and vital part of American democracy.

The Role of the Courts in Defining First Amendment Boundaries

The judiciary has played an indispensable role in shaping the interpretation of the First Amendment since its inception. While the amendment's text may seem straightforward, its application to real-world situations has often required careful judicial consideration to balance competing interests. Over the centuries, the courts—particularly the U.S. Supreme Court—have been called upon to interpret the First Amendment in ways that both protect individual liberties and address societal concerns. The resulting body of case law is a testament to the flexibility and adaptability of this fundamental protection, even as it continues to evolve.

From the earliest days of the republic, courts have struggled with how to define the limits of free speech. One of the first major tests of First Amendment protections came with the Alien and Sedition Acts of 1798, which made it a crime to criticize the government. The acts were controversial and were eventually allowed to expire, but they highlighted a key tension that persists to this day: How do we protect the right to criticize those in power while ensuring that speech does not undermine national security or public order?

In the 20th century, the Supreme Court began to more actively define the parameters of free speech. One of the landmark cases was *Schenck v. United States* (1919), which established the "clear and present danger" test. The case arose during World War I, when Charles Schenck was prosecuted for distributing leaflets opposing the draft. Justice Oliver Wendell Holmes, writing for the court, famously declared that free speech would not protect a man "falsely shouting fire in a theater and causing a panic." In *Schenck*, the court ruled that speech could be restricted if it posed a clear and present danger to national security. This ruling marked the first significant limitation on free speech and set a precedent for the balancing act between freedom and security.

However, the clear and present danger test evolved over time, particularly in cases that tested the limits of political speech. In *Brandenburg v. Ohio* (1969), the court established a more stringent standard, ruling that speech could only be restricted if it was "directed to inciting or producing imminent lawless action" and was likely to produce such action. This decision, which arose from the prosecution of a Ku Klux Klan leader for inflammatory speech, strengthened protections for even controversial or offensive speech, provided it did not directly incite violence. The *Brandenburg* ruling continues to serve as a guiding principle in determining when the government can limit speech without violating the First Amendment.

The courts have also had a profound impact on the freedom of the press. One of the most famous cases in this area is *New York Times Co. v. United States* (1971), commonly known as the Pentagon Papers case. The U.S. government sought to prevent the *New*

York Times and the *Washington Post* from publishing classified documents that detailed the government's actions during the Vietnam War. The Supreme Court ruled in favor of the newspapers, asserting that prior restraint—government action to prevent the publication of material—was unconstitutional unless there was a direct, immediate, and irreparable harm to national security. This case reinforced the idea that a free press is essential to a functioning democracy, serving as a check on government power and ensuring that the public is informed about its government's actions.

The free exercise of religion has also been a frequent subject of judicial interpretation. In *Employment Division v. Smith* (1990), the Supreme Court ruled that the government could enforce generally applicable laws even if they incidentally burdened religious practices. The case involved two Native Americans who were fired from their jobs for using peyote in a religious ceremony and were subsequently denied unemployment benefits. The court held that individuals could not claim exemption from laws simply because they conflicted with their religious beliefs. This decision sparked significant controversy and led to the passage of the Religious Freedom Restoration Act (RFRA) in 1993, which aimed to restore broader protections for religious exercise by requiring the government to demonstrate a compelling interest before imposing a substantial burden on religious practices.

The right to assembly and petition has also been shaped by landmark court decisions. For example, in *National Socialist Party of America v. Village of Skokie* (1977), the court upheld the right of a neo-Nazi group to march through a predominantly Jewish neighborhood, despite the offensive nature of their message. The court ruled that the government could not restrict the group's right to assemble and express their views simply because those views were repugnant to the majority. This decision underscored the principle that the First Amendment protects not only popular speech but also speech that is deeply unpopular or controversial.

Throughout its history, the judiciary has played a critical role in defining and defending the boundaries of First Amendment freedoms. While the courts have had to wrestle with difficult questions about how far these rights extend, their rulings have helped to clarify the limits of government authority and ensure that the First Amendment continues to serve as a robust safeguard of individual liberties. These judicial interpretations remain essential to maintaining the balance between freedom and order in a democratic society, ensuring that the principles enshrined in the Constitution remain relevant and resilient in an ever-changing world.

The Role of Free Speech in Social Movements

Free speech has been the beating heart of many of the most significant social movements in American history, providing activists and marginalized groups with a powerful tool to demand change. From the abolitionist movement to civil rights, women's suffrage to LGBTQ+ equality, the First Amendment's protection of speech, assembly, and petition has been central to the pursuit of justice. By allowing individuals and groups to voice dissent and challenge the status quo, free speech has not only enabled progress but also deepened the democratic process, ensuring that all voices—especially those previously silenced—have a chance to be heard.

One of the earliest and most impactful uses of free speech in a social movement was the abolitionist campaign of the 19th century. At a time when the institution of slavery was deeply entrenched in American society, abolitionists relied on pamphlets, speeches, newspapers, and public demonstrations to argue against the moral and legal legitimacy of slavery. Activists like Frederick Douglass, an escaped slave who became one of the most powerful voices of the movement, used the written and spoken word to expose the brutal realities of slavery. Through his speeches and his autobiographical works, such as *Narrative of the Life of Frederick Douglass, an American Slave*, Douglass not only educated the public but also inspired a growing movement dedicated to the abolition of slavery. His use of free speech was a form of resistance, empowering not only himself but others in the fight for equality.

The First Amendment also played a critical role in the women's suffrage movement of the late 19th and early 20th centuries. Suffragists like Susan B. Anthony and Elizabeth Cady Stanton harnessed the power of public speech, assembly, and petition to demand the right to vote for women. In 1848, the first Women's Rights Convention was held in Seneca Falls, New York, where activists drafted the Declaration of Sentiments, a document that used the framework of the Declaration of Independence to argue for women's equality. The movement grew through public speeches, marches, and civil disobedience, culminating in the passage of the 19th Amendment in 1920, which granted women the right to vote. The ability to organize, protest, and voice dissent—rights guaranteed by the First Amendment—were crucial in the suffragists' success.

The civil rights movement of the 1950s and 1960s is perhaps the most well-known example of free speech being used to effect transformative social change. Led by figures like Martin Luther King Jr., the movement sought to dismantle segregation and end racial discrimination in the United States. King's speeches, such as his iconic "I Have a Dream" address, galvanized the nation and gave a moral voice to the movement's demands for equality. The 1963 March on Washington for Jobs and Freedom, where King delivered his famous speech, was one of the largest demonstrations in American history, made possible by the right to assemble peacefully and petition the government. The civil rights movement demonstrated the power of free speech in challenging deeply rooted systems of oppression, and it forever changed the landscape of American society.

Activism in the LGBTQ+ community has similarly relied on the First Amendment to advance the cause of equality. Early advocates for LGBTQ+ rights faced extreme hostility and discrimination, but over time, the community's ability to organize and speak out became one of its most powerful tools. The 1969 Stonewall Riots in New York City, often cited as the catalyst for the modern LGBTQ+ rights movement, were a direct response to police brutality and discrimination against LGBTQ+ individuals. Following the riots, activists began to organize more openly, using free speech to advocate for legal protections and social acceptance. Organizations like the Gay Liberation Front and, later, ACT UP during the AIDS crisis of the 1980s, used protests, rallies, and public demonstrations to force the nation to confront issues of inequality and injustice.

The First Amendment has also been central to more recent movements like Black Lives Matter (BLM) and the Women's March. BLM, which began in response to the police killings of unarmed Black individuals, quickly grew into a national and global movement advocating for racial justice and police reform. Protests, social media campaigns, and public demonstrations—all forms of protected speech and assembly—became crucial tools in the movement's ability to bring attention to issues of systemic racism and inequality. The Women's March, which first took place in January 2017 in response to the inauguration of President Donald Trump, became one of the largest demonstrations in American history. It showcased the power of collective action and free speech in advocating for women's rights, reproductive freedom, and social justice.

These movements highlight the dynamic and transformative power of the First Amendment in shaping the course of American history. By protecting the right to speak out, protest, and petition the government, the First Amendment ensures that social change can happen from the ground up. It empowers individuals and groups who challenge unjust systems and demand that their voices be heard, even when those voices make those in power uncomfortable.

While free speech is not without its challenges—movements are often met with counter-protests, police repression, or attempts at silencing—the enduring legacy of these social movements demonstrates that the First Amendment is an essential tool for achieving justice. Social movements, in their purest form, are expressions of the democratic process at work. They are evidence of a society that values dialogue, dissent, and the right of individuals to challenge the established order. Through these movements, the First Amendment has proven its ability to be not just a legal protection but a driving force for progress and equality in the United States.

The Challenges to Free Speech in a Polarized Society

In today's increasingly polarized society, the challenges to free speech have taken on new dimensions, testing the very principles the First Amendment was designed to protect. While free speech is meant to ensure that all voices can be heard, it now faces intense scrutiny from various corners—ranging from the government to private entities, from political groups to social media platforms. These tensions raise fundamental questions about the limits of speech, the responsibilities of platforms that disseminate information, and how society can balance the protection of free expression with the growing demand for civility and accountability.

One of the most pressing challenges is the rise of hate speech and extremist rhetoric in public discourse. While the First Amendment protects the right to express unpopular or even offensive opinions, there is an ongoing debate about how far those protections should extend when speech becomes harmful. Hate speech, which targets individuals or groups based on race, religion, gender, or sexual orientation, has the potential to incite violence and create a climate of fear and hostility. However, U.S. courts have generally ruled that hate speech is protected under the First Amendment unless it directly incites violence or lawless action, as outlined in *Brandenburg v. Ohio* (1969). This principle has been a cornerstone of free speech jurisprudence, but it leaves society grappling with the question of how to address speech that, while legally permissible, contributes to the marginalization or dehumanization of vulnerable groups.

The digital age has further complicated the landscape of free speech. The advent of social media platforms like Facebook, Twitter, and YouTube has created new opportunities for individuals to express themselves and reach vast audiences. However, these platforms have also become battlegrounds for misinformation, harassment, and political manipulation. Private companies that control these platforms wield significant power over what speech is allowed and what is censored, leading to concerns about corporate overreach and the arbitrary enforcement of content policies. While the First Amendment protects individuals from government censorship, it does not apply to private companies, leaving users with limited recourse when their content is removed or restricted. This has led to debates about whether social media platforms should be treated as public utilities, subject to more stringent regulations, or whether they should retain their autonomy to moderate content as they see fit.

Another major challenge to free speech is the phenomenon of "cancel culture," where individuals or groups face public backlash, often on social media, for expressing controversial opinions or engaging in behavior deemed offensive. In some cases, this results in social ostracism, loss of employment, or damage to reputations. While proponents of cancel culture argue that it is a form of accountability for harmful speech or actions, critics contend that it stifles open dialogue and discourages people from expressing their views for fear of retribution. The First Amendment protects individuals from government action but does not shield them from the consequences of public opinion. Nonetheless, the rise of cancel culture raises important questions about the health of free speech in a society where disagreement can quickly escalate into social or professional punishment.

Universities, traditionally seen as bastions of free thought and expression, have also become flashpoints in the debate over free speech. In recent years, many college campuses have faced controversies over whether to allow speakers with controversial or offensive views. In some cases, student groups have protested or disrupted events, arguing that certain speakers promote hate or discrimination. Critics, however, argue that this shuts down important opportunities for dialogue and debate, undermining the very purpose of higher education. The challenge for universities is to strike a balance between protecting free speech and fostering an inclusive environment where all students feel safe and respected. This tension reflects a broader societal struggle over how to navigate the competing demands of free expression and social justice.

The role of the government in regulating speech is another critical issue. While the First Amendment prohibits government censorship, there are instances where the government has sought to limit speech in the name of national security, public safety, or other concerns. For example, during times of war or national crisis, the government has enacted laws that restrict speech deemed to be dangerous or subversive, such as the Espionage Act of 1917 or the PATRIOT Act following the 9/11 attacks. These laws have sparked debates over whether the government is justified in limiting speech to protect the public or whether such actions represent a dangerous encroachment on civil liberties. The balance between free speech and security remains a contentious issue, particularly in an era of terrorism and cyber warfare.

In addition to legal challenges, cultural forces also play a role in shaping the boundaries of free speech. The increasing polarization of American society has created echo chambers where individuals are more likely to encounter opinions that reinforce their existing beliefs rather than challenge them. This polarization has made civil discourse more difficult, as people with differing views often see each other as adversaries rather than participants in a shared democratic experiment. In such an environment, the marketplace of ideas—the concept that free speech allows the best ideas to rise to the top—becomes less effective, as people become more entrenched in their positions and less willing to engage with opposing viewpoints.

Despite these challenges, the First Amendment remains a powerful and essential protection for free speech in the United States. It allows for a diversity of ideas, fosters innovation, and enables individuals to challenge authority and seek justice. However, as society continues to grapple with the complexities of hate speech, digital platforms, cancel culture, and political polarization, the future of free speech will depend on how these issues are navigated. Ensuring that free speech thrives in a way that promotes both liberty and responsibility will require ongoing dialogue, legal refinement, and a renewed commitment to the principles of open debate and tolerance for dissenting views.

In the end, the challenges to free speech are not insurmountable, but they do require thoughtful consideration and a willingness to engage with the difficult questions that arise when liberty intersects with societal concerns. As the world continues to evolve, so too must our understanding of how to protect the vital freedoms enshrined in the First Amendment, ensuring that they remain resilient and relevant in the face of new and unforeseen challenges.

CHAPTER 17

Appendix: Important Documents and Resources

The First Amendment of the United States Constitution
The First Amendment, adopted in 1791 as part of the Bill of Rights, is the cornerstone of American democracy. It guarantees essential freedoms that allow individuals to express themselves, challenge authority, and advocate for change. The full text is as follows:

"Congress shall make no law respecting an establishment of religion, or prohibiting the free exercise thereof; or abridging the freedom of speech, or of the press; or the right of the people peaceably to assemble, and to petition the Government for a redress of grievances."

This succinct yet powerful amendment forms the foundation of the protections we have discussed throughout this book. Each clause—whether on religion, speech, the press, assembly, or petition—has been interpreted, challenged, and upheld in significant ways over the years.

Key Supreme Court Cases Discussed in This Book
To better understand how the First Amendment has been shaped over time, here is a list of landmark Supreme Court cases that have defined its scope and application. These cases reflect pivotal mo-

ments in American legal history where the principles of free speech, press, religion, assembly, and petition were tested:

1. **Schenck v. United States (1919)**
   Established the "clear and present danger" test, determining that speech which incites illegal actions or poses a direct threat to public safety is not protected.
2. **Brandenburg v. Ohio (1969)**
   Refined the "clear and present danger" test by ruling that speech advocating illegal action is protected unless it is likely to incite "imminent lawless action."
3. **New York Times Co. v. Sullivan (1964)**
   Established the "actual malice" standard for defamation cases involving public figures, greatly expanding freedom of the press.
4. **Tinker v. Des Moines Independent Community School District (1969)**
   Affirmed that students do not "shed their constitutional rights to freedom of speech or expression at the schoolhouse gate," setting an important precedent for student free speech.
5. **Citizens United v. Federal Election Commission (2010)**
   Expanded the rights of corporations and unions to engage in political speech, ruling that government restrictions on independent political expenditures violate the First Amendment.
6. **Texas v. Johnson (1989)**
   Held that flag burning constitutes symbolic speech protected by the First Amendment, affirming the right to express dissent through actions as well as words.
7. **Burwell v. Hobby Lobby Stores, Inc. (2014)**
   Decided that closely held for-profit corporations can refuse to

provide contraception coverage based on religious objections under the Religious Freedom Restoration Act.
8. **Morse v. Frederick (2007)**
Allowed schools to limit speech that promotes illegal drug use, establishing that student speech can be restricted in certain contexts without violating the First Amendment.
9. **Lemon v. Kurtzman (1971)**
Created the "Lemon test" for determining when government actions violate the Establishment Clause, requiring that actions must have a secular purpose and neither advance nor inhibit religion.
10. **Masterpiece Cakeshop v. Colorado Civil Rights Commission (2018)**
Addressed the conflict between religious beliefs and anti-discrimination laws, ruling in favor of a baker who refused to make a wedding cake for a same-sex couple due to his religious objections.

These cases, among others, demonstrate the evolving nature of the First Amendment and how the Supreme Court has played a crucial role in balancing individual freedoms with societal interests.

Resources for Further Reading

For readers interested in delving deeper into the history, philosophy, and legal battles surrounding the First Amendment, the following books and articles provide valuable insights:

- **"Free Speech: A History from Socrates to Social Media" by Jacob Mchangama**
  A comprehensive history of free speech, tracing its evolution from ancient Greece to the modern digital age.

- **"The Soul of the First Amendment" by Floyd Abrams**
  Offers an in-depth exploration of the First Amendment's centrality to American identity and its unique place in global democracy.
- **"Speaking Freely: Trials of the First Amendment" by Nat Hentoff**
  Chronicles Hentoff's personal experiences as a journalist and free speech advocate, offering a unique perspective on First Amendment battles.
- **"Freedom for the Thought That We Hate: A Biography of the First Amendment" by Anthony Lewis**
  A gripping narrative on how the First Amendment has been shaped by landmark cases and fierce public debate.
- **"The First Amendment Encyclopedia" (Middle Tennessee State University)**
  A free, online resource offering detailed entries on key First Amendment topics, cases, and figures.

Organizations Supporting First Amendment Rights

Several organizations are dedicated to defending and promoting First Amendment rights. Whether through legal advocacy, education, or public campaigns, these groups work to ensure that the freedoms guaranteed by the First Amendment remain protected:

- **The American Civil Liberties Union (ACLU)**
  A nonprofit organization that has been at the forefront of defending civil liberties, including free speech and religious freedoms, for over a century.
- **The Foundation for Individual Rights and Expression (FIRE)**

An organization dedicated to defending free speech rights on college campuses across the United States.
- **The Knight First Amendment Institute at Columbia University**
Focuses on defending free speech in the digital age and conducts research on how new technologies impact First Amendment freedoms.
- **The Reporters Committee for Freedom of the Press**
Provides pro bono legal support to journalists and news organizations, ensuring that the press remains free and independent.
- **The National Coalition Against Censorship (NCAC)**
Works to combat censorship in schools, libraries, and public institutions, promoting the free exchange of ideas in educational and cultural settings.

How to Get Involved

As a reader inspired by the First Amendment, you can take an active role in defending and promoting these essential freedoms. Here are a few ways to get involved:

- **Stay Informed**: Follow current events, legal cases, and public debates that affect First Amendment rights. Understanding the ongoing issues is the first step in protecting them.
- **Support Advocacy Groups**: Consider donating to or volunteering with organizations that champion free speech, religious freedom, and the other protections enshrined in the First Amendment.
- **Engage in Civil Discourse**: Practice free speech by participating in community discussions, attending public forums, and engaging in civil debates on important issues.

- **Contact Elected Officials**: Advocate for First Amendment rights by writing to or meeting with your elected representatives to express your views on free speech, press freedom, and religious liberty.
- **Exercise Your Rights**: The First Amendment is not just an abstract legal principle; it's a living right that can be exercised every day. Whether by speaking out on social issues, assembling with others to protest, or writing letters to the editor, make your voice heard.

By taking an active role in protecting and promoting First Amendment rights, we contribute to the ongoing defense of democracy and the preservation of liberty for future generations.

Milton Keynes UK
Ingram Content Group UK Ltd.
UKHW031634201124
451457UK00011B/222